To David + Trish

Thanks for being an
important part of my journey.
May yours continue to be
full of adventure, music +
mystery.

Love,

[signature]

OUT OF THE SIXTIES

My Journey in Search of My Self and the True Nature of Existence

JASHANANANDA

ISBN: 978-1-3044-0081-9 (sc)
ISBN: 978-1-4834-0675-6 (hc)
ISBN: 978-1-4834-0674-9 (e)

Library of Congress Control Number: 2014900315

Because of the dynamic nature of the Internet, any web addresses or links contained in this book may have changed since publication and may no longer be valid. The views expressed in this work are solely those of the author and do not necessarily reflect the views of the publisher, and the publisher hereby disclaims any responsibility for them.

Cover design is based on a painting by artist and poet Prartho Sereno.

Lulu Publishing Services rev. date: 4/14/2014

***

This book is dedicated to all the teachers

ahead on the path

and to my daughter Dawn

who left this world so early in life.

***

Prologue

Walking the Dog Part 1

August 26th, 1993

It's a Thursday and it's a most ordinary day, which becomes most extraordinary as it unfolds. I am working in my home office; as a cost saving measure the software company for which I work has closed their Denver office and has asked each of its employees to begin working from home. I miss the camaraderie of office life, and I also find it more difficult to separate home life from work life now. Still, working from home has its advantages. For one thing, my "commute" is reduced from almost an hour to less than two minutes.

Today I am learning about a new PC database my company is developing, and so I work a little longer than usual. Around 5:30, my eight-year-old daughter Dawn comes in, sits on my lap, and reminds me that it's time to quit working and play with her.

"I'm almost done, Dawn," I say to her gently. "Just give me a few more minutes."

My wife Jill has gotten home early from her job as a Psychotherapist and has started dinner, so when I finish my work dinner is nearly ready. After spending a little time with Dawn, I share a simple meal of grilled potatoes and veggie burgers with my family, and then Jill and I take a walk together. The temperature outside is cool because it has been raining much of the day, but the evening is pleasant enough. We walk up the street named

"Peacechance" in our mountain subdivision in the foothills just west of Denver, then onto the unpaved part of a street called "Whirlaway", and finally on around the big meadow and back home. In case you missed it, all the streets in this little piece of paradise are named after racehorses. We walk the usual loop around the "block", as we call it, but then take a long cut to have more time to talk. It's a beautiful evening strolling beside the wide-open meadow where elk often graze on the edge of a young Ponderosa pine forest. Birds are singing and we meet an occasional couple moving along in the other direction as we walk. Jill and I take turns talking, hoping that we can bridge the communication gap between us that has been widening over the summer.

I speak first and talk about my dreams and aspirations, my frustrations with my corporate job, and my true ambitions around music and writing. Jill speaks next and I feel myself reacting as she speaks about how she feels stifled and unable to change due to my lack of acceptance of her. As for my aspirations, she says that I have been saying the same thing for the last eighteen years. Well, I suppose that is true. I am still dreaming the same dreams, but I'm making progress with them. My music is improving and my confidence is growing. Yes, it's slow going, but that's how I am. It's my nature to make slow but steady progress.

After our talk we return home and back to the business of raising three children in the insular environment of the American suburb. Later in the evening a most remarkable and inexplicable thing happens. I walk out the front door as I do every night to walk our black and white Cocker Spaniel Maggie; only this time I notice something very strange. The moment I step outside, everything in my field of view begins shimmering. The trees, the grass, the rocks, even the mountains in the distance are all alive and super-charged with energy. Then, as I stand there staring in disbelief, I have the overwhelming perception that I am expanding. All at once I become huge... towering over everything as if I were now twenty or thirty feet tall, and I have the distinct impression that I can see over the next hill and then clear into the next county.

"What's going on? Am I tripping? Am I having a flashback?"

The experience I'm having is very much like those I have had on L.S.D., only this time I'm not on acid. In fact I haven't taken anything like that in almost twenty years.

"Is it something I ate?"

No. I don't think it can be anything I have eaten. Dinner was quite ordinary, and as I say, I haven't taken any magic pill, but here I am in an altered state of consciousness never the less. As I walk along this country road, I begin to feel embarrassed at being so expanded, so open and so vulnerable, but I soon forget about that as I become captivated by how beautiful everything is. The trees and the sky and grass are all glistening and pulsating with life, and I can see that all these things are really all one thing, or rather all one energy, and that I'm not separate from it. I have the strong sense that I am also that very same energy.

I return to the house full to overflowing with this vibrant aliveness and then approach Jill. I must sound pretty crazy as I try to explain to her what I am experiencing.

"I'm feeling really strange, like I've taken psychedelics or something. Everything looks so radiant and alive."

My wife, the psychotherapist, looks at me as if I were a bug under an entomologist's magnifying glass. I can see the concern on her face as she asks me the next question.

"How long have you been feeling this way?"

"I started having this feeling and these perceptions just a few minutes ago," I tell her, "when I went out to walk Maggie."

"How do you feel now?" She asks.

"I feel wonderful! It's my best psychedelic trip, and I'm not even on anything. Everything is so clear, so clean."

"Perhaps you're having a panic attack," Jill says later in the evening as my heightened perception continues. It's now well after midnight.

"Do I look panicked?" I ask as I sit calmly in my work chair by the computer. "I've never felt better in my life!"

"Well, something is happening to you," Jill replies.

"Maybe it's a spiritual awakening... you know, like Ram Dass used to talk about. After all my years of yoga practice maybe it's finally happening to me."

Jill doesn't say anything in response. She just looks at me with obvious concern as I sit down in one of our easy chairs and try to collect myself.

"I wonder how long it will last," I say mostly to myself.

Always in the past, I had a little blot or a tiny red see-through square to blame this experience on. "Take one and see the world. You can sleep in the morning." Coming down was always implied in taking L.S.D. With the little red tab there was always a timeframe, twelve hours and you're back to normal. But what about this experience? Since I haven't taken anything, there's nothing to wear off. But pill or not, I assume the experience won't last. The idea that for every high there's a low is so ingrained in my psyche.

"I better use it while I've got it," I tell myself.

Jill finally goes to bed, but I stay up for a couple of more hours in front of my computer and end up writing the prologue and the first draft of an outline for the first fourteen chapters of my autobiography. As I write I have the overwhelming feeling that if I record everything that has happened in my life leading to this moment, I will be able to understand the purpose of it all and what is happening to me now. In short, I'll solve this great mystery, which is my life. And so I begin.

Chapter 1

Incarnation:
A Trillion to One Chance

The great omnipresence takes a long, slow, quiet inhale. Just as slowly, breathing through her nose, she allows the breath to escape. Expanding outward in all directions, the universe is reborn. Scientists call this the big bang and see the universe expanding on to infinity. Dust particles consolidate into mighty galaxies and billions and billions of stars are born (as the late Carl Sagan was fond of saying). A small subset (only billions of these stars) form solar systems with planets orbiting them. On the edge of one insignificant spiral galaxy, there is a small star with nine planets revolving about it in various orbits. Like the three bears' porridge some are too hot to sustain life, and some are much too cold. Some have thousand-mile dense, toxic atmospheres, and one planet is just right (at least for the moment) for life as we know it. As we peer down through this planet's modest atmosphere, we can see mostly blue. Getting a little closer we notice some blotches of green, the landmasses. On one of these blotches called North America there is a cluster of tiny blue shapes. These shapes are actually the bodies of water we call the Great Lakes. A small land mass surrounded by these lakes can be seen like a hand facing upward in greeting. In the fleshy part of lower thumb muscle of this hand lies a small grouping of houses and buildings clustered around a center of learning called the University of Michigan. Of the billions of people on this tiny planet we wish to consider just one life, a life that started in this place called Ann Arbor. This is the life I know the best; this life is my own.

What are the odds that any one specific person comes into being?

Out of more than seven billion people on this planet, somehow two people, my mother and father, found each other. They didn't grow up together. One grew up in Boston, the other in Maryland. So, what were the thousands of little decisions that each made in the twenty plus years of their lives that led each to that moment where they met? A long debate over a chosen college. A chance meeting of a friend of a friend. The break up with an old girl friend. A decision not to cross the street or to cross the street at a specific moment. Perhaps, a near death by a drunk driver who at the last minute was talked into staying overnight at a friend's house. All these things, each trivial by themselves, determine a very specific outcome. If my mom hadn't lost that second baby, if they had decided to go out that night in December of 1948. Instead, they stayed home. If that one in a million sperm had not made the journey, or had been beaten out by another. If my dad had eaten a different meal, worn different pants... and on and on. The odds were pretty unlikely, and yet... here I am. If there is such a thing as fate, then perhaps I was destined to be.

If there is such a thing as reincarnation, perhaps I would have grabbed the next available vehicle if this one hadn't worked out. But, I wonder, would I have been *me*, the product of this genetic makeup, this environment and this astrological configuration? Would I still have this feeling inside, this awareness, that certain penetrating gaze? Who am I anyway? Just exactly what makes me unique? What makes me the *who* that I think I am? The answer to that question is the essence of my spiritual journey and the impetus for writing this book.

***

There's an age-old argument in Psychology about the relative importance of heredity versus environment in determining who we are. The question is just how much of what we are is determined by our genetic makeup and how much of it has to do with the environment in which we were raised? Thinking about the role heredity plays, I'm reminded of this old joke: A man decides that he wants a new suit.

His friend says, "Go see my brother-in-law. He's a great tailor and he can get you a suit for near whole-sale."

So the guy goes to this tailor. He has to take the train into the city, take the subway and then walk a few blocks to the tailor's store.

"Harry sent me," he says to the man behind the counter.

"Oh, my brother-in-law! How is that son-of-a-gun?"

"He's doing fine. Say listen, he says you can get me a really good deal on a suit."

"You bet! I've got just the thing for you." He goes into the back and brings out this coat. The man puts it on.

"It seems to hang a little funny."

"Oh, that's easy to fix. Just hunch over a little to the right." The man hunches over.

"Now it hangs okay, but the left sleeve seems a little long."

"No problem, just twist your body a little and hang your left arm down in front." The man complies and the suit coat fits perfectly.

"Shall I wrap it up for you?"

"No, I'll just wear it." So the man walks out of the store all hunched over and twisted with one arm dangling. Another man and a woman happen to be walking down the street at that moment.

The woman turns to the man and says, "Look at that, honey. That must be a great tailor. Look how well that suit fits that poor, deformed, crippled man!"

So... we seem to walk through our lives wearing our deformed hereditary suits as if they were precious family heirlooms.

My own *hereditary suit* is Scotch Irish and English on my Dad's side with some claims of nobility, and mostly Scandinavian on my mother's side. But, I have to say, when my parents told me about this, it seemed like it was a story about someone else. Maybe this is because I wasn't around my grandparents much growing up, or perhaps because my parents didn't observe any family traditions. Whatever the reason, I am left with the feeling that my heritage says very little about who I am. Perhaps its influence permeates me so deeply that I don't even notice it.

I must admit, though, that in one very specific way, I am aware of how my heredity has influenced the way I see the world. You see I'm red/green color deficient. It's an inherited trait passed down on my mother's side on the x-chromosome. What it amounts to is that I don't see colors the way others do. The way you know is by taking a color vision test. In the test there's a big circle filled with loads of small colored dots that are arranged in such a way that a number stands out of the circle and you can recognize it, that is unless you are red/green color deficient. Then you can't see the number. It's no fun taking the test if you're color deficient.

When people know I've got this trait, they almost always ask me, "So, what do you see? What does red look like to you?"

What can I say to them? "Here, have an eyeball. Take a look for yourself."

You see the only way to describe color is through the words we have for color. Clearly I see color differently than *normal* people, but who's to say that any of us see the same as any one else. The Native Americans have an expression about walking a mile in your brother's moccasins. How about a day looking through someone else's eyes, using another person's brain? Now that would be an enlightening experience! So clearly heredity plays a part in how we see the world. We obviously inherit certain perceptual propensities, and it also seems clear to me that we inherit certain mental traits that influence how we think about things.

So we can see at least some of the part heredity plays in who we are, but what part does our environment play. How much of who we are is shaped by that? Some people say that we are all just products of our environment. A book was written on the notion, "We are who we were when...." I'm sorry, I don't recall whose idea this was, but the idea is as follows: Our identity, that is, who we see ourselves as being, is a product of the world as it was in our formative years. Someone growing up in the depression has a different reality than someone growing up in the *roaring twenties*. Growing up in the 50's results in a different look at life than growing up in the 60's. Not only do we have a different attitude about long hair, but we approach life and our fellow men in a totally different way. They say that it is hard for people growing up in places like Harlem to break out, to see hope and prosperity in the world rather than crime and violence.

"You've got to understand, officer, he was neglected as a child, beaten, abandoned, unloved, taught no moral responsibility, etc...."

So which is more important? Heredity or Environment? What makes it most difficult to tease out the influences of the two is the fact that most of us were raised by our parents, thus the two influences overlap. To overcome this problem, researchers spent a lot of time studying adopted children, but the results of these studies are inconclusive at best.

Ok... so now we throw a monkey wrench into the works. Let's examine the child prodigy.

"He picked up a violin for the first time and just began to play it. It's as if he'd been playing for 40 years."

Genetic? None of the relatives can play an instrument. Environmental? No one at home plays. They don't even listen to music, and no one at day care plays. The only logical explanation is that he had played for many years ... before. Before what? Before this lifetime. In the last life he studied the violin. All his life he practiced. Yes... this implies reincarnation and a continuance of something from one lifetime to another... perhaps soul evolution. This new way of looking at things suggests that to some extent, we are who we are from the moment we are born, not from our genetics, but rather from some part of us that is beyond this body, this cellular makeup, or our experiences in this life. The implication is that who we are transcends this single life. Is it true? I really don't know. I do get the sense that my kids were very unique beings from the moment they were born. It seems to me beyond heredity, but there's no way to really be sure. One thing that is clear to me is that humans are very complex beings, and I believe it's useful to look at all the factors if one wants to get to the bottom of the question, "Who am I?"

There's a new age precept that each soul actually chooses his or her parents and the particular incarnation consciously in order to learn certain lessons here on earth, as if there were a sort of screening room somewhere in the spirit realm in which one could review potential situations:

"Hey Jashanananda, come check out this one," my friend says to me from the life selection room. "This couple wanting a second baby are both scientists and free thinkers."

"Hmmm. They seem to love each other," I say encouraged, "so it'll be a safe and nurturing environment. And they being Scientists I think they'll be supportive of me finding my own way."

"They don't have a religious background, though," my friend cautions, "so you'll have to search for that divine connection on your own."

"That could be good," I say. "That way I'd have no indoctrinated beliefs to let go of. I'll tell you, I've got a good feeling about this potential incarnation. I think that's the one!"

And so.... I was born. The place was Ann Arbor, Michigan and the date was September 11, 1949. This is what I'm told, and it's what's written on my birth certificate, although the little ink imprint of my two-inch foot, I do not recognize. I was born large (8 lbs 7 oz.) to a small Mother. I believe I was a bit reluctant to make my appearance. I sure didn't want to be the second Leo in the family, but now the time had come. I could put it off no longer and being a Virgo seemed safe enough.

A psychic channel (or the Entity she was channeling) told me I was a Native American medicine man, a Shaman, living in Canada in my last life. I really don't know about that, but in this life, I was to be a white, Anglo-Saxon born to a well-educated, middle class family of refined upbringing, born in the mid-west of America, in the middle of the 20th century, to middle of the road Republicans. Wow! What interesting karma. But, of course, I knew nothing about karma at the time, or at least I don't recall knowing.

There was nothing really extraordinary about my birth, although my Mother did say that I was very reluctant to come out. Her contractions started two weeks earlier, but I was in no hurry. I was, no doubt, afraid to take the plunge into that unknown world. I spoke with my mother recently when she was visiting, and another tidbit she mentioned was that I was supposed to be twin girls: Elizabeth and what was the other name? Hmmm, I don't recall. Something to think about, though, this twin girl thing!

My birth certificate says I was born at 7:59 A.M. I am definitely a morning person. I like to get up early so as to have time for my yoga practice and chanting. And being born in Ann Arbor seems appropriate. It's the only hippie town in the mid-west, a little piece of Berkeley right there near the Motor City. It was, perhaps, an omen of things to come.

I didn't know anything about astrology in 1949, nor did I for many years to come. The stars were there just the same. I read something recently that helped me see how the position of the planets at the time of my birth could actually have a physical effect on me. Apparently, the gravitational pull of the planets greatly influences the electromagnetic field that is generated by the sun, which in turn affects all of life on our planet. Whether this is the true explanation or not, I have found Astrology to be a very rich source of information about an individual.

Here's what I have discovered about myself from looking at the stars: When I was born, the Sun was in Virgo in my 12th house, this house representing my karma, the subconscious and my lesson in this life. Virgo being the ground, the earth, purity, and discrimination, and the Sun, being my source of life, my power and my self expression, my energy is focused on working through my karma (this life's tasks) by staying grounded and using my powers of discrimination to choose my experiences wisely and carefully.

My moon, the symbol of change, fluctuation and emotion, is placed in Taurus, the sign of the bull, which is slow, stubborn, stable, careful, reliable, and secure. Placed in the house of relationships (the 7th house), it indicates that I will be steady of emotion and loyal in marriage.

But what of my quest to find who I am? To find the true self? And what of the personality? How do others see me? One's rising sign helps shed light on these things. My rising sign is Libra, the mental sign of balance and harmony. I seek equilibrium, peace, harmony, and understanding and my path to self-actualization is through balance. I have three planets in Libra in the first house to strengthen its influence: Venus the goddess of beauty and love, Mercury, the great communicator, and Neptune my inspiration. Wow! I'm blown away just thinking about it. If I can't discover my true self with that configuration....

Neptune is a generational planet. It moves so slowly relative to our sky that it was in Libra from 1943 to 1957. This is the flower power generation: focused on peace and love, nonmaterialistic, and prone towards drugs. What this is to a generation is to me in heavy doses due to its prominent placement in my chart. Some say I'm stuck in the 60's. I was, am, and always will be a hippie (well perhaps not in 1949, but the potential was there).

There are other planets in my chart, of course: Saturn in Virgo in the eleventh house holding me back from making friends (manifesting as shyness in my younger years), Mars in Leo in the tenth house making me quite direct and assertive in the world, especially in my career, Jupiter by itself on the bottom of my chart in the fourth house in Capricorn. It is at home with my things, my bed, and the security of my blankets to protect me, where I am most expanded and creative.

The year was 1949, four years after the end of World War II. The U.S. was full of optimism and prosperity, and we were in the middle of the baby boom. The parents of this generation had been children during the depression, so, for them, security and having enough to eat were very important and not taken for granted.

"Clean up your plate. There are starving people in China." We were to hear these words as a sort of mantra as we were growing up.

This was the scientific era. No more breastfeeding. There was a more sterile, sanitary approach, the formula. The modern kitchen no longer had an icebox. An all-electric refrigerator was in many homes. There was central heat, radio programs like Amos and Andy, and lawns to mow in the newly forming suburbs. For guidance parents would read books like *Baby and Child Care* by Dr. Benjamin Spock (not the guy with pointed ears, the pediatrician). Spock was the first pediatrician to study psychoanalysis to try to understand children's needs and family dynamics, and he would tell a generation of parents to be more flexible and affectionate with their children, and to treat them as individuals. And so... into all of these circumstances, this individual was born... the odds a trillion to one.

Chapter 2

Out of Fear

"The bogeyman will get you if you don't watch out!"

This epitomizes my early childhood. I was scared, scared of everything, but mostly everything I didn't know about. Yes, the unknown was the scariest of all. I was talking with my father before he died and discovered that he was the same way. He had Alzheimer's and re-experienced a lot of those old fears as the disease progressed. My father was extremely bright: 220 IQ or something like that. I was never diagnosed with anywhere near that level of intelligence, but I believe that I, like my father, was very aware of my environment, perhaps aware of too much too soon. I couldn't handle it, and so I was fearful. I can see this same thing with my own kids as they were growing up. At a certain age (let's say two years old) Aaron, my oldest, had no fear of the slide at the local playground. He loved it. He would climb fearlessly up the ladder, get to the top, and without hesitation, come sliding down to my out-stretched arms.

"Weeeee."

The next year it was a completely different story. He took one look at that slide and became petrified. No way he was going down that thing.

We, his parents, encouraged him. "Come on Aaron. You can do it! You loved it last year!"

It was hard for us to accept his newfound fear, and so we coaxed him up the ladder. Slowly and methodically he put one reluctant foot after the other on the rungs. It was a tall slide, and there were lots of kids on the playground that day, and many were lining up at the ladder. As he crept up rung after rung, kids started climbing up behind him. By the time he had gotten to the top, there were kids all the way down the ladder and onto the playground. And then that moment came, the moment of reckoning. He looked down that long slide and freaked out! He froze in his tracks, just stood there. The other kids started yelling. We yelled up to him too.

"Come on, Aaron! Just slide on down."

It was no use. He was not going to do it. And so he turned and climbed back down the way he had come, squeezing by all the kids standing on the ladder behind him and then down past the long line of kids on the playground. What embarrassment. I don't know if he felt it, but I sure did! That had to be equal in embarrassment to a fraternity prank played on me in College, which left me with only a hand towel, a flight of stairs lined with people waiting for dinner, and a cold walk across campus to my clothes. It's funny how looking back on that memory, I feel as though it happened to someone else. It's somehow, no longer real.

Aaron probably doesn't even remember the incident on the slide, but I'm left wondering what changed for him from age two to age three? Why was he all of a sudden afraid? My thought is that the key to unlocking this mystery is found in awareness. He suddenly became aware of the danger. The height and the fall.

"Holy cow! A guy could get killed up here!"

They say that no man can look at God and live. The vision is too bright, the awareness too intense. A person would be scared to death. One's nerves would fry, like getting hit with 10,000 volts of electricity. Some of us were born with fewer filters than others. As a result, the awareness is greater, and so is the fear. It's funny that I'm saying this, because I now feel like I've become very insensitive, especially to messages from my body. There are so many things I don't even notice. For example, how do I feel right now? Am I hungry? Thirsty? Tired? Happy? Sad? Does that food upset me? Am I sensitive to garlic? Chocolate? Coffee? Sugar? Chemicals? What is my liver saying to me right now? My kidneys? Does it help to take vitamin supplements? My second wife, Chantal, who is French always knows what her liver is doing, while I can never even remember which side it's on.

But let me get back to my childhood fear. Perhaps it wasn't an awareness issue that caused the trepidation. Maybe, I was afraid all the time because I wasn't held, wasn't loved, wasn't comforted as much as I wanted to be. My mother was not a hugger, at least this was the story I told myself for a lot of my life. But the truth is that when I was eight or so I rejected her affection. I distinctly remember burying my head under the covers when she tried to kiss me goodnight. I couldn't handle the feelings it stirred in me. From that point on she became a sort of cheerleader. She would come into my room every morning, pull open the curtains, turn to me and ask, "What gay mad thing are you going to do today?" I'd usually just groan and bury myself under the covers, but I never forgot what she said.

In my early childhood my main occupation was holding on to my mother's skirts. You can see it in the pictures and hear it told by everyone in the family. As my mother went about her housework, there I was holding on for dear life, and if a stranger came to visit I hid in those same skirts. It was a haven. Years later, I stopped clinging to skirts. Instead, I started chasing them (girls who wore them, anyway). I still love skirts. I no longer chase them, now I wear them. It happened at a music festival. I was divorced and on my own at the festival and was standing in front of one of the clothing booths admiring a beautiful skirt.

"Hmm. That's so beautiful. I'd like to buy it, but who could I give it to?" I had no one in my life at the time.

Then I had an impulse. "I'll buy it for myself," I said and so I did.

When I started wearing the skirt, it caused quite a stir, I can tell you! Hmmm... that twin girl thing coming back? It seems I always had latent tendencies.

When I was four, so the story goes, my mother wanted to get back to work, and she thought it would be good for me to get out from under her skirts, so she took me to preschool. I was petrified. I screamed bloody murder and thought I would die! She left me anyway, and I settled down, more or less, but continued the show of terror for weeks. I had been abandoned out in the scary world, traumatized for life, or at least for a lot of it.

Okay! So now I've gone full circle and back to the environmental theory of who I am. The sensitivity/awareness theory was hereditary. The "my mom abandoned me at day care" theory is environmental. What is the karmic perspective? Looking at my Astrology chart, I notice that my moon's north node is in Aries in the seventh house. This means my "path" to freedom in this lifetime is through strengthening and asserting *self*, whereas in the past (South node in Libra in the first house), my identity was defined by others. Hmmm... asserting myself. That's the real scary part, where I have to stand alone and be seen in the big scary world.

So what's that bogeyman I was so scared of as a child? Well, I think, for me the bogeyman epitomized the fear of something lurking out there, something threatening my very existence: The dark, the unknown, the unpredictable. It's funny how children cope with these things. They must have a zone of safety to deal with the fear. For me it was my bed covers. (From mother's skirt to bed covers. It all makes sense now!) Yes, you see, I knew that if I could just get under the covers in my bed, I would be safe, neck down like a turtle in his shell. My head could be out. That was okay. My head had eyes to keep it safe, I guess. The trick for getting into bed at night was to get from the bedroom door where the light switch was to the bed and under the covers before some hideous monster could get me.

"Okay. Here goes. Flip off the switch and dive for it. Quick, pull up those covers. Ah, safe. The protective shield is in place."

Thank God I never had my covers get untucked from the bottom. I would have been devastated.

There was one time, however, when the covers almost didn't hold. It was early one Saturday morning when I was around eight years old. I was still sleeping, or at least close to it, when I heard a loud clanking sound outside my bedroom window.

"Clank, clank, thump, thump", followed by the most horrendous noise I'd ever heard, "Squeeeeeeek, squeeeeeeeek, Yeaaaarrp,

Yeaaaarp." The sound was actually an indescribably high-pitched whining.

My heart began to pound. My eyes were popping out of my head. The source of the sound was so close and so loud. All I could think was that "they" were coming for me! At the time I didn't know about U.F.O. abductions. If I had, there wouldn't have been much doubt in my mind about what was happening. At that very moment, the little men would be cutting through the glass, lifting me out of my bed, covers or not, and sweeping me off into the waiting saucer. Probing relentlessly, their hideous faces staring down upon my body. Well, it's certainly a good thing I didn't know about such things back then. That would have been more than I could bear.

But still, what was this sound? I wasn't dreaming. I was awake! It was real, whatever it was, and the desire to know was stronger than the fear, so I mustered up all the courage I had and left the safety of my covers. I didn't dare face whatever it was directly, so I decided on a safer course, to sneak around behind it. Ever so slowly I opened the bedroom door. I saw nothing, but I knew I'd have to head down the hall, across the living room, into the glass walled family room and outside the back door to really see what was making the sound. I didn't know how far I would get, but I had to try. Slowly I inched my way down the long hallway, past the first bathroom, past the second bathroom. As I arrived at the living room, I heard a door squeak open. I looked across the living room, through the glass walled family room, to the back door. The door was just closing, and there passing through the doorway was a ... well... a... a yellow thing... a creature, a yellow headed, yellow bodied, large sort of being.

"Oh my God. I've seen it!" I looked in utter disbelieve and total panic, and then... I had never run down that hall so fast. Like the Cowardly lion in the Wizard of Oz running from the great and powerful man behind the curtain, I ran down that hall, turned into my room and dived for the bed, the covers and safety.

"Whew."

All was quiet for a few long seconds, but my mind was racing. "What'll I do?"

And then... there it was again! "Squeeeeeeek, squeeeeeeeek, Yeaaaarrp, Yeaaaarp."

The shear panic, I hope you can imagine. Several minutes passed. The sound continued and my heart was nearly jumping out of my throat, but I knew I had to do an incredibly brave thing. I had no choice now but to face it head on. I could no longer stand the torment. And so I forced myself to rise up in that bed, turn towards the curtains, and with every ounce of internal strength I had, slowly, gently, almost imperceptibly crack the curtains a subatomic-particle's distance apart. I peeled back that curtain like a chromosome in the cell of an amoeba in the process of splitting. Would I survive it, or would I be dissolved by what I was about to see like Lot's wife looking back at what God had forbidden. At my moment of reckoning there before me was..............

MY BROTHER. That's right, it was just my brother there on a ladder, with his yellow rubber raincoat and hood, and he was simply washing my windows.

Fear's a funny thing. It's certainly a powerful motivator. The things we're most afraid of are the things we don't understand, the things we can't make sense of. I guess it's a deep routed genetic response. That which is unknown is dangerous. When we come to know it, we can predict its movements and can protect ourselves against its dangers. Fear gets the old adrenaline going. Flight or fight response they call it. We have a whole system called the autonomic nervous system just for this purpose, and a mind that is hell-bent on demystifying everything. And so we spend all of our childhood getting to know the world and the things in it so we can better anticipate its movements, making us better able to cope with and to adapt to what life throws at us.

The irony is that the same knowledge that helps us be prepared for life also makes us go to sleep in a way, to become unconscious of our world and its mysteries. My mind's naming and classifying of experience is the very thing that stops me from seeing things as they really are. Instead of really seeing, I end up dismissing much of what's before me. One glance and I say, "Oh yes, I know that." And then give it no more thought. I miss so much this way. I miss the magic, the absolute unpredictability... the total freedom of each moment, each person, and each situation.

"I'm sorry, did you say something? I wasn't paying attention. You see, I already know who you are, I know what you're going to do next, and even what you are thinking. I also know that's a chair over there, and out there is a tree. I know that sound is from a car passing by in the rain, that the other sound is that of raindrops hitting the window, and that there are people talking in the next room. I know that it will begin to get dark in about three hours, and that winter will last another couple of months."

But... when I really pay attention, I see that there are so many things I don't know, have no idea about in fact. I certainly had no idea that, years later, I'd marry a French woman from Algeria, and would live in Africa and then Costa Rica. I would never have guessed that the Berlin wall would crumble, and in fact I wouldn't even know whom I'd end up meeting on the street later that very day. If I lift the blinders of expectation and knowing from my perception, what else will I see? What will I hear? Will God speak to me? Will the Red Sea part? Will I suddenly find myself hurling through space at a thousand miles an hour? How exciting! How frightening!

So is this the choice? FEAR or SLEEP? Perhaps this feeling in the pit of my stomach is what keeps me alive. Maybe this longing, this fear, this anxiety is just God speaking to me. And what do I do with it? It seems I spend a lot of time just trying to plug it up, hide from it and dismiss it with my preconceived notions.

Chapter 3

The Watcher

Back in 1962, I was a watcher. It was a way to deal with the all-pervasive fear I had of everything around me. Even after my father took a job at Ohio State and we moved from Ann Arbor to Columbus, Ohio, my family still spent summers at our cottage in Michigan high upon a bluff overlooking the lake with the same name. It was there that I sat for hours just observing the life around me in that beautiful place. I thought that if I watched long enough, I would figure out what this crazy world was in which I was living and how the whole thing called life worked. There were bluffs, woods, meadows, a beach, lots of secret places and, most of all, insects. Instead of allowing these six-legged creatures to get the best of me... scared to go outside, scared to be inside, always scared of what might get me... instead of that, I began to explore this wild world. For hours and hours, I would loose myself in the mystery and wonder of nature's diverse ways. I sat and watched beetles navigate through the tall grass and caterpillars weave their cocoons. I marveled at the way dragonflies darted around, and how leafhoppers blended in so well with their environment.

At some point my brother got involved, and we started collecting insects. We had special glass cases (called Riker Mounts) for displaying the insects we caught and, of course, we had to kill the insects before mounting them. We did this by taking a jar and suspending a screen above a wad of cotton. This wad of cotton was doused with a good "healthy" dose of Carbon Tetrachloride (well, perhaps "healthy" is a poor choice of words here. There was nothing healthy about it). When we placed our specimen in the jar, it squirmed for a few seconds, but very soon became still. I don't recall my feelings about this, watching our insects die, but I do remember my awe of the life process. I also remember the joy I felt running through the fields with my brother with our nets catching Monarchs and Swallowtails, Green Darners, Katydids. There seemed to be no end to the variety. We found black Scarab beetles, gold plated Rhinoceros beetles, giant walking sticks and Cicadas who spent over twenty years underground only to rise up into my net and into my jar. I will never forget the amazing moths: the Polyphemus whose wings had big painted eyes, the Cecropia with its Arabian rug pattern and six-inch wing span, and the one and only Luna moth, the velvet green beauty that's only seen on a full-moon night in June. I've only seen the Luna moth twice in my life, once as a kid and another time much later when I was on an L.S.D. trip in the woods. I'll tell more about that later. My mother gave me the name of a book a while back when I was reminiscing with her about this green beauty. This was a book that her father had given her when she was a child and was called "The Girl of the Limberlost". The Luna moth played a key role. I'm going to try and search for a copy of the book (footnote: I just downloaded the Kindle edition of the book from Amazon for free! Amazing, after all these years, now I get to read it!)

The collecting of insects was a wondrous pursuit. Looking back on it, though, I don't know how I killed all those insects. I have tried to balance this Karma in my adult years by helping insects any time I have the opportunity. I help them across the street, remove them kindly from the house, and take them off sidewalks and onto bushes. I certainly could not kill them now... well except mosquitoes. With them it's "kill or be killed!"

When I lived in Louisiana a few years back, I used to capture the giant Palmetto bug (actually a three inch long cockroach, but it sounds better to call him a Palmetto bug). For some reason they liked to walk around on the ceiling and then drop down at the most inauspicious times. I would climb up on a well-placed chair and grab hold of this monstrous bug. Sometimes he would squeeze through my fingers and get away. More often, I would get hold of him, run for the door, open it (which was sometimes tricky with the bug clasped in my hands), and toss him out. I don't think this really did any good, though. He was so fast that he must have run back into the house even before I could get the door closed again. It's only a theory, because I never saw him do it. All I really know is that only a few minutes later there he'd be again on that ceiling. Here in Costa Rica where I now live, those same bugs are four to five inches long, so big I could almost hitch a saddle on them and go for a ride!

My Virgo disposition for collecting and categorizing prompted me to collect many other things in addition to insects, things that didn't need Carbon Tetrachloride. This included bottle caps (many of which we found on the dead end road by our Michigan cottage), stamps, coins (until I got hard up for money and spent them all), and even cereal box tops. My box top collection was fascinating because I could watch the trends in box sizes and keep track of price fluctuations. What I noticed during that time was that cereal boxes kept getting taller and skinnier, taller and skinnier over the years, until one day some marketing guy said, "Enough is enough," and introduced the new "space-saving" box (shorter and fatter, shorter and fatter), and slowly more and more brands came on board. Prices, of course always seemed to go up. The other wonderful thing about the box top collection was that if they ever had an offer on the back of the box like this: "Send $1.00 and 10,000 box tops to FREE CORVETTE OFFER," I'd have a head start and would certainly be the first on my block to get it. Who knew they'd stop using the box top and go with the UPC label for those special offers? There were no UPC labels back in those days of course. The scanner was a thing of the future.

It seems to me that all of these pursuits were about organizing chaos. If I could collect, organize and classify the stuff of the world, I would have some kind of control over it. There was also the endless pursuit of trying to make sense of things. Here's a very early

19

memory to illustrate this. My older brother played the piano and I distinctly remember trying to figure out how he knew where to put his hands. From where I stood, I looked up at all those white keys hanging over the keyboard (yes, I said looked up!) and could see no pattern, no labels, no clues at all. Try it yourself. Make yourself shorter than the piano keyboard, look up and see what you see. The truth is that sharps and flats exist only in another dimension, and in those days, and for many years to come, I only believed what I saw.

My brother Laird was four years older than I was and a Leo. The name "Laird" means lord, and the name definitely fit him. He was certainly the leader of our gang of two, and being so much younger than him, I deferred to him in most things. It was sometimes tough growing up in his shadow. Laird was an athlete, and he had a grade point average of 4.0 in school. I was no match for him in either capacity, and was often unfavorably compared to him, especially by my teachers.

But despite all of this, being the baby in the family had its advantages. For one thing, there was a lot less pressure on me, because there were fewer expectations, and I had a lot more room to be irresponsible. If Laird let his grades slip a little he would hear about it, but I could get mediocre grades, and it was accepted. While my brother was always struggling to get my Dad's respect, I could simply get along with him because I didn't have as much to prove.

I could get beat up by my brother, though, and that was not such a fun thing. I distinctly remember teasing Laird while he was playing baseball one time. I think I was hanging around and maybe threw some dirt where I shouldn't have. My brother came running out to where I was, pick me up by my feet and hung me upside down. Then dropped me on my head. I'm sure I went home crying. I don't know what happened to him for that. I guess it was hard for Laird to have a tag-along, snot nosed kid brother. Well, being the snot nosed kid brother wasn't all that great either, especially for my self-esteem.

There were times, though, when my brother and I were pals. This mainly happened in Michigan where there weren't any other kids around to be pals with. Laird's favorite game was something I think he invented called "Stairs Baseball". We played endless games of it. You see, my brother loved baseball. He loved to play the game, he loved to watch it and he loved to read about it. When he watched baseball on TV, he would watch two games at a time (flipping back and forth between channels) while he had another game going on the radio. His favorite team was the Detroit Tigers and he has remained a loyal fan throughout his life. I always thought the sport was boring. What I saw was just a bunch of men standing around chewing tobacco waiting for something to happen. I guess Laird dealt with the slow pace of the game by having three games going at once.

But even though I wasn't much into baseball, I enjoyed Stairs Baseball. Laird had a way of making it interesting and fun. In the game, there was only a pitcher and a batter so it was perfectly suited for two people. We used a tennis ball, and the batter's box was just at the bottom of the stairs that led to our porch above the garage. That way, when the ball was thrown, it would bounce off the stairs and back to the pitcher so no catcher was needed. What made it fun was that my brother was very creative with the game. Through his example, we made up rosters for each of our teams and the eighteen players each had a name, a personality and a batting style. We had left-handed and right-handed batters. Some guys held the bat high in the air and stood straight up at the plate. Others pulled the bat way back and hunched over. All the players had different mannerisms. We had sluggers and bunters, guys that pulled the ball and guys who often hit foul balls or struck out, and of course when the pitcher came to bat, he could never bat very well (which was historically accurate). Because of my brother's fascination with the sport and all the games we played of Stairs Baseball, I ended up learning quite a bit about how the game is played.

When we weren't playing baseball or chasing butterflies around the cottage, we would be at the beach. My dad built a set of stairs running down to the beach from the house, one hundred steep steps down the one hundred foot bluff to the sand. After the stairs were built, my brother and I could go to the beach by ourselves, and so we spent a lot more time there. There were days in our long summer vacations when we would be down at that beautiful sandy shore most of the day. We'd swim, make elaborate sand castles with motes and draw bridges, and spent hours building mighty dams for the little spring that seeped out of the bank and down to the great lake. Both the sand castle and dam building activities were great lessons in let-go as our great efforts to stop *Mother Nature* were always futile in the end.

One time the great Mother did more than just destroy our sand castles. One time she had us running for our lives. It was mid-afternoon one August day. Laird and I were down on the beach building one of our grand sand castles when Laird happened to look out toward the horizon.

"Do you see that thing out there?" he asked me pointing with his finger.

I strained to look where he was pointing, and I did see something, but couldn't tell what it was. After a few minutes we both noticed that whatever it was, it was getting bigger.

"I think it's a water spout," Laird said.

Just then we heard shouting. It was our mother standing at the top of the bluff yelling and pointing, "You better get up here, you two!"

We took one more look at the approaching twister before beginning our hundred-step climb to the top of the bluff. That waterspout was definitely getting closer and bigger. I was the first on the steps, but my brother was right behind me.

"Run... run," he shouted as he breathed down my neck.

I could feel the wind and the spray on my back and my heart pounding.

"It's getting closer, Bryan, run as fast as you can," yelled Laird with panic in his voice.

"Come on," my mother yelled from above.

I could see terror in her eyes as I ran. My lungs began to burn and my legs got heavy, but I kept running. Water began pelting my back, and the wind howled in my ears, but I never stopped to look back, just kept running, finally to the top. Then we all dashed for the house, threw ourselves in, and pulled shut the door. Just then the twister lifted up out of the water and disappeared into the sky. We later heard on the radio that it had gathered strength again and had become a major tornado, doing damage as far south as Lansing some 200 miles from us. I guess the updraft saved us. But, to this day, I still wish I had looked back... just once.

We never saw another twister and soon went back to our habit of heading *down* to the beach when the winds began to blow. You see, Lake Michigan was big enough that when the wind picked up, we could ride the waves. The whole family went. I loved the feeling of jumping into the wave, having it grab me and send me zooming to shore. The best time for waves was during storms, so when the skies were ominous and the rain began to fall, we'd grab our Styrofoam boards, race down those steps and throw ourselves into the cool water. After a couple hours of exhilaration, my mother would see my trembling body, chattering teeth and blue lips and decide it was time for everyone to get out. Then we'd drag ourselves up the long steps to the house and gather in the living room in front of the fireplace where my dad would make a perfect fire. On really special occasions we'd have hot cider, and then Dad would switch on the hi-fi and put on a record from his collection. Dad loved all kinds of music, but one of his favorites was Harry Belafonte.

Eventually and inevitably summer would come to an end, and we had to return home to Ohio. Soon my parents were back at work, and when not in school, Laird went back to playing with friends his own age, and I went back to being solitary. Yes, in grade school, I was a definite loner, and being that way I had some strange ideas. Let's face it, I was a strange kid. For one thing, I ate grass. I would go home for lunch (even though my parents weren't there), because I couldn't bear to be in the cafeteria at school. I had no friends. I would have to sit by myself and then I'd be picked on. So, instead, I chose to walk home. It was only about three blocks. I must have taken my lunch and then just brought it home. Maybe I ate in the backyard. I really don't remember. I also don't remember what I did at recess. I must have coped with that somehow. Well, anyway this one day, I must have forgotten my lunch. I got home and tried to get in the house, but it was locked.

I thought to myself, "I'll starve if I don't eat something." And so I tried eating grass.

I pulled up a small clump and put it in my mouth. I chewed and chewed and chewed.

"Cows and Horses eat this stuff," I reasoned, but it was no use. I couldn't swallow it. I searched my Mom's garden.

"Chives! They're eatable." As I munched on a handful of these spicy plants, I felt a relief. I wouldn't starve to death that day.

I wonder why I had no friends. I was too shy, I guess, or just too vulnerable, or maybe it was my breath from eating those chives! I never thought of that. Of course I had just moved from Michigan, so I was different. I can see now that I didn't really do anything to facilitate friendships. I didn't really try to fit in. I don't think I had any idea how to do that.

I remember one time in the playground, there was this nerd (another nerd, not me) who was getting severely picked on because he buttoned the top button of his shirt. Oh, God. The ultimate sin! As I watched this happen, I felt really bad for this kid. What did I do? I buttoned my top button and walked right up to the guys who were doing the harassing. It was solidarity at age ten. Power to the buttoned-up people.

This reminds me of the Dr. Seuss story about the two kinds of Sneetches. There were plain-bellied Sneetches and Sneetches with stars upon "thar's" (their bellies that is). The ones with the stars were putting down the ones without. Finally the ones without decided to take matters into their own hands. They were tired of getting picked on, and so they got paintbrushes and started painting stars on their bellies. The first group got really upset.

"How dare you paint stars on your bellies, you impostors!"

So they invented a machine that would remove stars, and they all had their stars taken off. That way they'd still know which Sneetches were which. Well then... the Sneetches who originally had no stars, began taking their newly painted stars off and then the ones who originally had stars put them back on, and so it went.

On again, off again, until all distinctions were totally blurred. Unfortunately, in my case, I was the only one to go for the new top-button trend. Just two nerds instead of one.

I did some kinky things when I was in sixth grade, too. Perhaps it was because I was a loner and a bit of an outcast, or maybe it was a way to express my budding interest in sex. When no one was around, I used to go into my mother's closet and put on her bras and dresses. I never got caught doing this, or at least my mother never confronted me about it. I would have been mortified if I'd been caught. Why did I do it? I guess I needed the excitement and dressing up like that gave me a bit of a naughty thrill. I wouldn't even consider stealing or shoplifting, defacing property or other destructive acts. My thrill seeking didn't have anger in it.

The other kinky thing I'd do was to run around outside naked. This was really a thrill. I'd take all my clothes off and sneak out of my bedroom window at night. Then I'd run through the yard, across the neighbor's backyard, and down to the streetlight at the corner. It was the middle of the night so the light was always flashing.

"A car's coming! Quick into the bushes," I'd say to myself, adrenaline pumping hard.

I never got caught in this one either. Thinking back on it, what would have happened if I had been caught? Years of therapy? No. I don't think so. It wasn't really done that much then. Not for kids. That came later. But, even without therapy, being caught would have been very embarrassing, that's for sure! I still wonder what motivated me to do these things. I can't blame it on TV sex and violence like I can for my kids behavior. I can still get in touch with the feeling of excitement it gave me to run around naked like that, though. Actually the phenomenon became quite popular on college campuses in the 70's. It was called "streaking".

Ok, so you've heard all my deep dark secrets, things I never told anyone... and I feel better. They're not nearly so dark and perverted now that I shared them. Thanks so much for listening.

Chapter 4

Towards a Sense of Belonging

One of my friends during sixth grade was a guy named Mike. He was a poorly dressed, tall, skinny, scrappy, ill tempered, boastful.... Come to think of it, why was I friends with this guy? All I can say is that in sixth grade I took what I could get as far as friends go, and for some reason Mike was it. One of main things we did together was play football along with some other guys, and inevitably Mike would loose his temper and fists would start flying. It was definitely a stormy friendship! One day, he passed me a note in school with a drawing of a guy with a protruding rear end. It was labeled "Blackbutt" and was suppose to be a portrait of me, I guess (my last name was Blackwell). I sent it back with an equally graphic sketch of his rear end and labeled it "Flatbutt" (remember he was tall and skinny). Well, wouldn't you know, I got caught trying to pass the note back to him. The teacher seized it and then made me take the note home for a parent's signature. Someone teased me as I was walking home that afternoon and stole the note. I'm not sure what happened then. I either got it back or drew another one. I can tell you one thing for sure, my parents never saw the note. I was convinced that I would've been killed or worse (mortified) if what I thought were my prim and proper parents saw my dirty butt pictures. I'm sure I forged their signatures, but it's funny about memory. It seems to change over time, changing perspective as my overall awareness increases. What really happened, I guess I'll never know.

There is one memory of Mike that was a happy one, and I remember it distinctly. His family may have been poor, but his dad ran a drive-in movie theater one summer, and Mike invited me one time. I'll never forget it. I saw "How the West Was Won", an epic saga with Debbie Reynolds. That was the clincher. I took one look at Debbie on the big screen, and I fell hopelessly in love. God! I can still feel that crushing feeling in the center of my chest and that longing to be the one she was kissing. Well... this certainly was not the last time I had such feelings. There were many crushes ahead for this pure virgin Virgo with Venus in Libra in the first house, but the rush of feelings that night in front of the big screen was the first.

***

Somehow, I survived my early childhood, but seventh grade didn't find me any better adjusted. In fact, I had only one friend in seventh grade and he was in France for the year. Just my luck, I guess. Luck? Did I use that word? I hear a voice of protest at the idea of luck. "No such thing", my mind declares. You see, I was brought up in a family where science was the religion and I was taught that this physical world and the laws that govern it were the only reality. In that reality, everything had a cause that could be determined with enough investigation. In other words, there was always a logical explanation for everything.

Our family bibles were the dictionary and the encyclopedia and many dinnertime discussions ended in the consultation of one of them. Our debates always had something to do with truth and reality, and the worldview that was espoused was objective and scientific. As the story goes, we are mammals evolved from apes. We are born, we live and then we die. How do we deal with this fact? Well, it's up to us to do something meaningful while we are alive to create a legacy for those that follow. To make a contribution to human kind was life's purpose. In our family view, people who believed in God, divine providence or even luck were merely superstitious. Although they certainly were not communists, my parents would probably have agreed with Karl Marx when he said that religion was just the opiate of the masses.

Now days, my perspective is a bit different. Now I would more likely say: "Everything has divine purpose and is the balance of karma." In this view what comes into one's life is just what he has chosen for himself to learn the next great lesson.

This of course is a belief just like the belief that Jesus died for our sins or that everything follows the laws of science. With my atheistic background, you might ask where I got the belief that there is a divine conspiracy for my benefit? As you will discover as my story unfolds, this change in perspective was a result of my personal experiences and my studies in Eastern philosophy in my early 20's. I don't really know that there's a divine purpose to everything, of course. I took this on as an external belief, but I must say that seeing things this way has made it easier to deal with the ups and downs of life.

So what do I really know about the world and my place in it? I close my eyes and sit. I allow my thoughts to wander over this crazy life and all that has happened in it to this point, and I wonder, "My God! Did I create the whole damn thing out of my unconsciousness?" It seems like the whole mess was just one big blunder lived by a sleepwalker tumbling down the stairs of life. Some stairs were padded. Some were not. Either way, it seems like I was just a victim of gravity.

"Wake up! And take a step in a chosen direction for a change!" I hear someone shout from deep inside me.

"Where will it lead?" says another voice. The one I call *me* most often.

"Wherever you want to go," the first voice retorts.

"And where is that?" asks *me*.

No answer... and with the perspective in mind that perhaps I created this whole situation, I'll continue on with my story, and maybe, just maybe, in the telling of it, I'll see the point of it, once and for all.

But, in seventh grade I wasn't a philosopher. I was much more pragmatic. I didn't feel the hand of destiny. I just thought that there was something wrong with me. I wasn't really conscious of this belief, but I was very busy trying to cope with it. Despite my negative self-image, I was considered reasonably smart in junior high and so I was placed in an advanced group at school. I took all of my classes in seventh grade with this group. It's funny, you'd think there'd be some nice kids in this class, but it wasn't to be. At least no one was nice to me. Thinking back on this, I wonder what it was about me that brought about this reaction in my classmates. My family certainly wasn't the richest one in the upper middle class suburban environment where we lived, and so I was teased for the clothes I wore. I guess I dressed like a nerd, and I appeared vulnerable. I did have a reprieve though, a secret life, a place where life was grand.

Somehow my parents must have sensed my unpopularity with my classmates, and so they enrolled me in a ballroom dance class that none of my classmates attended. It was called Cotillion, and it was run by a woman named Mrs. Potts. There was one other kid from my school who went to this dance school, but he wasn't from my class. Ned Millington the Third was his name and he lived in my neighborhood. Ned and I became some form of friends, although at times he was an obnoxious, spoiled brat. He didn't have parents for some reason, so he was raised by his aunt, Mrs. Maxwell. Come to think of it she must not have really been his aunt. She was really old and crotchety. I suppose maybe she was his great aunt. All I can remember about her was her big black car and her stern looking face framed in gray hair peering over the steering wheel. You see, she drove us to the dance school some of the time. It was during these trips to Cotillion that I discovered that Ned's great aunt was quite a bigot. I remember her complaining about Jews that had come into the neighborhood. She was horrified. God knows what she would have thought about Blacks or Atheists. I never let on that I was a non-believer and the issue of Blacks never came up. You see there were no Blacks in our neighborhood. Not a single one. For years I would find this racial group somewhat foreign as a result. I'd always stood up for them intellectually, declaring their rights and what not, but I was afraid of them. Years later, that would all change when I lived, worked and traveled in sub-Saharan Africa.

I said that my parents only believed in science, but that's not entirely true. There was one strong belief that was beyond the reach of science that was also highly valued in the family. It was something that was never really spoken about, but never the less permeated the atmosphere of my childhood. That transcendent conviction was that of the power and importance of love. This was demonstrated most strongly in the personal love between my mother and father. The two of them were devoted to each other and inseparable, spending nearly every waking and sleeping moment together. They worked together and they played together, often to the exclusion of the rest of the world. In fact they had almost no outside friends. Even I felt excluded from the love of this powerful twosome and, as spiritual teacher Leonard Jacobson would suggest years later, due to the fact that my parents were not really present for me, I developed substitute needs. In my case, it was an obsession with girls. I wanted the love I saw my parents living, and I was constantly yearning for it. This tendency was reinforced by the culture of the early sixties, typified by the movies of people like Walt Disney and Doris Day. There was always a happy-ever-after ending in those movies that idealized romantic love, and this view remained in the background of my psyche for many years to come.

But back in 1963, although I yearned for their company, I was still really afraid of girls, and so when my parents told me they enrolled me in dance classes, I was petrified. I'll never forget the evening of that first night of Cotillion. I screamed bloody murder to my parents.

"Oh, God! Don't make me go! I'll just die. I can't do it. I'm going to hate it! If you make me go, I'll have a heart attack!"

I didn't want to go, in case you couldn't tell. I was really scared. There would be girls there for God's sake! It was a fate worse than death (even thought it was what I secretly longed for). I remember so vividly the experience of being dropped off there with Ned, and I can even imagine holding onto the car door, my parents prying my fingers off, and them dragging me in there kicking and screaming. I don't think I really did that, but it was certainly how I felt. As I said before, there were hardly any kids from my school there.

"They all come from the Catholic School," Ned informed me as we walked into the building.

And then, there they were, all the Catholic girls standing along one wall in party dresses and white gloves. Ned and I were directed to stand along the other wall with the rest of the boys. Mrs. Potts was quite a character. She was a stuffy old lady who thrived on formality. The boys were all dressed in coats and ties and the girls had formal dresses and white gloves, as I mentioned.

Mrs. Potts stepped forward, held herself in a dignified way and addressed us.

"Ok, boys. Each of you is to select a partner and offer your arm to her. Girls you are to take his arm and then together form a line for the introductions."

It was the moment of reckoning. We couldn't go into the dance hall until we had selected a partner... a girl!

"God. I can't do this!" I screamed inside.

But Ned was a bit more sure of himself than I was, and when he moved ahead this gave me courage. He picked a girl, and so I picked her friend. We had to introduce ourselves and then offer our arms for escorting. I moved forward, made the required introduction and offered my arm. The girl took it. God! I didn't die! I thought for sure I would, but I didn't. In fact, she accepted my approach and now we were walking together! The whole experience was like being in a dream. Was it really happening to me?

After choosing my partner, I was required to present her to Mrs. Potts with a formal introduction before entering the dance floor. As we lined up to do this, my throat became dry. I was sure my voice was lost down some deep cavity, never to be found. Would I make a fool of myself? Would I say something stupid? Would I be able to say the girl's name? Once again, I was gripped in fear... the worst kind of fright, that of social embarrassment.

"Good evening Mrs. Potts, may I present ..." and then I looked down at the girl's name tag pinned delicately onto her dress, and suddenly this wave of horror overtook me. Her first name was Mary Lou, which was okay, but her last name was spelled Z-S-C-H-A-C-H.

"Good evening Mrs. Potts, may I present Mary Lou ah.. ah...." I muttered something under my breath and we were in. Mary Lou smiled at me and told me how it was supposed to be pronounced; "Jauch", like "Frère Jacques" in the French nursery rhyme. Her smile somehow made it all right. When I finally got a good look at her, I realized Mary Lou was very pretty, and she turned out to be very sweet. God, I'm getting goose bumps even now thinking about her. I can still feel her small hand in mine in those soft white gloves and the smell of her perfume. And, amazingly enough, she seemed to like me. This was a start of a beautiful romance.

After that night, I looked forward every week to our being together, and Mary Lou's dance card always had my name on every dance. Now, this was actually against the rules. You were supposed to mix, and there was this really weird, nerdy looking high school kid who worked for Mrs. Potts, had a creepy low voice, wore a foam rubber bow tie, and made a habit of walking around the dance floor harassing people, Mary Lou and me especially, telling us we had to switch partners! Well, I'd switch with Ned for a minute or two and then go right back to Mary Lou when the guy turned his back. It was hopeless trying to separate us. We were lost in each other.

Incidentally, a few years later I took a summer job as a landscape maintenance man. Another guy and I were being driven to our first job by a tall man with a really low voice.

"There's something very familiar about this guy", I thought to myself as I studied his face in the rearview mirror. Then I suddenly realized it was he, the guy from Cotillion. When I asked him about it, he opened up his glove box and there was that foam rubber tie. As for the low voice, it turned out he was the son of an undertaker!

I didn't dare tell my parents I loved Cotillion, since I'd put up such a fuss and didn't want to hear the words, "I told you so". I suppose they knew, though. My pretended protest every week must have seemed a bit thin. I carried Mary Lou's picture for years after that, and although she didn't return to Cotillion the next year, went to Catholic schools through high school and I never saw her again, I called her once years later. She had become a cheerleader and was popular. Our time had passed, but I'll never forget Mary Lou, my first love.

***

In ninth grade, things started to turn around for me. For the past two years of school, I had been stuck in the same class with the same kids, but in ninth grade, I had classes with other kids. I sat next to a cool looking but not terribly bright girl in study hall who called me Brain instead of Brian (which was still a misspelling of my real name). I remember one time she stole my pen and put it in the top pocket of her blouse. Then she dared me to reach in and get it. I couldn't even consider reaching in there, but boy I sure wanted to. What a tease she was. Her last name must have started with a "B". That's the only reason I can think of why we would be sitting next to each other. These were little things, but little things do lead to bigger things, and that was certainly true for me.

Chapter 5

Finally Fitting In

The summer before tenth grade was my first great summer in Ohio. I spent the whole summer hanging out in my new friend John Johnston's neighborhood. At last I had a sense of belonging. I was there so much that I often took meals there. You'd think I'd moved in. One thing that made it great was that there were lots of kids my age in the neighborhood, unlike on my street. John's dad was a Psychiatrist and it seems like they had a lot of money, so John had a lot of expensive toys. For one thing he had a lot of recording equipment, and we spent hours recording the top 40 off the radio, which we listened to religiously. This was an amazing time for popular music. It was the onset of what was called *The British Invasion*, and so the music of the Beach Boys, Jan & Dean and Ricky Nelson was being mixed with music from groups like the Beatles, the Searchers, the Dave Clark Five and the Rolling Stones.

There were lots of other things going on in John's neighborhood that summer as well. Everyone in the neighborhood helped built a float for the Fourth of July parade and one of the older boys played the guitar and sang rock and roll on the float. One rather overweight girl who probably wouldn't have been popular under other circumstances had a pool, so all the kids in the neighborhood gathered over at her house. We played games like Marco Polo and pool tag. It was a great way to beat the Midwestern summer heat.

I also had a brief romantic interlude that summer, when I met an eighth grader named Kathy who was visiting for the Fourth of July.

After the festivities, I remember timidly cornering her in someone's garage and stealing a quick kiss. After that, I was walking on air. She left the next day and I never heard from her again, but I had had my moment.

Looking back with adult awareness, I think perhaps John was gay. He was a gentle, kind soul, but not the least bit interested in girls. Along with his recording work, and a fixation he had with a microphone he had to bug the telephone, he played the organ. I remember thinking his playing was a bit square, but he enjoyed it just the same.

In tenth grade, I was finally in high school and there were so many new faces. Each of my classes was with different kids. I even had a class with mostly upperclassmen (or women as the case may be). In that class, I sat next to a senior girl who said I was cute. It was a real boost in my self-esteem! One of the older guys in that same class was in a rock and roll band. I have no idea what the class was. Makes one wonder what we really learn in school. Anyway, the band was called the Cheerful Earful. I went to see them once and it was a wild scene... everyone dressed in colorful clothes and dancing.

The year was 1964 and the British Invasion was really getting in to high gear. The fashion of Carnaby Street, a very *mod* street in London, was taking off in the U.S. I dove head first into this new fad, spending most of my allowance and sometimes even my lunch money on mod clothing. I began wearing lots of paisley and also had a pair of tight, hip hugging, orange bellbottom pants, a wide belt (at least an inch and a half wide), and a bright red shirt with yellow poke-a-dots. I loved that stuff. The biggest problem was trying to sit down in those pants. That and trying to keep my shirt tucked in. If I have any regrets in life one might be that I don't have those clothes any more. Years later, I visited that famous street in London. At that time a paisley shirt sold for over two hundred dollars in one of the shops there!

At the time of the "British Invasion", anything that was British was cool... and I was definitely into cool. I had finally awakened from my nerdy slumber and I had just one thing on my mind: girls, although I didn't understand them. Understand them? I didn't even know they were human. I thought they were Goddesses you worshipped from afar. I made brief and daring contacts like with the girl in the garage on the fourth of July, but that would eventually change.

About that time I made a friend named Larry who felt exactly the same way I did about the female race. We were both obsessed. We hung around a lot together then. He lived close to school and I used to go over there every day after class. We both loved watching the Monkeys and Batman on TV, and when we weren't together we talked on the phone to each other for hours. We were around each other so much that we often would say the same thing at the same time. We even kind of looked alike. Later we were to discover that philosophically, politically and metaphysically, we were miles apart. But, in tenth grade we were inseparable.

On one particular night in the fall of that year, Larry and I went to a High school football game together. I don't remember the game at all. It wasn't that I didn't care about football. I was into it as much as anyone. But the thing is... we met some girls... even walked them home. The one I was with was named Karen. It turns out they were only eighth graders, but they were real, not just our fantasies. Larry only lasted a month with his girl, but I dated Karen for seven months. She was my first steady girlfriend. We didn't go out much. Instead, we used to spend a lot of time in her basement playing pool, listening to music and necking. Eventually, her father decided that she was too young for a serious relationship and I stopped seeing her.

That's when Larry and I started dreaming about being rock stars, pretending that we played guitars and that we were the Monkeys. Instead of guitars though, we played fireplace utensils. Yes, it's true. I got my musical start on fireplace pokers and shovels. Later that year, I bought an electric guitar. I couldn't play it, but I enjoyed just strapping it on and pretending. I wonder why I didn't take lessons? I guess, at that time I was more interested in looking cool than actually playing music.

That spring, I went out for the track team. That changed my life once again. I stretched my physical limits and got respectability and respect. I wasn't in the *in* crowd, but I was in a pretty good *out* crowd. Let me start at the beginning.

When I first went out for track, I was just a kid. I remember looking at the seniors in awe. These guys were the great ones. Some of them, like one guy I remember named Skeet Hopkins, were sprinters and also football heroes. They were big strong Greek god types. Well the girls certainly saw them that way. I wasn't big and powerful enough to be a sprinter, and I didn't have the stamina to be a distance runner so I found my niche in the middle: one lap around the track, 440 yards or a quarter of a mile. The coach was an old guy named Larkins. We called him Larks. He had a unique way with people.

"Now, now, look at me boy. Look at me," he would say while gesturing with his left hand in a half pointing manner. He couldn't quite remember my name. He used to call me Blackburn. "Now Blackburn, look at me boy, look at me."

The real slave driver of the coaching staff was the assistant coach, Marv Croston. The name was appropriate. He was a cross man, and oddly enough he was also the cross-country coach, always looking for recruits. He decided that a 440 man really had to run cross-country as well as track to be any good, and so after track season in tenth grade, he pressured me to join the cross-country team. This meant practicing every day all summer long! Now track was one thing and a fair amount of work running sprints and jogging and running more sprints, but cross-country was another matter altogether. The sport was grueling. We'd start practice fairly early in the morning. I don't really remember how early, but before it got too hot, which wasn't so easy in Ohio in the summer time. We'd run ten miles down to the river and back. We'd run sprints, run a 440, walk a 440, run a 440. Run a mile and then jog another mile. At the end of a practice we were all ready to drop. How did I stand it?

Well... a positive effect of all this hard work and shared misery was that a group of us got to be very good friends. We hung out a lot after practice and we had parties, we played Frisbee football, made movies with someone's super-8 movie camera and in general had some great times. We were not really the "cool" guys in school. Cross-country was not the "cool" sport. But we were good friends, and that's when I learned that having good friends was even better than being cool.

The next fall, I ran in some cross-country meets and kept getting stronger and stronger. I was not a distance runner, but did pretty well. I remember running a 10:40 two-mile one time at a meet. This was my all time personal best, finally breaking the eleven-minute mark.

Well, it turned out that Mr. Croston was right about what it took to excel in track. By the time track season came around, my cross-country training paid off. There were two twins who had beaten me out the year before for a slot on the junior varsity team, and frankly, they weren't very nice about it. The varsity superstars from the year before were gone and there were varsity mile relay slots to be filled. Suddenly, I found myself as fast or faster than the twins. I made the mile relay team and it was those twins, one senior and myself running for the glory of the school. Here I was stepping into the shoes of the great Skeet Hopkins! In some ways, it was hard to take.

It reminds me of something that happened when I was in second grade. I remember walking in the hall of our school and seeing my brother the big sixth grader actually talking to a patrol boy. There he was, my brother, talking to one of the coolest kids in school, a patrol boy. He had the cool belt, he had a whistle, he had a badge. He even had a flag. Four years later, I became a patrol boy, but somehow it wasn't the same. When I was a patrol boy, it wasn't a great and wonderful thing. It was just little old insignificant me being a patrol boy. I hadn't changed. Well, the same thing happened with track. It was still just me in that mile relay. Even when I started collecting ribbons and trophies, it was still just me getting that stuff. But still, even if I couldn't fully let in the feelings of success, there were positive consequences. My popularity was increasing and I was developing some confidence, at least I suppose I must have been. I didn't really notice it, but that spring of my junior year I had a letter jacket, so I guess I was cool. The life lesson there might be that you finally get what you desire when you no longer need it.

That next summer, a friend from the cross-country team invited me down to his neighborhood near one of the public pools, and I spent a lot of time down there getting to know several of the neighborhood girls as a result. For some reason, all the girls I met down there were Catholic and from large families, some with as many as nine or ten kids. This had some interesting advantages. If one girl didn't work out, I could always try a sister or two. At last, I was truly happy. I had friends, I had a sense of belonging, and I even seemed to be popular with the girls. Now, at age 16, that meant I was okay.

As my senior year of school started, I decided to drop out of Cross-country. It wasn't really my thing and it was interfering with my budding social life. Larry and I were still good friends, and this also gave me a little more time to hang out with him again. We played one-on-one football in his yard, and we continued to talk on the phone together for hours. Then I met a girl named Robin. She took my relationship with girls to a whole new level. She was wild, free and assertive. Robin had recently broken up with a guy named Bill who wore a leather jacket, smoked cigarettes behind the bleachers at school and maybe even had a motorcycle. He was what the rest of us called a *hood*, someone with greased back hair who drank alcohol and engaged in questionable activities.

I, on the other hand, was certainly not a *hood*, but I wasn't a conformist either. In fact, that Beatle haircut of mine kept growing and it eventually became an *issue* at school. Frankly, school became a battleground for social change. While the school had policies against long hair on boys and short skirts on girls, the fashions of the young were turning toward just those things. I can't tell you how many times I, a model student in every other way, would be hauled into the principal's office for this silly thing.

"Your hair is not allowed to touch the back of your collar, go over your ears or eyebrows. You'll have to get it cut!" the vice-principal would tell me in one of those impromptu meetings.

I complained to my mother that it was a violation of rights, but she didn't want to cause trouble and jeopardize my education, so she said that we could take action after I graduated. I think she knew that by then it wouldn't matter to me. Still, my hair continued to be a sort of badge of belonging for me throughout my life. I suppose it still is a big piece of my identity.

But now let me return to something even more important than my hair... my love life. Robin had broken up with Bill the *hood*, and now she was with me, and she was by far the cutest, wildest, fastest girl I had ever been with. God was she provocative, and I fell hard. I got my first hickey while dating her: my first, second, third, fourth.... One night, I stayed at her house necking until four in the morning. My parents were waiting up. Boy did I get yelled at. One night she spent the night at my house. It was one of those times when my parents were out of town and had left me alone. I was pretty excited about this, and had high expectations. Things did not work out the way I had planned, though. For some reason my friend Larry came over. I think he felt it was his moral responsibility to keep Robin and I from having sex. Well he succeeded. She spent a large part of the night talking to him. I got really upset and irrationally jealous and threatened to stab myself with the scissors if she didn't stop talking to Larry and be with me. I had really lost it. That was the beginning of the end of my relationship with Robin.

God, what a girl she was, though. I still think of her from time to time. It's amazing how strong these feelings and urges were inside of me. Hormones were raging, of course. I was reaching sexual maturity. But I still had so much to learn about love. I really had no clue... just felt the obsession to find someone... out there. One thing I can say is that each relationship I had took me a little deeper into the mystery of what it is to love, and eventually I touched the truth... that "I" am that love. But I didn't realize that for many years to come.

Chapter 6

Love and Identity

I had just graduated from High School, and it was now the summer of 1967, known in the media as the "Summer of Love". The term originated with the formation of the Council for the Summer of Love in the spring of that year as a response to the convergence of young people on the Haight-Ashbury district of San Francisco. The Council supported a free health clinic and organized housing, food, sanitation, music and arts for the influx of young people to that great city. All this is to say, that that summer there was a generational movement and a *love happening* on a grand scale.

As young people from all over the United States were gathering on the west coast, I was preparing for my own personal summer of love. I had no idea what was going on in San Francisco at the time. I was focused on something much closer to home, a girl named Lana. Just saying her name brings up the image of her beautiful red hair, sincere green eyes, and slim figure in my mind, and gives me butterflies in my stomach. Before this relationship, I had just been in love with love, but this one was different. Lana was the sweetest person I had ever known.

"You make every day like Christmas", she used to say to me.

The way I met her was unusual for me. I had heard that Robin's old boy friend, Bill the *hood* had just broken up with his latest girl friend and I knew he had good taste in girls. I had seen the girl around, she seemed nice and I knew she was available, so I made the move. I think I approached her in school. I wish I could remember more. I can't imagine how I got up the nerve. Me, "Mr. Rehearsed phone calls", "Mr. Dial the first few numbers and hang up", "Mr. Scared to death of girls." But somehow I did muster up the courage. I guess I was feeling more confident at that time, and besides she was a grade behind me in school so she was less intimidating. Well, miracle of miracles, she said yes, we went out, and she was an absolute angel. It didn't take long for us to fall in love. It was at the senior prom, or more specifically the barn party afterwards. I remember lying on that blanket in the hay and kissing for the first time. *I Think We're Alone Now* was being broadcast on the sound system. It became *our song*. What a summer we had! We spent almost every minute of it together: talking, walking, boating, bike riding, kissing.

She had a couch in her basement where the record player was, and we spent a lot of time there listening to the romantic music of a singing group called the Lettermen. Lana loved the Lettermen, and there was also a poet she loved named Rod McKuen. We listened to some of his records too. It was all very romantic. I remember it all so vividly, like it's happening all over again. There we are on that couch, snuggling close, just about to kiss. A Lettermen record is playing on the stereo. We lean toward each other bringing our lips close... and then, out of nowhere, Lana's three sisters coming jumping out from behind the couch.

"Caught you!" They shout in unison. It's their favorite game.

As I write this, I can still feel Lana sitting there next to me in those tight white jeans she used to wear. I can see her cute figure, her long auburn hair and that angelic face. God, I'm really getting wrapped up in this. My memory of it is so strong now... I can feel her in my arms... I can hear her voice, I can smell her perfume. How does the mind store such vivid memory clusters so neatly tucked away for so many years just ready to pop out like they're doing right now? God. I've got to get my mind off this. I'm going to relive our break up, and then I'm going to cry. I was so heartbroken when she left me. I guess the timing of our relationship just wasn't right or maybe it just wasn't meant to last.

While my little personal drama was heating up, that summer also saw some of the worst violence in U.S. cities in the country's history — this was because of the race riots that occurred in places such as Detroit and Newark. This aspect of the summer of 1967 is often called "The Long, Hot Summer". The cause of this violence is generally attributed to racial discrimination against African-Americans and the frustration and anger it inspired in black people. Frankly, I wasn't affected much by these events. I had other things on my mind. What consumed my attention was the fact that summer was coming to an end, and I would have to say goodbye to my beloved Lana and head off to college.

College started in the middle of September, so I would have to leave on my eighteenth birthday. It would be the first time I'd be away from home for more than a few days. My plan was to attend the College of Wooster, a very small Presbyterian College in a very small town in Northern Ohio. It's a little strange that I chose that college, considering it was Presbyterian and very conservative. I know my parents really believed in the liberal arts education and were encouraging me to attend a small college, and the admissions counselor at the school was very inviting. All I had to do was say, "Yes." But mostly I think I felt I could handle life there. I felt safe and protected in the small conservative atmosphere of the place. But still, why did I leave my girl friend and go away? Did I secretly recognize that this was just a passing relationship? No, I don't think that was it. I just don't think I saw any alternative. Everything was already in place before I had even met Lana. I was already accepted at this college, and I simply didn't know I had any say in the matter. Looking back over my life I see this as a repeated pattern. I didn't see all the choices I had. But then again, maybe I didn't really have the freedom to choose. Perhaps I was just following my destiny.

So this brings up the issue of free will versus destiny. One view is that everything has to be the way it is. From that vantage point, every event is tied to every other event and locked into some inevitable flow. It's all interconnected, and nothing happens that isn't part of some grand script. A corollary to this view for optimistic fatalists is that everything works out for the best, and if we could just step back and rise above the day-to-day events, we would see the purpose, the plan and how it all fits together. The other view, espousing free will, says that in every moment I have the freedom of choice. I can do this or do that and it's totally up to me to direct my life.

Whether I'm free to choose or not, one thing is certainly true. What I do at this very moment will start a chain of events that will effect not only the rest of my life, but the lives of all those with whom I come into contact, and all the lives of the people with whom those people come into contact and on and on until the whole world is affected. (I later learn a name for this. It's called the *Butterfly Effect*). Now imagine that each of us, each of the billions of us on this planet, chooses something new at this very moment. Wow, that would be something. We could change the world, right now! And... that's the reality. That's the way it really is! Well... maybe.

To take another look at the idea of destiny, let me contemplate the notion of the fated relationship. As a case in point, I consider the movie *Sleepless in Seattle*, one of my favorites for some reason. In this movie there are two people who are drawn to each other from opposite sides of the country through a series of circumstances. When they finally meet each other at the end of the movie, there is something perfect about the meeting, as if they were meant to be together... as if it were their destiny. I've watched the movie many times, and often after it was over I would wonder, "Is there a magic person out there for me? The perfect soul mate? The one and only? My other half?"

Along the subject of "my other half," Carl Jung talked in his writings about something he called the anima and the animus. The idea is that every person has his or her other half, the latent part, the feminine for males and the masculine for females. But, Jung saw that other half as being inside each one of us, often buried in the subconscious. In his view, the external soul mate is nothing more than a projection of that perfect other half hiding inside.

Throughout my life I often felt like I missed out somehow, didn't wait for that perfect someone, sold myself short, and just didn't believe in myself enough to find her. Oh yes, I had seen that perfect someone now and then, but the timing was wrong or the circumstances were just a little off, or I didn't dare approach her. The feeling was often like two ships passing in the night, just missing each other, fated to drift through the endless sea of life, always listening for foghorns in the mist, and wondering what might have been. On the other hand, perhaps there are no love ships, and everything I've ever longed for is right here... inside me.

As an adolescent, I was always in love with love: the idea of love, the feeling of love, but not in love with a particular person. The girl was almost inconsequential. Later, I thought I was in love with a particular person, and that the person mattered, tragically mattered, especially when the relationship ended. Had I grown in my understanding from adolescence, or was I just being blinded by attachment? If love is really just something inside me, does the recipient matter?

***

It was September 10, 1967. After saying goodbye to Lana, my good buddy Larry and I went out for one last game of miniature golf before I left for college. This was one of our favorite activities together, and it seemed important to do it one last time. I don't remember the game, but I do remember that afterwards Larry and I were sitting in an all-night donut shop eating what you find is such places and sipping milk through straws when the clock struck midnight and I was at last of legal drinking age (for 3.2% beer anyway). I glanced down at the milk carton as I gurgled its last drop up into my straw and chuckled to myself. Yes, I was a wild man, alright, a college man... really showing the stuff he was made of on his big step into manhood.

The next morning, I piled my things into the car and we headed off to college. Although my age said otherwise, I was still so naive. I'd be living away from home for the first time in my life, and I was scared. It seems the unknown always scared me. It's funny, but I don't remember my parents being there. I half remember that maybe my brother drove me to school. In any case, I don't remember much comforting, and I felt like I was going off to war or something.

The world had sent a man to the moon, and now it was sending me to college. The Vietnam War was beginning to escalate, and the Beatles had just put out their landmark album, *Sergeant Pepper*, a tribute to love and a shift in consciousness. The country was about to bust apart. As for me, I was a very conservative guy. I hadn't even tasted my first beer yet. I was a virgin in a virgin world, at a Christian college where the girls had a ten o'clock curfew, and opposite sex room visitations, much less coed dorms, were a thing of the far distant future. There was even a mandatory Chapel attendance.

I'll never forget first meeting my roommate. Talk about incompatibility! He was a motorcycle jock from Ann Arbor who wore black leather, hardly ever spoke to me, and liked to sleep with the window wide open even in the dead of winter. The only thing we had in common was that we both knew Bruce Van Vlack in third grade. The funny thing is that we both claimed him as our best friend in that grade.

Well, passive avoidance got me through that year, and I gradually, slowly, cautiously began exploring the world as much as I could and still hold on to my High School love at home who was now a senior. I wonder what her senior year was like. I know she missed me. All her letters said so. God, I was so insecure that first year. I practically spent the whole year living from letter to letter from my beloved Lana. But, despite my insecurity, I did make some friends and I even pledged a local fraternity. I remember staying up all night with one friend named Dave. He had been valedictorian of my high school graduating class. As it turned out, he was gay, but probably not when he was in high school. Anyway, he and I and his roommate stayed up all night studying for some kind of class exam. I honestly don't remember any of the subject matter. I do remember Dave's piano playing, though. He was a master of chord embellishments. I can still hear one of his favorite songs, *Cherish*, playing in my head. And then, around three of four in the morning, Dave's roommate began reciting poetry and we all became absolutely silly.

"Who chased the clouds away... 't was Love." Author unknown.

It was soon after that night that I met Lou, the greatest Latin lover and bull-shitter I was to ever know. He was a lady killer from Columbia and considerably older and... in retrospect, what the hell was he doing in my little provincial College in the middle of Ohio? Lou was everything I was not. He was a man of the world. He was confident, suave and mature. He even shaved! For some reason, we became great friends and he talked me into pledging a fraternity that didn't have the best reputation, but because of Lou's magnanimous acceptance of me, I felt like I belonged there.

I remember the many nights Lou and I would walk down to the local pizza place at three o'clock in the morning. "I'm buying," Lou would announce. After all the pizza was eaten and the place was closing their doors, I'd inevitably have to help Lou to his feet after he got stinking drunk and depressed on Slow Gin fizzes and just wanted to sit in the corner and cry. But once I got him up and out the door, we'd always start singing at the top of our lungs on those crazy walks back home.

I didn't find out why he was crying for quite some time. It turns out, Lou had this sort of secret girl friend that he would go off and see, a mysterious love affair. It wasn't until the end of my sophomore year that I discovered that this secret girl friend of his was a boy friend! Yes, Lou was gay. I was his roommate for a whole year and didn't even know. That's why he got drunk and cried on slow gin fizzes. I wonder what he's doing today. I hope AIDs hasn't gotten him.

But let me get back to my naive, sheltered, idyllic dream world of a life. I remember as if it were yesterday those long walks to the mailroom on the other side of campus.

"Did I get a letter from her today?"

I looked forward to those letters so much. I can still smell the perfume she used to put on those pretty lavender envelopes addressed with perfect penmanship. God, I loved those letters. One day she sent me her picture in the cute, striped blouse.

Wow! I haven't had these memories in years. I can smell those letters so vividly and even feel the pang of separation in my heart... and the adrenaline rushing through my body as I read those devastating words of her "Dear John" letter.

It's amazing how intensely alive those feelings still are so many years later, and this leads me to think that perhaps time is not real, and that everything I ever experienced is still right here, right now. For example, when I haven't seen someone in years and then we're together again. At first it's strange to be with that person. He or she looks different and acts different. But then, after only a few minutes, something clicks in and it's as if no time has passed at all... like one of us has just ducked into the kitchen to get a glass of water or something. All those years of growing and changing and becoming someone, and here we are and nothing has changed at all. Some essential "I" is still here and unchanged, eternal.

Chapter 7

The Times They are a Changing

One of the most intense experiences of my life occurred during that first year of college. I was just finishing a weeklong fraternity initiation that involved all sorts of hazing and humiliation. Yes, there were life goldfish involved, but that was the least of it. I won't go into detail, but suffice it to say that it was rightly named *Hell Week*. It was the last day of the ordeal and all the pledges were gathered in one room. Suddenly, I was pulled out of the group, blindfolded and taken to some basement room somewhere. As I sat there in the dark some guys began yelling in my face, "You've failed your initiation and you've let down all the other pledges. Because of you no one will be initiated this year."

I didn't really understand what I had done, but I felt absolutely horrible.

Then I heard another voice say, "Prepare yourself for your punishment," and then two guys grabbed me and guided me down a long corridor into what felt like a large room. There was a long moment of quiet accompanied by a feeling inside me of intense fear, and then someone started removing my blindfold. I remember the moment so distinctly. As the blindfold was coming off, my vision was a bit blurry at first. Then, slowly, my eyes began to adapt to the light. There was someone standing in front of me, smiling... no, not just someone. It was Lana.

"Lana?" I cried out in utter confusion.

Then she ran up to me with hugs and kisses, and the world was instantly transformed from hell to heaven.

"What? Where? How?" For those first few seconds I was so disoriented, but then I looked around and realized I was in the middle of a party. Was it my first out-of-body experience? It felt more like my first in-the-body experience.

"Lou called and invited me," Lana said sweetly.

"And I had to do a lot of talking to convince her mother it was okay," Lou said shaking my hand. My face cracked open in a huge grin, but I couldn't formulate any words.

"Looking at you now, I can see it was worth it," Lou added matching my grin with his.

God! What a guy Lou was! What a great friend, and that was a wonderful weekend. Lana was properly attended to, and nothing her mother would not approve of occurred (that happened later), but having her there was such a gift. I loved her so much. I can count on the fingers of one hand the number of times I have been that happy. Yes, this was one of those peak experiences when the love and good feelings just welled up in me, my heart was wide open, my mind was quiet, and I was totally present and in the moment. At the time I didn't think of it as spiritual, but now I see it for its transcendental quality.

After a joy filled visit with my beloved girlfriend, I put her on the bus home to Columbus, and we were back to writing letters and longing for each other once again. If we're making note of spiritual lessons, here's one to be counted: happiness, no matter how total, is a transient thing. As my joy began to fade, young love in a long distance relationship was helping me to get in touch with longing. Years later, spiritual teacher, Gangaji, would invite all of us who were gathered before her to enter that longing, as she said, "not the story of the longing, but the longing itself", and I would think back to this time in 1968 when I was deeply into those feelings, and the story.

While I was busy feeling the effects of love at a distance, there were some strong political stirrings in America. Anti-Vietnam war sentiments were on the rise along with increases in racial tensions, and then the proverbial shit hit the fan. On April 4th, 1968, Martin Luther King, Jr., a prominent leader of the civil rights movement, was assassinated in Memphis, Tennessee. This event precipitated riots in over a hundred cities. Meanwhile, the war in Vietnam was escalating, and war protests were on the rise. Later in that year, President Johnson announced he would not seek reelection and there was much excitement from the younger generation about the possibility of nominating Bobby Kennedy, a peace candidate and brother of the late President, for that most important political office.

There was something new arising in the world at this time in history, something that seemed vitally important to young Americans. It was a movement towards love and freedom, both personal and collective, and the breaking down of cultural boundaries. It was a shift in consciousness trying to happen on a global scale, like a fever catching hold of young people, which resulted in them coming together in large numbers just to celebrate life and love one another. At the same time, hate and violence were coming to the forefront as well. As a result of television, these darker forces could no longer be hidden. Instead, they were being called forth to be healed and released from the collective awareness so that a new consciousness could evolve.

A popular music group of the sixties, the Youngbloods, would capture the sentiment of the times and create an anthem for our generation: "C'mon people now, smile on your brother. Ev'rybody get together, try and love one another right now, right now, right now!"

Although I wasn't aware of it yet, I was grooming myself for this shift in consciousness by opening to love in the only way I knew how... through the love of a girl. In the spring of 1968, I was busy counting the days until I would be with Lana again, and at last spring turned to summer and she and I were reunited. We had a fantastic summer together, although I was pretty busy with a 40-hour a week job at an Army Supply depot. I got the job by taking the civil service exam. A friend who worked at the post office suggested I take the exam as a way to get a good paying government job, and he was right. But oh boy, what a place to work! The security was so intense at the depot that it took me over a half day on my first day of work just to get through the red tape to be placed at my desk, and then what I was given to do was the most boring thing I have ever had to do in my entire life! My job was to take invoices for tanks and tank parts and parts of tank parts I suppose, although there were no descriptions on the invoices, and check them to make sure they were done properly. I had a calculator, and my job was to add up the numbers and make sure they checked with the total. That was it. That was the job... and not once was there a bad invoice.

There was a big clock on the wall in front of my desk and my eyes wondered to it hopefully every few minutes throughout each day of that long summer.

"Is it time for lunch yet? How can a clock move so slowly?"

There was another spiritual lesson hidden in that moment. "Time is relative, not absolute." If I'd really thought about it then, I'd have realized that this was proof that time was an illusion, but in that moment it all seemed far too real.

The ladies I worked with were amazed at my speed and asked that I slow down a bit.

"Don't go so fast. We don't want to run out of invoices." a woman probably in her fifties pleaded. 'Besides you're making us look bad,' I could almost hear her say.

I looked over at her, sitting at her desk just across from me, and my eyes settled on a small plaque on her desk. I read the words engraved on the plaque: "This award is given to Shirley Hawthorn for thirty years of continuous service."

"Oh my God!" I cried out inside... even though I was a non-believer.

Thirty years! She'd been doing this same God awful boring job for thirty years! I couldn't comprehend it. I knew then like I never knew before why I was in College. I had no idea what I wanted to do, but I sure knew what I didn't want to do! I just couldn't fathom that kind of eternity, thirty years adding numbers. Of course, now I know the secret. Just take each moment as it presents itself. It could be a great meditation, but I wasn't ready for that at the time.

For transportation that summer, I bought a motor scooter from Sears. I remember the day it arrived. It came in a wooden crate that had "GENOVA" stamped on the side. An Italian motor scooter was about to be mine. I unboxed the bike, and followed the instructions included to mount the front wheel, breaks, handlebars, etc. That scooter and I were in for some great times. After I got a little practice on the scooter, I began riding it to work, right down Main Street through downtown Columbus to the other side of town. It often rained, but usually only on the way home.

As I was working at the depot, the inconceivable happened. On June 5, 1968, our beloved Bobby Kennedy, the hope of a new generation, was shot and killed shortly after midnight. It seemed that the whole world was coming apart. Later that summer at the Democratic national convention, things really got crazy as fighting broke out between demonstrators and the Chicago Police Department who were assisted by the Illinois National Guard. Much to the disappointment of the youth gathered in Chicago and around television sets all over the country, Hubert Humphrey, an establishment candidate, won the nomination and would run against Richard Nixon for President in November. No political change was in sight, which frustrated all of us who desperately wanted that change.

When I went back to school that fall, I took the scooter. The first year in school I took the bus back home once a month to see Lana, but this year, things would be different. She was going to College too. Lana was attending Bowling Green State University about a hundred and twenty miles due West of Wooster and on no bus route. That's where the scooter came in handy, and what a ride it was! The scooter couldn't get much over forty miles per hour on its own, but I had perfected the art of slip-streaming. Whenever a truck passed me, I would get sucked into its *wake*, a kind of partial vacuum created by the mass of the truck. If I stayed close enough, I could grab on to this air space and get the scooter up to forty-five, forty-seven, I even got it over fifty once or twice. I could usually hold on to this position for about fifteen or twenty minutes before gravity or wind resistance or speed differential would finally overcome the force and pull us apart. When that happened, I'd just wait for the next truck to pass and go through the whole process again. Riding the scooter in the dead of winter was really an experience! To try to stay warm, I would wear almost all the clothes I had. On one trip in late February, this consisted of three pairs of pants, four shirts and a winter coat. I remember vividly arriving in Bowling Green that time, chilled to the bone. I stopped the bike in front of the dorm and when I climbed off, I had no legs. I looked down and could see them stuck there. That was a relief. But my legs were completely numb so for all practical purposes, I had no legs, no feet, and no ground. It was as if I were suspended in nothingness. Taking a step was a weird experience. I had to look down as I stepped to be sure my leg was extended and then shift my weight based on what my eyes were telling me. Then I dragged the next leg forward. Laboriously I stepped into the dorm lobby in this manner and went up to the desk. My mouth was numb as well, and as a result, I could hardly get it to form the words.

"I... I'm here to see Lana, please." I mumbled.

I had a seat and waited for her to come to the lobby. I wasn't allowed back in her room, not in those days, except when they were having an open house. Even then, all doors had to stay open. There was also a rule in the lobby: four feet on the floor at all times. There I sat gradually thawing out, going out of numbness into pain, the glorious feeling of life surging back into my body. And then, there she was. I stood as best I could and we embraced.

"I missed you."

"It's great to see you!"

But each visit became more difficult as she got more involved in college life. One weekend I arrived to discover that she had begun drinking alcohol. At the time I didn't drink and had a self-righteous attitude about it. Well, I drank that weekend: to show her I could, to try to keep my girl, to punish myself, to punish her. Whatever the reason, the punishment was Scotch and Coke... on the golf course. I got so drunk. I was so sick. I don't think I ever drank Scotch again after that night. The next day I rode back to Wooster feeling miserable on multiple levels, but life went on and more global concerns began to overshadow my own post adolescent pain.

***

As Bob Dylan, a spokesman for those times so clearly stated, "The times they are a changing."

This was even true in a small, conservative northern Ohio community and eventually I got involved in this movement for change. The first thing I did for the cause was to participate in an antiwar demonstration and draft card burning. I'll never forget it.

"Come on. You don't believe in war do you?" encouraged a friend. No, I didn't believe in war, but of course I was still on my college deferment. In spite of that, my friend convinced me to go and I walked downtown with him to check out the scene. There was a crowd of about forty or fifty people gathered around a small bonfire down in front of the county courthouse. People were carrying signs and chanting, "Hell no! We won't go." Then people started taking out their wallets, finding their draft cards, and throwing them into the fire. The chanting got louder and angrier, and I became mesmerized by the widespread display of passion. I don't remember if I threw my draft card in to that fire, but I was definitely swept up in the sentiment.

The next week at our Wednesday morning "chapel" meeting, the comedian Dick Gregory came to speak. Once a large man, he was quite thin now. He was in the middle of a forty day hunger fast to protest the Vietnam War, and he spoke passionately. He told us that if we weren't taking action, we were part of the problem. I was pulled into the cause like metal to a magnet... the youth cause... the cause of love and freedom, equality and brotherhood. We were the "flower-power" generation, and the feeling of it all had a certain transcendent quality. Yes! Certainly the times they were a changing! I was beginning to be a seeker of something. Of course, it was very much an external something, at this point. People weren't really turning inward ... yet.

Then came the final element to seal my identification with the *tribe*. One Friday evening near the end of the 1969 school year, I walked into a friend's room in our fraternity.

"Here, try this," he said passing me a hand-rolled cigarette.

"No thanks, I don't smoke," I said naively.

"This isn't tobacco!" he said as he took a big drag off the cigarette, held his breath and handed the cigarette to me. "Inhale and hold it in as long as you can."

I took the cigarette, took a puff and immediately began coughing and passed it on. The *joint* came around again and I took another puff... a little more carefully this time and managed to hold in the smoke for a few seconds. I had heard about marijuana, and was curious, but nothing happened for me that night. I was a bit disappointed, because I longed to bust out of my mental prison, but even though I didn't *get off*, I still felt the camaraderie that sharing marijuana created. For one thing, we passed it around from one person to another in a circle of friends, always sharing equally. Then of course, since marijuana was illegal, smoking it created a conspiratorial bond, which made all of us partaking of it a bit subversive. We were sharing a secret, and that brought us closer, and because it was against the law this caused us to begin distrusting the establishment. This led to the popular motto, "Don't trust anyone over thirty." And of course, when I finally did start having personal experiences with marijuana, the heightened awareness that I experienced on the drug would add to the feeling of intimacy with those I trusted, but also intensify a feeling of paranoia toward anyone I didn't.

Chapter 8

Dear John and the Tear Gas

As time went by, my relationship with Lana became increasingly more difficult to maintain. Much as I wanted to hold on to her, I was losing her to College life. I wanted to stop her from changing, from growing, and as a result I was jealous of everything she did and everyone with whom she spent time. I'd always been afraid of the things I didn't know and couldn't control, and now it seemed like my whole life was out of control. I reacted by hiding behind a veil of conservatism, but I couldn't hide forever. Strangely enough, despite all that was happening or because of it, our relationship was about to take another intimate step. We were about to discover sex!

I'd seen a lot of Cary Grant movies growing up, so I knew how to set the stage, and now Lana and I were going to be together for the weekend. My parents were out of town, and so we had our chance. She got a ride to Columbus, and so did I. I went all out in preparation, putting special sheets on the foldout bed in the basement, and decorating the room with streamers. I had candlelight and fishnets and Champagne and a romantic dinner ready (probably frozen pot pies. that's all I knew how to cook). I can't remember what else I did, but it was a big production. This was going to be the night, the first time for us both. She came to the door, and I led her down the steps. Tommy James was playing on the stereo. I remember undressing her, undressing myself and feeling an innocent embarrassment. What a beautiful yet modest and petite young body she had. Protection? We used nature's cycles, foolhardy in retrospect. Two weeks later when she missed her period, we had a few weeks of soul searching. I was prepared to marry her. My life would certainly have turned out differently, if I had. What would I have become without those years of lone introspection? I could very well have been stuck in 1968. Ah, but let me get back to the magic of that moment.

We sat before each other in nature's full splendor, skin touching skin, her fair complexion intertwined with mine. We were two virgin explorers searching for the Promised Land. The penetration, gentle as it was, hurt her and she cried, but then held me so tight I thought she'd squeeze right through me.

***

That summer, 700 miles away, 500,000 people gathered in a muddy field somewhere in upstate New York to celebrate peace, love and Rock and Roll. The place was called Woodstock. Swami Satchidananda, an Indian spiritual teacher, gave the invocation and the rest was the stuff of legend. I only heard about the festival after it was over, and it would be several years before I would encounter the Swami again. I still had a long unfoldment ahead before I was ready for that meeting.

While all of that was happening, I was focused on just one person, and now that she was home from college and away from other influences, and we had taken that deep step into further intimacy, relations between us were better. But soon summer turned again to fall. By then, I'd had enough of my small, safe cocoon called Wooster and felt like I was ready to experience something bigger, more dynamic.

I transferred to Ohio State University and shared a three-bedroom apartment with two guys from Cleveland. One was a Chess nerd who drove a BMW and had a very shy girlfriend who was taller than him by three or four inches, which is not saying much because he couldn't have been much taller than five foot even. The other guy, Doug, was a bit of a drinker and sort of a jock, not really my type, but he was friendly enough and turned out to be a considerate roommate.

Lana came down a lot at first. Those weekend sex binges were so intense. But they weren't going to last. She got more and more involved at Bowling Green, and finally stopped coming. What came instead was the "Dear John" letter:

"Dear Bryan,

I will always care a lot for you, but...."

I could feel the rushing blood into my head. The words were standing out on the page as if they were the announcement of World War III. I see the words, and somewhere back inside myself, I can see myself looking at myself reading the words I can't believe I'm reading. The worst had come to pass. I had lost her. The adrenaline surged through my body and right out through the top of my head, and I had a distinct feeling that I was falling forward off a great precipice.

"... I think it would be best if we see other people...." the letter continued.

"She's met someone else and it's over between us," I thought. I ached so badly, I thought my heart would fall right out of my chest cavity. I felt like a fish out of water, gasping for breath. I was an alien in an alien land. In short, I was utterly lost. She was my world.

"What will I do now? How can I ever live without her? How can I ever find happiness again?" Well, it did take quite awhile!

***

After the crushing blow of the "Dear John" letter, there were some really lonely times. This is when I entered my drunken period. It was convenient that my roommate Doug liked to drink. We drank in the apartment and drank in the bars, and one time when I was blitzed out of my mind, I tried to pick up a girl on the street. She slapped me, I think. I was just too drunk to be sure what happened, but I was so desperate for female companionship. When I was near the emotional bottom, Doug suggested we attend a fraternity party.

"Hey Bryan, the Beta Theta Pi are having a party tonight with free booze! I've got a friend in that fraternity and he's invited us. Let's go check it out!"

I realized I needed to get out of the hole I was in, so I agreed to go.

The party was actually what they called a *rush party*, the name they gave to parties they held once a year to meet potential new fraternity members. In fact the whole rushing process involved lots of parties and lots of drinking. At some point potential candidates were selected and then individually wooed by the fraternity. Since there were several fraternities rushing at the same time, the whole process became quite competitive. Because I had been in a fraternity at Wooster that had historic ties with the Beta's, I was selected as a candidate. For some reason, Doug was not.

Once I pledged Beta Theta Pi, the "party was over", so to speak. What followed was the long-drawn-out process of being a pledge, a person of sub-human status. Over those months, we pledges became quite close. There's nothing like a little adversity and a common enemy to bring people together. Although it was not always fun being a pledge, at least it helped take my mind off of Lana.

Then came hell week. They put us through a lot of shit... demeaning, physically hard and sometimes dangerous (chugging beers by opening the top and then the bottom into our months). They went easy on me because I was older, but I still got sucked in and totally wrapped up in it. It brought me even closer to my fellow pledges, but I never forgave some of the others for their meanness.

This was a jock fraternity, at least in part. Four of the five starting Ohio State basketball players were in the fraternity. One guy was seven feet tall and another was six feet ten. These people were animals. They didn't even fit in their beds. While these guys barked orders, we pledges cleaned bathrooms with toothbrushes, recited the back of beer cans: "From the glass lined tanks of old Latrobe ....", recited the Greek alphabet backwards and forwards, and in the end, without sleep and physically exhausted, I was made to feel, once again, like I personally screwed up everything and made the entire pledge class fail the initiation (only, of course for it be revealed that we had really all made it). It's hard to believe I bought the whole charade for the second time, but at long last I was a full-fledged member.

That spring the parties were intense, drunken binges, and every party ended with all the guys doing some kind of macho dance they called "gatoring," which involved jumping up in the air and banging our chests against each other. I can't believe I was part of that.

The last party of the year was a big bash out at a lake and started in the early afternoon. The guys in charge of the alcohol mixed fruit juice with every possible type of alcohol in huge trashcans and we drank all day long. And of course, when the party was over, we all drove home! I don't know how we lived through it. Someone was watching over us, I guess. The name of the game was "obliteration," just what the doctor ordered for my aching heart.

I dated a lot of girls during that time, mostly blind dates with someone's sorority sister. Perhaps, because of all the drinking, most encounters were shallow and meaningless. There was one sorority girl I had a crush on. I can't remember her name, but I remember that she was short and really cute. She lived at home and had a little yapping dog. I was really interested in her, but it turned out she was just stringing me along and dumped me when she found something better to amuse herself.

That's when I turned my attention to something more reliable to love, my car. I had a white, 1964 Corvair convertible and I spent hours washing and waxing it. It was the only time in my life that I spent time caring for a car. It was an activity my roommate and I shared, and I suppose that was the key to it, like when I was a kid spending all those hours playing baseball with my brother just because he liked it. I was and always will be a bit of a chameleon. Years later, when I perfected the art, people would often say to me, "We have so much in common. We like all the same things." This is a trait of mine. With three planets in Libra in the first house, I am very other oriented and have a tendency to loose myself there.

One time, when the car was all washed and waxed, a fraternity brother set me up with this sexpot of a girl. She was a fraternity man's dream date. She was loose and free and she wanted to have sex, no questions asked. Her body was so beautiful that when we went to bed, I was so overwhelmed that I climaxed prematurely. I felt so bad about that. I wanted her so much, and I was so caught up in the fantasy of her that I couldn't really be present with the reality of her. A year later, she came to my apartment for a visit, and I hoped for a chance to redeem myself, but she had decided to be faithful to her boyfriend and give up her nymphomanic ways. She had even brought along a chaperone just to be sure she didn't give in to temptation. After she left, I was filled with regret and thoughts about what might have been. The truth of the matter is that there was really no might-have-been accept maybe a one-night stand with this girl. Even though there was a strong chemistry between us, she had a boyfriend. But somehow with the deep loneliness I felt and the longing to be with someone, I was blinded to the realities. I turned once again to alcohol.

I was certainly drinking a lot of alcohol in those days. Why was I drinking? Well, it was definitely a way to connect with people and to go along with the crowd. After all it was a college past time and the cultural drug of choice to deal with our feelings of separation and despair. There was a change in consciousness that resulted. It disengaged the rational mind for a time, and helped me forget my troubles and numb the pain of my heartbreak. And I seemed to be a happy drunk. I really let myself go into the experience, and it was a time when I was free of the pain of the past and the fear of what lay ahead. But ultimately, the practice was not fulfilling, and the times would eventually demand more from me.

At about this same time, I had a sort of academic identity crisis. I had been a math major up to this point. It was a logical, rational, exacting pursuit and I had been good at it. But one Friday afternoon, I was sitting in my theoretical Matrix Algebra Class, when suddenly a "switch" turned off in my mind.

"What is he talking about?" I wondered to myself. I realized I didn't have a clue.

Just then he said to us, "I hope you turn in your homework today so I have something to do over the weekend." At least that's what I remember him saying.

"What a geek! What kind of future is this for me?" I wondered almost aloud.

Bright and early Monday morning, I marched into the administration building and switched my major to Psychology. Why Psychology? Well, I believe it was because I was becoming more and more confused about who I was and what I wanted. My identity was in transition, and I thought Psychology might have answers to the questions I was having about myself. I knew the discipline dealt with feelings and motivations and consciousness... real personal issues. It would certain have to be more interesting than Mathematics!

That spring, as my interests were shifting, things really started heating up on the political front. Troupes were being sent in record numbers to Viet Nam, and college campuses were becoming a focal point for anti-war demonstrations. As a result, large groups began congregating on the Ohio State campus to protest the war and there were "outside agitators" as the media called them... a group called the S.D.S., the Students for a Democratic Society. I became intrigued. What were they saying? What was going on? What were we doing in Viet Nam? Someone said it was the fault of the Military Industrial Complex. Another said it was due to corporate greed. One day, I found myself down on campus in the middle of a crowd that was chanting, "No more War, no more war," over and over.

Someone shouted. "Let's go to the ROTZ building! They're growing the military right there! Come on. Let's go."

Suddenly the crowd started moving and the chanting got louder as we approached the ROTZ steps.

"No more war! No more War! Come on, let's smash something! Throw bricks!"

Just then someone threw a brick and broke a window, and I suddenly felt the energy of the crowd as a mindless being, totally out of control. It was all very scary, and I wanted no part in the violence.

As an aside, I see now how the issue of *control* has played a big part in my life and my spiritual journey. As a fearful child, I put a lot of energy into controlling my environment, and later when things got out of *control* in my relationship with Lana, I couldn't deal with my feelings of insecurity and jealousy. Although drinking brought about a loss of control of my actions, it actually helped me stay in control of my feelings. But now here I was... in the middle of an angry mob that was totally out of control!

"Shit! This is getting out of hand," I said to myself and pulled away from the crowd.

Things were getting out of hand for sure! Then, as I stepped out of the crowd and looked behind me, I saw... soldiers with guns... and tanks!

"My God! I can't believe there are tanks coming down the street!"

There was a standoff... and then, all at once, the crowd dispersed, and there were lots of people running in every direction. Suddenly, there were cops all along the streets, and they started tossing tear gas canisters. As I ran towards home, I saw the police toss a canister through a window into a guy's apartment leaving nothing but glass and smoke. Then one of them tossed a canister through a fraternity window and a bed caught on fire.

"The police are out of control!" I thought to myself as I ran on down the street back to my apartment.

There was the smell of teargas everywhere I turned, and my eyes were stinging so bad that I thought the pain would never go away... and the smell, I would never forget that smell. I got to my door, my heart practically pounding out of my chest, I fumbled with the keys, burst into my apartment and threw myself onto the couch. As I began to catch my breath, I turned on the TV to see what was happening.

My roommate came down stairs when he heard the commotion. On the TV screen were images of tanks and soldiers and mobs of people, and someone was making an announcement.

"Governor Rhodes has called out the National Guard as riots are breaking out on all the major Ohio campuses... this just in. At Kent State, four students have been shot and killed by Ohio National Guardsmen...."

"What if you knew her and found her dead on the ground... four dead in Ohio." -- Crosby, Stills and Nash.

I couldn't believe it. Those bastards had killed four students, shot them down in cold blood. Damn war! Stupid military!

This was a turning point for me. This was the moment when I rejected the establishment, the dominant culture of the land, and joined the counter-culture. I had just left my society, and I would spend years dealing with it with mistrust and judgment with the prevailing feeling of being on the outside looking in, like Ebenezer Scrooge looking in Tiny Tim's window on Christmas day. It's hard to say how this split with society affected my spiritual journey. In one way, having lost my ties to the dominant culture freed me up to experiment on the fringes of society, leading to many discoveries and ultimately a shift in consciousness. But, on the other hand, there had been a price to pay, and it would take me many years to heal that schism of mistrust inside me and the nagging feeling that I was doing something wrong all the time.

The next day, it was announced that the university was closing for the rest of the year. My college transcripts for that time with their mark of "pass/fail" instead of grades for that quarter stood as an ever-present reminder of what had happened.

Chapter 9

Opening to a New Experience

I was ready for something new, and as circumstance would have it, I had my chance. That summer I was given a great invitation by my friend, John Sunburg. He was a friend of mine from Wooster who had two nicknames. One was the name *Sunshine*. He'd had this one since he was a kid, because of his amazing smile and of course it was kind of like Sunburg. John was an easy-going guy, and loved everyone, but he was also a good student. Even though he was conservative in his appearance, with short well-combed hair and collared shirts, and conservative in his ways, a serious and focused student destined to work in industry, he was good-natured and treated everyone as a friend.

In college, he acquired the second nickname, *Party* because he was always ready for one. His college dorm room was always decorated with fishnets and he had a strobe light that was synchronized with the music he played. There was always lots of alcohol (Schlitz malt liquor was his favorite) and a good supply of Goldfish pretzels at John's place. The pretzels were perfect for tossing up into the air and into someone's mouth. Whose mouth? It didn't matter. We threw them everywhere.

After Lana and I began to have problems, John and I did some serious drinking up in that *party* room of his, and we stayed in touch after I left Wooster. He was still grateful that I introduced him to a girl I was seeing before I left. I can't remember her name. She was a local high school student I met at a party. First John's roommate danced with her. And then I did and I did again and again and then she and I hung out together for several months. She was an intense kisser. She and I, my roommate Lou and this girl I had a crush on with long straight hair and the most beautiful Bambi eyes, a girl whom we affectionately nicknamed *Walleye*, would double date. It's kind of funny that I had a crush on *Walleye* and yet my roommate was the one dating her. As I recall, I was too shy to make the move on her, so Lou did, just to show me how it was done, I guess. He dated her the whole time I was with the high school girl. I'm not sure what he was trying to prove since he was gay. When I left Wooster, I didn't want the high school girl to be sad, so I introduced her to Party. I'm not sure I did her a favor. They were having sex before long and then when he left for graduate school, she was heartbroken.

Now this brings me back to what I meant to talk about. As I said, John and I had stayed in touch and somehow despite all the partying, he managed to graduate with honors. Now he was going to Santa Cruz, California to attend graduate school in Chemistry and he asked me to come along for the summer. I had one more year of College before graduation and I decided this would be a good time for a trip. I knew we'd have a great time. So, off we went in his brand new Plymouth Duster. It was June of 1970 and I was finally California bound. This was a dream come true for me. I had been *California Dreaming* for a long time.

"All the leaves brown and the sky is gray... California Dreaming on such a winters day...." --- The Mamas and Papas.

I was enamored with the West Coast as early as 1965, when I listened to the surfer music of Jan and Dean, heard the Beach Boys singing "I wish they all could be California girls....", watched Annette Funicello and Frankie Avalon in *Beach Blanket Bingo*, and faithfully followed the T.V. antics of *Gidget*. They all romanticized that paradise that was California. I knew it was the place to be... and at last I was going.

I don't remember much of the drive out. I do remember going to the Great Salt Lake and driving out onto this desolate island where there was supposed to be camping. It was the most God forsaken place I had ever seen. No trees, hardly any plant growth, just rocks and salt and dirt. It turned out that the campsites were tucked behind large boulders providing a little bit of shade. This place advertised showers. Well it did have a shower of sorts. All the fresh water was trucked in so the shower consisted of a big barrel of water suspended above the ground. Pull the rope and down it came. That was the shower. Right out in the open. No privacy, but then there wasn't another soul out on this island. Yes, it was an eerie, otherworldly place.

So much for the interlude. Next stop California! I'm not sure what we did when we first got to Santa Cruz. Graduate school didn't start for John until fall, so we had all summer. Somehow we found this old rundown apartment only a block from the beach for fifty dollars a month. The building was part of an inheritance and had not been lived in for several years. In exchange for staying there, we paid the fifty dollars and also had to help with the renovation. I remember doing lots of painting and laying ceramic tiles in the apartment bathroom. Well this work took us about two hours a day. The rest of the time I spent surfing and looking for girls. Boy did I go about looking for girls the wrong way! And oh yes, I also managed to get thrown in jail. But let me tell one thing at a time.

It's amazing how all this stuff is just flooding out of my mind all at once. I can still hear Mungo Jerry's *In the Summer Time* playing on the radio. I can see the palm trees and the pounding surf and I see myself hanging out on our little porch with Party and a few other friends he picked up along the way. The memory of that time is so vivid like it's happening all over again. And so is the loneliness and the pain of rejection I felt looking for love in all the wrong places. I was so stupid. I kept going up to girls who were sunbathing with there bikini tops unfastened and trying to start a meaningful relationship. Of course they all told me to buzz off. They were in a vulnerable position and I was harassing them, but all I could see was that it was California just three years after the summer of love where the girls were wild and free love was waiting to happen.

Well, free love would wait awhile longer to happen, at least for me, but there was surfing. I bought myself a surfboard, used and cheap, and every morning really early, I walked down the beach past the volleyball courts and the boardwalk to the surfing beach to catch the low tide. The fog was thick. The water was cold. But low tide, especially the early morning low tide, was when the surfing happened, and I was a surfer that summer. I wasn't a great surfer. In fact it took me most of the summer to learn to stand up on the board. But I was there. I was doing it. Jan and Dean would have been proud. The place I was surfing was one of the top winter surfing spots in the world. In the summer it was tame, but the waves were well formed and broke evenly and consistently. You see, ideal surfing conditions are created by some natural barrier. It may be an extended sand bar, a reef, or in this case a point of land jetting seaward. An ocean swell becomes a breaking wave when the bottom of the swell actually drags on the ocean floor making the column of water associated with it top heavy. Ideal surfing spots have a long drawn out curl, usually in one direction. A peninsula can be ideal for making this happen, and Santa Cruz had a perfect one.

Given the right conditions, a surfer can ride the wave just in front of the break or even inside the curl, all the way from the tip of the peninsula to the beach a half a mile down. What he doesn't want the wave to do is collapse on him. Then, all he has is white water to ride (if the wave didn't crash over his head and cause him to wipe out). Moving back and forth on the board changes the surfer's speed and allows him to move quicker when the wave is breaking faster or slow down if he's getting too far ahead of the break. Hanging ten is when the surfer walks all the way out to the end of the board such that all ten toes are actually hanging off the front. This maneuver can only be done when the surfer is in exactly the right spot on the wave. Surfing is a great sport! It's my favorite. There's so much variety. Not only can you approach a wave in different ways, different places have different conditions, and conditions vary from day to day, but every wave is unique. No wave is ever the same as another! Now that's variety. You can really feel the power of nature when you're surfing, too. You have to be very observant and very patient, getting in the right place, feeling the wave building and knowing when to go, getting in sync with the wave. You are definitely going with the flow in this sport. It's a very yin/yang energy balance kind of thing. And besides it's cool. So what else could you ask for? How about a whole summer doing it? That's what the summer of 1970 was for me.

When we weren't surfing or looking for female companionship, we were usually partying. Party was twenty-one and this was an age twenty-one drinking state. I was only twenty. He bought the liquor and we did plenty of drinking. One night we got hooked up with a long haired guy who had an American flag on the back of his shirt and two marines with shaved heads, who were shipping out the next day for Viet Nam. Well, I'll tell you those two marines were in the mood for drinking! After we got quite drunk, we decided to go for a walk on the boardwalk. Santa Cruz had a great one with a roller coaster, games, cotton candy and girls, so the five of us came sauntering toward that monument of good times, singing pretty loudly and having a staggeringly good time. Oh, did I mention to you that I was kind of growing my hair out that summer. From tenth grade and the Beatle haircut, my hair was now evolving into a more early-seventies Beatle haircut (a la George Harrison or Jesus Christ). So on to the boardwalk we came, two marines, a chemistry student, and two longhairs.

Unbeknownst to us, at that moment a call was being placed to the security people of the boardwalk alerting them to some troublemakers that were apparently on the boardwalk. The stage was set. Before we knew what hit us, two of us were grabbed from behind and dragged off to the security office. Guess which two? Not the two military guys. Not my friend Party. No, it was the guy with the American flag and me, the other guy with the long hair. I probably could have reasoned with them, but it was too late. My "friend" began insulting and verbally abusing the ones who grabbed us. The next thing I knew, they were locking us in the city jail! Behind bars! Fortunately for my friend, I had no identification on me. I lied about my age, or else he could have been charged with aiding to the delinquency of a minor. As it was, we were charged with being drunk in public and left to spend the night in jail. Well,

OUT OF THE SIXTIES

let me tell you, we played it to the hilt. After the bars clanged shut, we looked around at our stark but clean environment, a concrete floor, two concrete slabs for bunks, and a latrine. We stood there imagining what it would be like to be there for thirty days, five years, or thirty years. Then we took the metal cups that they had given us and began rattling them against the bars as we paced back and forth, sang *We shall overcome*, and were generally real nuisances. I don't know how long we were in there. I don't remember sleeping. But, eventually, John came with the bail money, thirty-five dollars apiece, and we were free at last, "God almighty, we are free at last". We later had to appear in court, plead guilty and say we'd never do it again. Since it was our first offense, we forfeited the thirty-five dollars, but the incident was to be stricken from our records after six months. Thus ended my short career as a criminal.

Chapter 10

The Threshold of a Dream

Soon after our deep bonding experience in the *clango*r, my jail friend and I decided to take a trip down the coast to Mexico. He had a little Datsun 2000, and I was an eager passenger. We packed light and still had to tie some stuff on the back of this little sports car. When I climbed in, I was reminded of those cars you ride at Disneyland, only this car had more than a go-cart engine and we weren't following a track. Instead, we were driving down Route One, a highway that winds along spectacular cliffs and provides some of the most beautiful scenery in the whole world. After going through the sleepy little town of Salinas, known as the artichoke capital of the world, and passing acres and acres of cultivated farmland, we arrived in the beautiful town of Carmel by the Sea. We parked in a lot by the ocean and walked out on to one of the whitest sand beaches I have ever seen. This day the beach was full of marines on what I imagined was their last leave before shipping out to Viet Nam. I don't know if I thought about it at the time, but some of those guys probably did not come back from their trip to Southeast Asia. Others would return physically or, more commonly, mentally scarred for life. As I watched these young men enjoying the sunshine, I thought about our war in Viet Nam. I couldn't understand why we were fighting there, but it wasn't until later that the whole thing would become more personal to me.

From Carmel, we headed south to Big Sur. We followed the windy road along the steep cliffs high above the crashing waves of the Pacific Ocean, catching breathtaking glimpses along the way. Then we saw a sign announcing that we were entering Pfeiffer Big Sur State Park. As we came around the next bend, I was totally amazed by what I saw. There along the highway were... young people everywhere. Most of them had long hair and they were so outrageously dressed with cool crazy hats, multicolored patchwork vests... patchwork everything really... with lots of embroidery. These young people were the free spirits known as "hippies". The word "hippie" apparently came from *hipster*, and was initially used to describe beatniks who had moved into New York City's Greenwich Village and San Francisco's Haight-Ashbury district. The term "hip" from which hipster was derived, appears to have come from African American jive slang and meant "sophisticated, currently fashionable, and fully up-to-date". And so they were... fashionably unfashionable. Some had so many patches on their jeans one could hardly find the denim. Some had big Afros and others had hair half way down their backs. It didn't matter what gender they were. And they were all just hanging out by the road. As we rounded the curve, we saw one guy with a long braid and thick beard playing a guitar and several people dancing around him with flowers in their hair. Then we saw one guy sitting by the side of the road in a cross-legged yoga posture, apparently hitchhiking, with his eyes closed and his arms held out, the thumb of his right hand indicating that he wanted a ride south while the thumb of his left hand was asking a ride north. I guess it didn't matter to him which way he went. He just wanted to go... wherever fate would take him. Unfortunately we couldn't give him a ride. We just barely had room for ourselves in our little two-seater Datsun.

After leaving the hippies of Big Sur, we continued driving south, passed uneventfully through ritzy Santa Barbara, and then spent an intense few hours driving through LA. It's the only place I know that has a rush hour at three in the morning.

We were ready to sleep by the time we got to San Diego. We pulled off the highway near La Jolla, home of Richard Millhouse Nixon our honorable president of the United States at the time, and searched for a suitable spot to crash. We finally found a place to pull over in a semi-deserted spot along a bluff by the ocean. It was getting dark when we got out the sleeping bags and bedded down on a patch of grass about five feet wide between the railroad tracks and the cliff leading to the ocean below. Gradually, we drifted off to sleep with the pounding of the surf below lulling us ever so gently, peacefully, relaxingly... and then....

"My God. What's happening!?"

I woke up to one of the loudest sounds I have ever heard. Looking up all I saw was a blinding light. Then the sound got louder and louder and the light got bigger and brighter. Was it the end of the world? An alien abduction? At last my eyes began to adjust to the light, and I could see that it was just a train coming down the tracks no more than a few feet from us. My heart continued to pound late into the night and it wasn't until near dawn that I finally drifted back off to sleep.

The next day we went to beautiful beach and rented two little half size air mattresses. There were ten-foot waves breaking close to shore and the mattresses were a great way to ride them. To get out past the breaking waves, we had to walk out to just about where they broke, then toss the mattresses up in the air and dive under. When we surfaced we hoped that the wave had passed and that our mattresses had cleared the top. Then we climbed on, paddled out a little further and then waited for that perfect wave. There was a constant barrage that day so we didn't wait long. Time and time again the giant wave would catch hold of my mattress, and I would zoom down the face of it.

The shallow water was packed with kids that day.

"Look out! I'm coming through!" I yelled each time.

Amazingly enough, everyone in my path always ducked out of my way just in time. How did they know I was coming? Oh yea. I forgot. There was a ten-foot wave right behind me.

The ride always ended with me zooming all the way onto the beach. Then I would flip off the mattress and tumble onto the sand, pull myself up, empty a few pounds of sand from my bathing suit pockets, and then run back out in the water to catch another wave. I was at it for hours. It was so much fun.

At last we left San Diego heading south and the next stop was Tijuana, Mexico. Of course, we had to get across the border first. The border police looked at us a bit suspiciously, but let us through without any trouble. The first thing I noticed when we entered Mexico was the incredible pervasive poverty... in stark contrast to conditions on the other side of the border. There, along the road, as we continued driving through the city, was a sprawling shanty town of cardboard box *houses* spread out for miles in the dust, and whenever we would stop in traffic, kids would come up to us to wash our windows and try to sell us stuff. I have to say, it was overwhelming. Years later, I would recall this experience and not be as shocked as I encountered similar conditions traveling in Sub-Saharan Africa.

We decided to go on past Tijuana to Ensenada in the hope that things would be less intense there. We had also heard that everything was a bit cheaper in Ensenada although I really had no intention of buying anything. I guess that explains why I only spent all the money I had!

But I'm getting ahead of myself, again. I keep doing that. You see, I know out it all turns out. I wish I knew how my present events turn out. That could be very useful. Hmmm. On second thought, think of the amazing fact that I don't know what's going to happen next. The possibilities are endless. In fact, maybe the story of the present hasn't even been written yet... which would seem to give me a lot of poetic freedom. This reminds me of an experience I had once being on a high place. It was the 14th floor of an Embassy Suites Hotel somewhere, during my time working in corporate America. I was looking out over the balcony all the way down to the lobby far below, and I thought to myself, "I could just decide to walk up to that balcony and jump off. I've got that freedom. I could do it. I could also choose not to do it. I've got that freedom!" Was I Crazy? I don't think so. If I had jumped, now that would have been crazy. But the question remains. Did I really have that freedom? Or did I just think I did? In any case, I'm awestruck by how much potential there is in any given moment, and I realize that pure potentiality is even more valuable than knowledge of the future. Now the past, that's something else again. Sometimes I wish

I could rewrite that. Sometimes I think I have. The truth is that my perception of the past is not really the same as the real past. My memory of it is based on selected perception, partial recollection, and a biased understanding. In short my reality of the past is simply that, merely my reality. I have a story called "The Water Bed Story". If you keep reading, you'll get to experience it. My kids have heard it, but doubt its authenticity. They've got a lot of nerve. I keep telling them that every detail is absolutely true, exactly how it happened. Well, at least it was my recollection of my selected perception of what seemed to me had happened. Let's face it; you've got your reality. I've got mine. I like mine for the most part.

So anyway, back to my reality of the summer of 1970. There we were, my new friend and I driving through Mexico and coming into Ensenada, one of the great bargain capitals of the World, and I was in the world's greatest position. I had no intention of buying anything! We found a parking place along the road and walked a couple of blocks into the heart of the marketplace. The streets were lined with little shops and bustling with tourists. We went in and out of lots of stores and looked at a lot of stuff. Everywhere the shopkeepers wanted to dicker.

"For you I'll give a deal!"

We were in one store and I was looking at a beautiful, fringed, tan leather jacket... think *Easy Rider*. I immediately fell in love with it.

"I'll let you have it for fifty dollars," the owner said, seeing my interest.

"No, no", I said. (I only had twenty-five to my name). "I'm just looking."

"Okay, this is my last offer, forty-five dollars," he countered.

"Sorry, I'm not buying today," I told him and then started leaving the store.

"Okay. Thirty-five dollars," the man said as we were leaving.

I waved the man off, left the store and started walking down the street. A couple of minutes later the man came out of his store and started following me down the street.

"Twenty-five dollars", he said at last, holding up the jacket.

"Okay", I said and went back and bought the jacket.

What a great price! I spent everything I had, but I had this great, all leather, tan jacket with the hippie fringe. I loved that jacket and wore it for years.

And so, off we went, I in my new leather jacket, the two us back across the border in a little red Datsun 2000. We had no illegal drugs, so the border search didn't bother us. I'm not sure how the next event occurred. We must have been out hiking somewhere. What happened was that my friend hurt his foot, sprained it actually, so he could no longer drive his stick shift, five-speed sports car.

"You're going to have to drive," he said holding the door open for me.

"Me?"

I'd never even driven a stick shift car, much less a sports car, but there we were on Route One, on a winding mountainous road along the spectacular cliffs of Big Sur, and I was taking over the wheel. What a fabulous crash course! Actually, I did okay. In fact, I did better than okay, and absolutely loved it. Driving that machine was effortless. The car had amazing power; she hugged the road like a paint stripe and slipped in and out of gears like a knife through warm butter. I can still feel the breeze in my hair and the roar of the engine. What a thrill.

"Hmmm. I might have to buy one of these myself some day," I mused as we cruised back through Big Sur.

As we came to the sign for the state park, we saw the same people hanging out by the road with their long hair and colorful clothes, and we saw the same guy hitchhiking with thumbs extended in both directions as we passed through heading north. It seemed like they were in some other dimension... somehow immune to the changes that time brings. I loved hippies for that... and seeing them, I yearned for the freedom they seemed to have.

But I had a different agenda ahead. I was to drive my friend's car back to Santa Cruz, take an airplane back home to finish college in Ohio, almost get drafted, attend graduate school... and then .... Well you'll find out.

***

But before leaving Santa Cruz, I decided I really wanted to try some Marijuana. You'll recall that I had tried it once the previous year in someone's dorm room back in Ohio, but really didn't get off on it. I just choked a lot and didn't inhale, as Bill Clinton would tell us he had done years later when he was running for President. But unlike Mr. Clinton, I decided that I really wanted to try pot again, and I figured that California was the place to do it. The thing was I didn't have any Marijuana and didn't know anyone who did, so I figured I needed to go out and *score* some. To do that, I went down to the boardwalk where I had previously been arrested (crazy in retrospect!), and just hung out there asking people who passed by if they had any for sale. Time after time, I came up empty. I must have looked like a nark or something, because no one wanted to sell me some pot.

Finally somebody I asked said, "No pot man, but I've got some great acid! It's windowpane, the purest stuff around."

At this point I'd take anything, so I bought the hit of L.S.D. I think I paid three dollars for this tiny little red square not much bigger than a grain of oatmeal.

"Take half. You should have a nice trip," he added as I was walking away with my score.

I was a bit scared of the L.S.D. I'd heard a lot of ominous stories about the stuff, but I was also quite curious, so I stashed it away in a safe place waiting for the right time to take it. That little red tab would stay stashed for five months. I kept waiting for the right moment, but the right moment never came.

In September of 1970, I said goodbye to California and returned to Ohio State University for my senior year in College. I went back to my beer drinking conservative roommate, my mainstream jock fraternity, my rational mind and my lucid life, but I didn't go back empty handed. I had spent a night in jail and felt the cruel injustice of the establishment, I had a vivid picture in my mind and a warm place in my heart for the Big Sur hippies and their life of abandonment, I had my own cool fringed hippie leather jacket, and I had a hit of L.S.D. stashed away, waiting to reveal its secrets.

***

There were a few other changes that were to show themselves in my senior year of college. In the spring of the past year, you may recall, I switched my major to Psychology, and so my senior year was filled with Psychology courses. I had a lot of catching up to do to graduate that year, and so I totally immersed myself in it. Meanwhile, my hair continued to grow and I didn't exactly fit the fraternity image any more. There was a small faction of other fraternity members who were also a bit on the fringe and we hung out together. The jocks of the fraternity didn't exactly approve. I met Nick at that time. He was a fellow pledge at my fraternity and he played the guitar, and coincidently, his girl friend, Lori, was a really good friend of my old girl friend Lana's sister. In fact I had met Lori at Lana's house once. Nick and Lori and I would eventually become great friends and Nick would be instrumental in my finally learning to play the guitar.

Meanwhile, I was getting deeply involved in my Psychology classes and taking part in some very questionable experiments. In one of these experiments we asked students to administer shock to their classmates as part of a lesson in behavior modification. Like in Hitler's Germany, many people administered what they thought was cruel punishment just because they were told to. Of course, the shock wasn't real, but they didn't know that!

While I was learning a lot about human nature in my classes, I spent most of my free time eating pizza and hanging out with my friends at a place called the South Berg, a basement bar in the south end of campus where we listened to endless playings of Led Zeppelin's "Whole lot of Love."

Meanwhile, the bedroom of my apartment was going through some changes to reflect my shift in consciousness. I had completely covered the walls and ceiling with black-light posters. There were psychedelic posters of infinite spirals and even a big day-glow picture of Jimi Hendrix. I remember lying on my bed listening to Santana while those black light posters, doorways into other dimensions, lay dormant, just waiting to be activated.

I had put those posters up naively... not knowing I was on a threshold... and about to plunge into a great perceptual mystery from which I would never really return.

Chapter 11

Journey into the Unknown

Trip 1: "The Freeing of the Perceptual Machinery"

One Friday night, I was sitting around watching T.V. with my roommate. It was a typical low consciousness evening. For some reason, my mind drifted to the little red tab sitting in my dresser drawer. The one I had bought in Santa Cruz the previous summer.

"You know," I thought to myself, "It's never going to be the right moment to take that acid."

Before I knew it, I was heading up those stairs to my bedroom. It was not pre-meditated. It just happened.

"Just take half, you'll have a nice trip." Those words from the guy who sold me the L.S.D. still echoed in my head. I pulled open my dresser drawer, found the little plastic bag that I had neatly stashed with my underwear, carefully removed the red tab from the bag and cut it in half with a pair of scissors.

"Ok. Here goes," I said to myself and took a deep breath to give myself courage. Then I placed one of the halves on my tongue, putting the other back in the little plastic bag and back in my drawer. I walked back down the stairs and went back to watching T.V. I didn't say anything to my roommate, just sat quietly on the coach... sat and waited... and waited... and waited some more. I noticed a feeling of butterflies in my stomach from being a bit scared, but nothing else happened. After waiting a half an hour, I went up stairs and took the other half. Frankly, I didn't really expect much to happen with such a small pill. Besides it seemed to me that nothing was ever as good as it was cracked up to be. This was my attitude about most things. You see I had a long history of disappointment. I'm not sure why. Perhaps it was my idealism. I imagined the ultimate, the perfect and complete experience and then had a lot of letdowns. I was sure I wouldn't *get off* on the L.S.D. But there was that one time when I was fourteen. I wasn't let down then. That time life lived up to my expectations and even exceeded them.

I was on a trip to Switzerland with my parents, and we were going to Zermatt. I'd seen the town in the Walt Disney movie Third Man on the Mountain. In the movie, there was an incredible view from town of the Matterhorn, the most beautiful mountain in the world. When we arrived in Zermatt my dad pointed it out to me.

"There it is. The Matterhorn."

I looked up to where he pointed to see a less than impressive small little peak on the far ridge.

"That can't be it. It's not the way it looked in the movie," I whined.

By now my parents were used to this reaction from me and attempted to placate me, but I couldn't let go of my disappointment. That night we stayed in a quaint little inn with big fluffy down comforters on the beds. My brother and I shared one room and my parents were in the adjoining room. We had a great balcony that looked out over the town square and the mountains beyond, and there was a picturesque old church nearby with a tall bell tower. We were really tired from the journey and still suffering from jet lag as a result of our long flight from the U.S., so we went to bed fairly early. The next thing I knew the church bells were ringing in the bell tower.

"Dong."

It must have been one o'clock in the morning. I groaned and went back to sleep.

"Dong, dong."

"Now it was two o'clock," I thought.

"Dong, dong, dong."

Three o'clock.

"Dong, dong, dong, dong, dong, dong...."

At four o'clock the bells were going crazy. My brother Laird and I pulled ourselves out of bed, he pulled the curtains back from the sliding glass door that opened on to the balcony, and we looked out to see what was going on. There, before us in all its magnificent splendor, was the most beautiful mountain I had ever seen, and the sun was just lighting the top of it. The clouds that had hidden it earlier had all rolled away, and I could almost hear angels singing I was so taken with the mountain's majestic beauty. We both just stared at the mountain in awe as the sunlight slowly grew to cover its entire Eastern face.

"It's even better than in the movie!" I exclaimed.

By four-thirty the whole mountain was sparkling, and that's when we went to wake up our parents to share our discovery. By 6:00 A.M., the mountain was completely covered by clouds again, but I had had my perfect moment when life more than lived up to expectation.

But I wasn't thinking about the Matterhorn as I sat on that couch in my apartment in 1971. I was just thinking, "Nothing's going to happen."

After watching a little more T.V., I casually told my roommate, Doug, what I had done. He absolutely freaked out!

"You did what! Oh my God. What should we do?"

The stage was set... and then... a few minutes later................. The world as I knew it began to dissolve. I began to GETTTT OFFFFF!

I first noticed feeling just a little bit funny in the pit of my stomach... and then... I noticed the room was becoming distorted. The walls were beginning to bend... in fact everything in my perception became fluid... morphing in and out of solidity. In that moment, everything began softening and dissolving, and I started seeing cartoon figures on everything.

"Hmmm. A very interesting drug." I thought out loud. "Good thing I know I took something or I'd be thinking I was going crazy."

Then I got the notion to approach the experience as a scientist.

"Hmmm. Let's test the powers of this perceptual drug."

I looked around for an object and settled on a light fixture outside my living room window. I stared at it for some time, and after a while everything else dropped away. There was only the light fixture and me. Nothing else existed.

"Can I turn that light fixture into something else?" I wondered. "A hook, maybe?"

I focused my intent and stared at that fixture with determination.

"Ah... Yes, there! It's no longer a light. It's a hook. Amazing!"

Then it was back to being a light fixture again.

"How about this picture on the wall?" It was a picture of a ship in the ocean. "Can I make the ship move?"

Suddenly, before my eyes, the ship came alive, and it was rolling with the waves. The waves were ebbing and flowing, and the ship was bobbing up and down!

"Wow! Incredible. What else can I do?"

There was a black-light poster on the wall in the dining room. It had a spiral pattern. I began to stare at the poster... down into the spiral. I stared for a while and then I began moving into the picture. In... in... in... in.

I was traveling... deeper and deeper... In, in, in... free falling deeper and deeper... through the inner space of the poster. I was transfixed for eons... lifetimes... unfathomable amounts of forever... deeper... deeper... deeper.

Another lifetime later, I became vaguely aware of my roommate watching me. I looked over from somewhere deep inside... inside what, I did not know, but from somewhere. Wherever I was, I could see Doug as if he were so very far away... way out there.... As I tried to make my perceptual way toward him, I felt that I was in some kind of a bubble and that he was way out beyond the bubble... in some other reality. I tried to tell him what was happening, but I couldn't even begin to bridge the gap between us, could not float the words out of my bubble. He was just too far out there, way beyond me, out in another world. I must have shown some concern on my face, or maybe Doug heard my attempts to get through to him. For whatever reason, he decided that he needed some backup, someone with experience in psychedelics.

"I'm going to go ask our neighbors to come over. I know they've tripped before. Maybe they can help."

Doug's words hung in the air out beyond me somewhere. Then he opened the door on the very edge of my reality and suddenly stepped out of the world, gone for what seemed like forever. I turned my attention back into the poster, down, down, down... way down....

Another eon later, I was pulled back out by a sound... a door opening. Yes, the door out of the world opened, and two really weird looking guys walked in with Doug.

"Look, our neighbors have come over to see you."

These two very strange guys with long straggly hair walked over and peered into the bubble at me.

"You okay?" one of them asked.

I turned and looked at them.... as if I were looking through one of those fish eye lenses in a fun house. What I saw was a grotesquely distorted head with a great big protruding, cartoon nose. The words were pouring out of a pair of big lips and kind of echoing through the thick substance of the bubble, barely penetrating. I must have looked rather unfriendly, because these guys didn't stay long.

"Whew. That was weird!" I thought to myself after they left. "Okay. Let's see. Back to testing my powers. Hey, let's see if I can turn on this black-light poster without the black light. Okay. Concentrate. Fix your gaze. Keep staring. Keep staring. That's it. There.... the inside is beginning to glow."

I kept staring and ever so slowly the center of the poster became brighter and brighter.

"Okay, now move out slowly. Brighter, brighter, brighter... That's it! Oops! I lost it. It's dark again."

It took enormous amounts of concentration, but I discovered that I could set a perceptual intention and then manifest what I intended. But my powers of perception were one thing and actually affecting reality was another. What I wanted next was some positive, concrete evidence that I could manipulate something in the real, tangible, physical world through my mind... that it wasn't all just an hallucination. I looked around for something to affect. There on the wall, across the room was a nail.

"Hmmm. I wonder if I can make that nail in the wall there across the room come out of the wall and fall to the ground."

I figured, if I could actually make the nail fall to the floor, I could then walk over and touch it there, handle it, even pick it up, and then I'd know that, like Uri Geller and the bending spoons, I also had real mental powers, not just crazy, drug induced imaginings.

"Okay. Set the intention and concentrate. That's it, now keep staring. Keep staring."

There before my eyes the nail began to bend. That's right, I could see the nail transforming under my gaze. In fact, I could even see the wall curving out a bit... and then the nail began to stretch out of the wall, like something I'd seen in a cartoon.

"That's it. It's bending. Yes! It's starting to come. Now it's wiggling. Yea, just a little bit more!"

If I could just get that nail to come all the way out of the wall and fall on the floor, then I'd have positive proof that all this was really happening, that the whole phenomenon wasn't just in my mind. I'd know that what I was perceiving was real and that reality was much vaster and much more mysterious than I had ever thought. Now I exerted all the will and concentration I could muster.

"Come on baby. You can do it! That's it... I see it moving. Just a little more. Come on. Concentrate."

If I could just pull a little harder... I could get it to drop.

At last, I slumped over in exhaustion. I just couldn't quite get that nail to come all the way out and drop to the floor. I have no idea what my roommate was doing during this time. Hopefully, he had gone to bed!

After a long moment of disappointment, I decided to listen to some music in the headphones. I sat in a big overstuffed chair while Grand Funk Railroad's "I'm Getting Closer to my Home" was playing in my ears.

The sounds were so rich and beautifully intricate, and then the song was ending... endlessly ending. Grand Funk kept singing the words over and over, "I'm getting closer to my home," but we weren't getting any closer. We were caught in some endless loop that went on and on for what seemed like hours. Then I glanced up at a painting hanging on the wall, and there, synchronized with the music, were movie credits rolling down the painting as if it were a movie screen. "Produced by ...." "Directed by ...." I tried to read the words, but I couldn't quite focus on the names.

I often have this same experience in dreams. I might have a message I am trying to read and I'd see the words there before me, but I just couldn't quite make them out. In the dream as soon as my mind tried to catch the details and discern the *real* content of the message, the whole message would wash away. Back in my living room the credits continued to roll down the painting, but it was as if there just wasn't enough information being presented to get the names of those involved.

At last it was getting very late, and I was tired of the game. I became restless flitting from one thing to another. I wanted to sleep, but I was so speedy, so amped up. I was *buzzing*, as the saying goes, like a bee that drank coffee.

"Will I ever sleep again?" I thought to myself. "Maybe I'll never come down and I'll be like this for the rest of my life."

But, at last the mind surrendered and the body crashed. The next day life was back to normal, and yet I would never look at the world the same way again. I had cracked open the doors of perception. Even if I had failed to completely alter reality, I would never again hold to the idea that "seeing is believing".

Chapter 12

The Luck of the Draw

That spring, more tensions on the Ohio State Campus prompted the university to close its doors for the rest of the year. Final exams were canceled, and suddenly I was done with college. What a way to graduate! But now there was a new concern. Now that I had graduated from college, I no longer had a student deferment from the army draft. At the time, there was a lottery for the draft that was based on birth date. Every year in this period of history, the days of the year were randomly picked to determine that day's ranking in the draft. Number ones were the first to be drafted, then number twos, and so on until enough people were drafted to fill the army. The first year of the draft was 1970, and the number that was reached in that year was 195. In the summer of 1971 the numbers were drawn for the next year. My heart pounded as I listened to my fate being called out on television.

"Number 1 is... September 14th."

"Whew. That was close!"

"Number 2 is... April 24th. Number 3 is...."

They continued calling as I sat on the edge of my seat. "Number 72 is... September 10th." Another close call!

After much suspense, they called "Number 158 is... September 11th."

There it was. My number was 158. I would be drafted. It was just a matter of time. What would I do? I knew I couldn't fight. I couldn't kill. Would I go to Canada? (By 1973, 70,000 young men would move to Canada). If I went to Canada, I knew that there was a strong possibility that I would never be able to return to the U.S. I didn't know if I could do something so final, but I didn't know what else to do, either. Conscientious objector status was very difficult to get. I really wondered what was going to happen, and I felt powerless to do anything about it. As I was debating all this in my mind, my notice came in the mail to report for my physical. I'll never forget all those guys lined up in their underwear.

"Turn your head and cough.... Okay. Next."

Some people told the draft board they were gay. Some tried to get doctors to write letters for them. I just went with what fate was dealing as if it were all beyond my control. I passed the exam, and I was now draft status 1A. All I could do was wait to be called. That was quite a summer. I kept thinking that maybe it was my last summer, certainly my last summer in innocence. I'll tell you one thing. I partied hard.

The first thing I did was hop in my little Corvair and drive seven hundred miles nonstop to McCrea Louisiana for the *Celebration of Life* rock festival. It was billed as a sort of *mini-Woodstock*, and more than 50,000 rock fans from around the nation converged on this small island in the middle of the Atchafalaya River. For three days we camped, listened to the music, smoked pot and played naked in the mud. It was great to bathe in the vibes of what I would consider a spiritual event of our generation... drugs, sex, and rock and roll.

Actually, I don't remember any sex, but there was a great feeling of openness and camaraderie as we lived together, played together, and partied together to the music of Pink Floyd, Ike & Tina Turner, the Beach Boys, Boz Scaggs, Chuck Berry, B. B. King, Melanie, Brownsville Station, the Allman Brothers, Stephen Stills & Neil Young, Country Joe McDonald, and John Sebastian. Neither Joplin nor Hendrix made it. They both died in the fall of 1970. And this was Dwayne Allman's last major concert before he died. Jim Morrison of the Doors died just two weeks after the festival ended. Drugs helped to open a generation of young people to a new way of living and being, but there were definitely some casualties.

When I returned from the festival, my parents were off in Europe, so I let go of my apartment and moved home. This is when Nick and Lori, their friend Harry, and I got really close. Every evening, we got together to play music. That's when I really started smoking a lot of pot. Harry brought over his big water pipe (called a bong, because of the effect it had on consciousness), which we kept stoked, and all four of us began to melt into each other as that summer stretched out into eternity. The pot we smoked was quite strong, and it really helped us all drop into the present moment. There was an intensity and vibrancy to everything we were experiencing, including each other and especially the music. We must have listened to Paul McCartney's new album, *Ram*, three hundred times. We listened from way down inside our beings until every note was deeply imprinted into our brains.

Then, after we'd smoked enough pot to be transported to another reality altogether, we'd get out the guitars. I had just bought a Yamaha guitar for eighty dollars at a local music store and Nick and Harry, who played pretty well, were kind enough to let me play along. Lori, the English major, was in charge of getting the words to the songs we were playing. She gathered and printed hundreds of songs for us, all the popular tunes of the time. We played songs like *Honkey Tonk Woman* from the Rolling Stones, *Wild World* by Cat Stevens, *Brown Eyed Girl* from Van Morrison, *Desperado* and *Tequila Sunrise* by the Eagles. We played for hours at a time, and there was a magic chemistry between us all, like nothing I had ever experienced before, nor since. We merged into one being. In fact we even had a name for us. Using our combined names, we called ourselves "BlackLori ScarGard Well Stoned and Erogenous Jones", and we were all of that! That summer, not only did I have an amazing bonding experience that transcended time, I actually learned to play the guitar!

One day in the middle of that amazing summer, this crazy-moody-long-long-blonde-haired-shy-friend-of-Lori's named Lisa came and joined us at my house. She had L.S.D.

"Anybody want to take this?" She asked, pulling a small foil packet from one of the pockets of her bib-overalls.

"Yea. I'll take some," I told her. I'd had such an interesting trip the first time and wanted to do some more inner exploring. As it turned out, it was just the two of us who took the acid.

Trip 2 or there abouts: "The View from Off the Treadmill"

After we dropped the acid, we continued to party with Nick, Lori and Harry. We smoked lots of pot and played guitars as usual. Then, at some point, I noticed that Nick, Lori and Harry kept wanting to smoke more pot.

"What for?" I wondered. "Who needs it?"

I felt totally complete and satisfied... and wide-awake. Then, after a while, I noticed everyone was crashed out on one or another of the couches in my house. That is, everyone except Lisa, me and Jimi Hendrix. Yes Jimi Hendrix! Lisa had brought his album, *Are you Experienced?* And as we listened I was totally blown away. I had listened to Hendrix before, but this time... for the first time, I actually heard his genius. My God, he was amazing! I was caught in the nuances of his musical phrasing for what seemed like lifetimes.

Eventually, the others dragged themselves out to their cars and went home, Hendrix had finished, and then there we were, Lisa and I alone together. That's when I realized I really didn't know Lisa, and she also realized that she didn't know me. We were both suddenly so shy, and of course our discomfort was intensified by the L.S.D. We both felt so vulnerable, so exposed... like being turned inside out. It was so awkward!

"... If you can just get your mind together, we'll hold hands and watch the sun rise from the bottom of the sea..." Jimi's words were still reverberating. "If you can just get your mind together...."

We decided to take a walk in the night air. We stepped out of the door into the warm July night and began walking. Down the street, up another... we walked and walked and talked and talked. The activity really helped relieve the tension, and before long we were totally present in the walking and talking. Nothing and no one else existed in the whole world. There we were, just the two of us, a few feet of sidewalk in front of us, and the memory of the few feet of sidewalk behind us. After what seemed like forever, we came to a large field. We walked out into the middle of the field and sat on a large log that was lying there. When we stopped, everything stopped... and then... there we were.......

.... suspended in time, out under a universe of stars... a dazzling array of vastness....

An eternity later, the stars began to fade and the sky began to lighten.

"What's happening? What is it?" Ah.... the sun! It was beginning to rise... It was a new day, and it felt like the first day of our lives.

"... If you can just get your mind together, we'll hold hands and watch the sun rise from the bottom of the sea...."

What a miracle! What a glorious spectacle!

..... and thennnnnnnnn ....

"Now what? What's that sound? What's coming?"

Cars! Cars were coming. First one, then another, and then several more. Then more and more cars. They were everywhere... filling all the streets around the field. As we kept watching, lines of cars materialized in front of stop signs and at traffic lights. Everyone was hurrying, hustling, honking.....

"Where are they all going, what on earth for, and what's the hurry?"

Then I was suddenly struck with a realization. It was rush hour. All these people were going to work!

"Wow, what a rush!"

And, yet there we sat... in the middle of that field... watching the rat race unfold. It all seemed like some strange game... weird, weird, insane game. Each person in his own honking, smoking, hustling, little rectangular tin box. Trying to get somewhere... to do something!

"Disgusting!"
"Absurd!"
And we ......
.... suspended .... watching...
...like the fool on the hill....

Exhaustion finally overtook us, and we walked back down the streets on which we had come and back into the world, but my relationship to time was forever altered.

I thought about Lisa for quite some time after our bonding. Lisa didn't like herself much and I felt so much compassion for her.

I wanted to say to her, "I like you even if you don't."

***

In the latter part of the summer of 1971, Harry and I took a camping trip to the Laurentian Mountains of Quebec. It was there that I wrote my first song with some help from Harry. It was called *Being Buffaloed* [1], and was a bit of a satire on hunting the magnificent beast.

***

President Nixon somehow saved my life that summer. Yes, it could be true! The draft law expired sometime during that crazy pot smoking, going out of our minds, BlackLori ScarGuard Well Stoned summer. While we were catapulting ourselves into our own reality, back in the *real world*, the law that would send me to fight in Southeast Asia or force me to leave my beautiful country had expired, and the bill to renew it was sitting on Dick Nixon's oval office desk. Maybe it was just the result of bureaucracy, maybe he had other things on his mind, or maybe, just maybe the fates were watching over me. Whatever the reason, it took Nixon two or three months to sign the new bill into effect. That was two or three months when no one was getting drafted. As I said before, my number was 158. They had gotten to somewhere around 130 when the law expired. Once he signed the bill, the draft continued. Would the delay slow the draft enough? As it turned out, it did. They only reached 143. Somehow, I knew before the end of summer. I don't remember how or when, but all of a sudden I realized I wouldn't be drafted, and I can't tell you how relieved I was.

But then at the last minute, I realized I needed to get it together to continue my education. Of course, I was going to graduate school.

My brother had a Ph.D. My dad had a Ph.D. My uncle had a Ph.D. My grandfather had a Ph.D. It wasn't a question of whether I would or not, but where was I going. My dad pulled some strings, I filled out an application, and two weeks later I was in: graduate school in Social Psychology at, of all places, Bowling Green State University. Yes, I finally ended up in Bowling Green, but much too late for the relationship with my old girl friend, Lana. She was still there finishing up her senior year, but we were miles apart now. She was a well-dressed, conservative sorority sister and I was fast becoming a longhaired hippie graduate student. I ran into her a couple of times, but it was always awkward, and we really had nothing to say to each other. Her sister, Dawn, was a different story. She was attending Bowling Green too, but she was not into sororities. Instead she hung out with the hippie fringe and was now a pot smoker. We connected a few times. I even had a bit of a crush on her at one point, but she would always see me as her sister's old boyfriend.

As part of the Graduate assistantship, I was given a job working for an experimental Clinical Psychologist who was a visiting professor from California. The assistantship came with a small stipend. As I began to learn about the professor's work, I discovered that he was doing drug research on rats. The procedure involved killing the rats, grinding up their brains and running them through a centrifuge.

When I heard about it, I knew that I could not do this work. I could not be involved in killing these little animals. He appreciated my position and let me just handle and weigh the rats. I handled so many rats that quarter that I became allergic to cedar chips! The next quarter I got a teaching assistantship, which I liked a lot more.

Since my acceptance at Bowling Green was such a last minute thing, all I could find for housing was a room in a boarding house. Actually, I had to share the room with someone. The person I never really got to know and have no recollection of. That first quarter of graduate school was hell. I had no privacy and no real place to call home, but little by little I began to get to know my boarding house neighbors, Stephen, Michael and Ben. When I think back on that time, I remember what crazy friends we became and the hours and hours we spent just hanging out together. Of course, the drugs we were taking intensified everything and helped bring us into the eternal present.

Chapter 13

My Crazy Friends and a Big Leak

"Trips of Abandon": Spring of 1972

That first year of Graduate School, I was living on the second floor of a rooming house with five rooms. The first person I met there was Stephen. He was a most unusual person, with or without the pot we were smoking. Stephen was a nerd I guess you could say. He was as blind as a sea turtle without his triple thickness glasses, and he was as skinny as a stick insect. I can still see him walking about the rooming house as if it were yesterday, a bit stooped over with his blondish hair flopped down over his face. He was the natural old man, even shuffling his feet a bit like Chaplin. I could almost imagine him twirling a cane. Stephen was an actor and a master of characters, especially the old man, somehow his true persona. He was also a real pack rat. In fact, Stephen's small room just down the hall from me was more like a museum than a room. He had a big old wooden desk, which took up a large part of his room and was full of little compartments. The desk reminded me of something Ebenezer Scrooge would have had. The remainder of the space was filled with old props from years of University theater productions, which made visiting Stephen's room a real trip, and somewhere amongst it all was his small bed.

Stephen and I soon became great friends, partly because he loved to get stoned on pot and take L.S.D. He was often my motor scooter partner on those occasions. Riding like the wind, singing the entire forty-five minute Jethro Tull song *Thick as a Brick* at the top of our lungs, light as the wind that carried us, Stephen and I were crazy, reckless, and free; riding through the world on what we called "Scott Scooter," the three of us, Stephen, me and that trusty scooter were true friends.

"Monkeys in a tree, climbing Man's monoliths
    Like a wise owl perched above
    Watching those dedicated students enter the barren wasteland of higher learning...
        ... And off again.
        A one act play
    And then riding like the wind to the four corners
    of the globe!
        A wave of paranoia...
        A cop car following...
        'Quick, down the side street!'
        Racing like an antelope...
                smelling danger...
                faster, faster.
                Down there,
                turn here.
            Through the alley
                up the street!
        Park it.
        Up the stairs... Quick. Run.
        Quickly, quickly
        Close the door.
        ....AH SAFE.... (and very high on acid)"

What I noticed from this little trip was how I viewed the world from such a self-centered, self-conscious perspective. In this little episode, I made up a whole story about being chased by the police and then all my perceptions helped support this paranoid delusion; at least I think it was a paranoid delusion. Hmmm. Maybe the cops really were after us! In any case, I was beginning to understand the mind of the Psychotic.

That's why I ended up volunteering at a drug drop-in center called Karma that year. I'd hang out at the center and help people who were freaking out on acid. My main therapeutic method was to "go with" what the client was experiencing. Rather than resist their delusions and reflect reality like most therapists did, I climbed into their psychosis with them... accompanied them on their trips and basically said, "Wow, this is cool!" I guess you could say I helped the clients reframe their experiences in a more positive light. Frankly, it worked, and we all had fun in the process! One night I guy came in to the center claiming he was Jeremy Clyde of the famous sixties rock duo, Chad and Jeremy. I ended up taking Jeremy home to my house, and we spent all night playing old Chad and Jeremy songs on our guitars. He left town the next day, and I never did find out if he really was Jeremy Clyde. I like to believe he was, but either way, we had a great time that night.

Another of my boarding house mates was Michael. He lived just across the hall from Stephen. Now there was an interesting guy. Unlike Stephen, Michael was a serious student, and so he studied a lot. He was Czechoslovakian, and he loved classical music. He particularly loved classical music with a twist, like *Switched on Bach*, a sort of Baroque music gone electric, and he also loved Frank Zappa, a crazy acidhead musician with an affinity for the bizarre. Michael had by far the best sound system in the house, and when he was taking a break from studying, he'd really crank it up. When he wasn't playing his Psychedelic classical, he'd put on the Rolling Stones' song, *Sympathy for the Devil* at full volume. I can't hear that song without an image of Michael's face flashing into my mind.

I ran into Michael years later in Denver, Colorado. He had become a stockbroker, and in his spare time he chanted the Japanese Buddhist mantra, *Namu Myōhō Renge Kyō* with a group of people that seemed to me to be "Spiritual Materialists."

Then there was Ben. What a freak he was. Ben was a free spirit just traveling across the country when he came to us. He stopped in to see a girl who was a student at BG, then rented a room in our boarding house for a month at a time, and then just stayed... all year. He wasn't going to school or anything, he was just hanging out. One of his great talents was that he could smoke a joint like no one else could. He got every last molecule of smoke. This was his technique: he took a long toke on the joint, and then, while still holding his breath in, he would take the joint out of his mouth, turn it around so the smoking part was under his nose, and through an amazing mastery of breath control suck in that last little bit of smoke through his nose before passing the joint on.

"Don't Bogart that joint my friend, pass it over to me," someone would often say to him as he was savoring the nuances.

Ben would eventually marry that girl he was visiting at Bowling Green, cut his long hair, put on a business suit, and get a prestigious engineering job. Then after twenty years or more of marriage he would leave his straight job, leave his marriage, and go off with an exotic dancer. The last thing I heard was that he had bought a sailboat and was living his dream of sailing in the Caribbean.

We had many inspired times together in that boarding house, while I, at the same time, was trying to focus a bit on my graduate studies in Social Psychology. By the end of the first quarter my roommate with whom I never connected moved out, finally leaving me with the room to myself. As the second quarter of graduate school commenced, I had a great space, had some great friends, my studies were going well, and I was teaching Introductory Psychology instead of handling condemned rats. Things were definitely looking up. That's when I bought a king-size waterbed.

My room was the large one at the end of the upstairs hall and had a window that opened to the front porch roof. When my roommate left, I had the landlord remove and bunk beds, and I set up my new waterbed. I had no frame and no liner, just the bed... a giant sack of water sitting on the hardwood floor. I borrowed a hose to fill the bed from my first-floor neighbors just before they moved out. It took several hours and untold numbers of gallons of water. In my math-major days, I probably could have worked out just how many gallons, but I put my mind to other things these days. I didn't have a heater for the bed, so I laid down two thick blankets between the bed and the bottom sheet. The cold still seeped in, but I didn't care. I loved the adventure and comfort of floating on the water. My housemates loved it too. The waterbed soon became a sort of social center, and it was quite common to have two or three of us lounged out on it at any particular moment. It was great to smoke some pot and loose oneself in the rhythmic movement it generated. We even played the party game, Twister, on that bed. Yep. Someone would invite some girls over and before we knew it we were laying the vinyl mat down on the bed and someone would begin spinning.

"Left foot red... right hand blue... left hand red...."

Inevitably we would all end up in a big puppy pile, tumbling and sloshing around on my bed of water. The waterbed held up amazingly well... until....

One morning, I woke up and noticed there was a soggy corner in my blankets. I pulled up the sheets and the two insulating blankets to investigate. There, along one of the corner seams of the vinyl... was a small leak.

"Hey guys, I need some help in here," I called out from my bedroom door. Stephen and Michael both heard me and came to my aid.

"The leak is right there in the corner," I explained. "Let's see if we can prop that part up, maybe take some of the pressure off."

Michael and I tugged at the corner of the waterbed and Stephen slipped some books underneath it. The trickle seemed to lessen, but not stop.

"I think you're going to have to drain it," said Michael.

The only way to drain a waterbed is to hook up a hose to it, run the water as if filling it, shut off the water, and disconnect the hose from the faucet. Gravity then pulls the water out of the hose and onto the ground creating a vacuum in the hose, which then continues to pull at the water from the waterbed until the bed is completely drained. This would all be fairly easy... if we had a hose.

"A hose. I've gotta find a hose, quick," I yelled.

I ran down the hall, out the door and down the back steps.

"I wonder who has a hose," I thought as I ran.

The downstairs neighbor had moved out, so I knocked on the next-door neighbor's house. Music was blaring. I knocked harder. A young, longhaired guy came to the door.

"Uh... waterbed's got a leak. I gotta find a hose... quick. You have one?"

"No, man. Sorry."

I knocked on another door, getting more frantic... same answer.

"No man. We don't have a hose."

The neighborhood was full of college students! No one had a hose. I looked around... up and down the street. Then I saw it... a little old house... white picket fence, paint peeling, grass overgrown in the yard, blinds pulled.

"Maybe, they've got a hose!"

I ran down the street, opened the gate in little white picket fence, and went up to the porch. I knocked... and waited, knocked again and waited some more. After awhile, I could here a very faint sound from inside... a shuffling sound.

"Shuffle, shuffle, shuffle, shuffle."

I was beside myself with a sense of urgency, but still I waited.

"Shuffle, shuffle, shuffle, shuffle."

At long last the door creaked open... ever so slowly... and a hunched over, decrepit old man poked his head out the door.

"Yessss?"

"Uh... my waterbed. It's got a leak. I need a hose real bad... and quick. Can I borrow your hose?"

"My what?" He retorted, hand cupped to his ear.

"A hose. I need to borrow your hose."

"Did you say you needed a hose?" he asked and then added, "Come to the back door. I've got a hose." He vanished inside and the door creaked shut.

I raced around to the back while visualizing the larger and larger leak in my waterbed, those hundreds of gallons of water rushing through the floorboards rotting out the plaster, and then pouring down into the downstairs apartment. My heart was beating a mile an minute.

"Shuffle, shuffle, shuffle, shuffle."

I was in suspended animation.

"Shuffle, shuffle, shuffle, shuffle, shuffle, shuffle."

At last the back door creaked open, the little old man leaned out and pointed to the side yard. "It's over there. Put it back when you're done, please."

I thanked him and raced over to where he had pointed. I didn't see it at first, but then as I got closer, I saw the hose curled around in the tall grass.

"Fantastic!"

I ran over to the spot where it lay and picked it up. The hose came up into my hands exactly as it had lain in the grass. The coil was perfectly preserved like those trees in the Petrified Forest. The hose was stiff as a board. I looked down at the spot from where I had taken the hose and saw a bare patch of ground exactly matching the shape of the hose.

"This hose has not been used in a very long time," I realized, "But it's a hose!"

I grabbed the hose and ran for the boarding house, upstairs and down the hall to my room. There was a big spot of water on the floor, which I mopped up with some towels and then I got to work. I opened the window and pulled at the hose trying to straighten it enough to lower one end of it down to the ground below. Stephen and Michael were both down there trying to reach it as I crawled out on the front porch roof and dangled it down. At last Michael grabbed the end, and we managed to straighten it out. I attached my end to the waterbed. Michael attached the other end to the spigot, and Stephen turned on the water.

Then I heard Michael cry out, "Shit! I'm drowning down here!"

I peered out over the roof to see a veritable fountain there along the wall. Water was coming out of at least a dozen places.

"We're never gonna get our vacuum this way," Michael said turning off the water.

"We need some tape!" I exclaimed.

Stephen said he had some. I met him at his room, and he dug through the cubbyholes in that mighty desk of his and at last held up a roll of masking tape. I wrapped the tape around several obvious breeches in the hose, and we tried again. The hose was still leaking, but not so badly. I listened for the water to reach the bed, and then when we finally heard it, we had Michael shut off the water and disconnect the hose. Water began trickling out the bottom.

"We did it!" yelled Stephen.

Just then the trickle stopped.

"More tape. We need more tape," I yelled.

We used up the rest of the roll, winding it around that hose in all the places where we had seen water.

"Ok! Let's try again," I hollered, and we repeated the process.

Although water was still seeping out the sides of the hose, the tape held, and this time the water continued to pour out of the bottom. After twenty minutes, the bed was noticeably lower... and then, when the bed was about eighty percent drained, the water stopped flowing from the hose.

"I guess that's as much as we're going to get out with this hose," I reasoned. "If we can just drag the bed up to the window, maybe we can drain the rest of the water out onto the roof."

Michael, Stephen and I all lifted.

"Uhhhh," we all grunted as we lifted a section of the bed only to have the water roll down to another section. It was like herding salamanders. Then we tried folding up the bed so that all the remaining water was trapped in one area.

"Okay. Let's all lift together. Uhhhhhhh."

We had the water contained, and we were gradually making our way up the wall to the window.

"That's it! Keep pushing!"

We pushed with every ounce of strength we had and finally got it up to the window... and then....

"Oh no!"

The bed got away from us!

"Bullllumm, bulllumm, bulllumm," it began rolling. We reached out, but too late. It was picking up speed as it rolled... down the roof and then... off... out of sight... only to be followed by a large "Bawump!"

The three of us crawled out to the edge of the roof and looked down to see a large pile of vinyl lying in the broken and twisted remains of the rose garden. My waterbed days had come to an end.

Chapter 14

On the Cross

The following spring, Ben's girl friend Cindy approached me as I was walking to class.

"I'm making a movie for my film class... and you would be perfect for the leading role," she said excitely.

"Oh yeah, what's the movie about?" I asked, my curiosity piqued at the prospect of being a movie star. I'd been in the movies before, but never in a starring role. My roommate Lou at Wooster had made a film. It was a spoof on James Bond movies in which I was an extra who died seven times! My most memorable death was when I was shot and then fell to the ground from a second story window. I was sore for a week from that stunt.

"It's an old story with a bit of a twist," she explained. "It's about the crucifixion of Jesus, only this time, he hammers in his own nails, with the help of God."

"And you want me to play...?"

"Jesus, of course," she said.

It was the long brown hair and beard, I guess. I did look the part, and I was an expert at dying, so I agreed. Cindy wanted to have Jesus crucified on a hill, but Bowling Green was... well... the name says it all... a bowling green. Well, at least it was flat enough to be one. But there was one spot on campus that might work. It was a place where they had ski lessons in the winter and was made by an earthmover when they were building the on-ramp for the freeway. Someone had the road crew dig a small pond and pile the dirt up beside it. The mound they created was about twenty feet high and was less than fifty yards from interstate 75. We called it Bill's Hill.

The filming was to be one Saturday morning. I arrived at Bill's Hill and was asked to wear a tattered cloth and a wreath of thorns. As Cindy began filming, I was instructed to pick up the cross they had made for me, and drag it up to the top of Bill's Hill as Ben and Michael and Stephen followed behind as my disciples. When we got to the top, we set up the cross by placing it in a hole that we had dug and I climbed up onto it with the help of a ladder.

"Here," Cindy said handing me a hammer and a large nail. I placed the nail between the fingers of my left hand, and as she filmed I began driving the nail into the cross. God's hand then reached down from above (Michael on the ladder out of sight of the camera), and *He* hammered in the other nail. A pretty young woman playing Mary Magdalene then held a joint to my lips with a very long roach clip, I took a toke, and my spirit ascended into heaven. The End.

I could now add "Crucified on Bill's Hill" to my list of accomplishments for this lifetime. To this day, I wonder what the people thought who were driving down the freeway that day.

***

The next year, I answered an ad posted on a University bulletin board for "roommate wanted", left the boarding house, and shared an apartment with someone who would remain one of my best friends throughout my life. Bill was his name, and he was a graduate student in the speech department specializing in human communications. He was intelligent, articulate, in touch with his feelings and quite present. Bill had big brown, puppy dog eyes and a warm smile. He had had polio in childhood, which gave him an atrophied right arm, but his right hand was unaffected. As a result, this hand had to navigate on its own to be of use to him. This was a truly amazing thing to watch. (a bit like watching cousin *It* in the T.V. show the Adams Family who was simply a hand with no body). The combined effect of Bill's disability, his almost Bambi-like innocence, and his little-boy mischievousness, made Bill an irresistible friend. Bill was also what I would call a connoisseur. You see he was used to having a lot more money than I was. I made $3,000 a year on my stipend, which I considered to be a lot of money, but Bill had actually worked as a social worker for a couple years before going back to school and had saved money. Well, I'll tell you this, he knew how to spend it. He loved fine food and would always buy the best cheese, and the best bread. He also insisted on the very best marijuana. The marijuana, of which he always had an ample supply, he got from his friend Jerry, a fellow communications student and local pot dealer.

It was through Bill that I met Jerry and his wife, Fran, who would prove to be a major influence in my life and my spiritual journey [2].

Fran was a Graduate student in the Counseling Department and a therapist at the University counseling center. At that time, the department was run by a man who had studied with Fritz Perls, the famous Gestalt therapist. The focus of Gestalt therapy was on the *experiential present moment*, and it was grounded on the belief that everyone is caught in webs of relationships; thus, it is only possible to know ourselves against the background of our relationships to the *other*.

Gestalt therapy focused on process and emphasized what was being done, thought, and felt in the present moment. Thus, it became known as the therapy of "I-thou in the here and now". One of the main methods for exploring the Gestalt was the encounter group, where one was encouraged to "let it all hang out... express your feelings... and come to your senses."

I felt myself drawn to this experiential and confrontational approach to Psychology, and over the course of that next year, I began spending more and more time hanging out at the counseling center and participating in these groups. This culminated in a twenty-four hour marathon encounter group: ten people in a room together for twenty-four hours with no sleep just relating as real as possible. It was while participating in these groups that I began developing a major crush on Fran. The combination of her sharp intellect, bubbly personality, and stunning good looks really hooked me. But, sadly, she was married, so I did the only thing I could under the circumstances. I started dating her best friend, Kimberly, another therapist at the center. Kimberly was alive, expressive, passionate and very in touch with her feelings. I was swept up in her way of being *real*, and I guess you could say I intimately embraced what my colleagues in the Psychology department called the *touchy feely* types.

As I was exploring this free-flow, experiential side of Psychology, I still had a foot in academia. After all, I was in a Ph.D. program in Social Psychology. The trouble was that this particular Psychology department had a strong behaviorist perspective. At that time, Psychology was struggling to be considered science, and therefore shied away from anything experiential. From the behaviorist view, man was just a response mechanism, or at least what could be known and studied about man's psyche were only his behaviors. The discipline had embraced physics as its model for the study of the human mind, and so it rejected anything that could not be seen from the outside. Behaviorists believed that humans were conditioned very much like other animals, and as a result an enormous amount of research in Psychology was done on rats. My area of study was no exception. So here I was twenty-three years old and becoming more and more curious about what made me tick, how I related to others, and who I really was, spending my time reviewing behavioral theories and studying rat and monkey behavior.

Frankly, I was much more interested in how we were uniquely human than how we were like rats, and I certainly did not want to be a mere observer in the process. I wanted to be an active participant. As the year progressed, I gravitated more and more toward the counseling center, where I could explore my senses and my feelings, communicate authentically, and discover who I really was in relation to those around me. I could see that this was where the *social* in Social Psychology was really practiced, by direct encounter. In the Gestalt groups I came face to face with repressed feelings, social masks, and what it meant to be truly authentic with other people. In other words, I was learning to be real!

I tried to bring these interests back to my Psychology study, and it became a major focus in my Master's thesis. I worked for nine months on a theoretical dissertation that explored the topic of emotions from the psychological, behavioral, and physiological levels. I even included some little known information from Freud's early physiological studies of synaptic loops in the brain. At long last I presented my masterpiece to the thesis committee, but they refused to read it. They said the proposal was too long and was not essentially experimental. I was crushed. I felt rejected and not understood and began wondering if there was something wrong with me. I questioned my capability and my self-worth and was flooded with self-doubt. I felt beat down. Then I turned from defeat to cynical compliance.

"I'll give them what they want," I told myself.

And so I sat down and wrote a completely new proposal on a completely new topic. It was a proposal for what I considered to be a stupid, meaningless, trivial little social psychology experiment. I took an existing experiment and changed one variable. It was two days' work. I don't even remember what the experiment was about. I submitted the new proposal to the thesis board.

"Now you're getting the idea!" they said. "This is much better. You just need to iron out a few details."

I can still feel the adrenalin rush through my veins at hearing these words!

"If this is what you think is better, then I quit!" I yelled, threw the paper across the desk and stormed out! The next day I quit graduate school. (Hmmm. I wonder now if I really came across that strong. That's certainly how I felt, but I wonder if I had that kind of courage. What I know for sure is that I did indeed drop out of graduate school.)

As I let go my prospects for a Ph.D., I told myself I didn't have time to waste on academic pursuits any more, and I felt the truth of it. Something inside was calling me. In that one act I had broken with my long family tradition in academia (brother, father, uncle, grandfather all PhD's), and I no longer had a road map for my life. I was on an uncharted course into unknown territory. My inner journey in search of my self and the true nature of existence began in earnest that day.

Chapter 15

Uncharted Territory

Following my inner calling, I began reading certain books. The first important book I remember reading was Aldous Huxley's *The Doors of Perception*, in which he described his experience of taking Mescalin for the first time.

He told us how he was so absorbed in the process of looking and so amazed by what he saw, that he couldn't be aware of anything else, and that everything was inexpressibly wonderful to the point of being terrifying. Huxley so clearly elucidated the other realms and experiences of reality. I was captivated, and as if I were hearing from Columbus after returning from America or Edmund Hillary after going to the South Pole, I was stirred to go exploring. But first, I read more from this journalist pioneer. He went on to tell us how he was shaken out of the ruts of ordinary perception and shown a world not as it appears to someone obsessed with words and ideas, but as they are experienced directly and unconditionally by something greater. As I read this I realized that I had glimpsed some of these realms myself, but now I had new resolve to look deeper. Then Huxley began describing the common features of the other realms. He talked about the special quality of light that was often experienced, and how everything was brilliantly illuminated, seeming to shine from within. When I read this, I thought about my first L.S.D. trip with the glowing black-light poster. Then he went on to describe the recognition on the drug of a heightened significance to all of life, as if everything experienced had a message to convey. I was to have this feeling again and again in my trips. As I understand it, this is very much the way a Psychotic views the world all the time, but hopefully without the paranoia. Lastly, he described the special classes of objects that turned up in the Psychedelic experience including living geometrical forms, animals and even archetypal figures.

While reading Huxley, I came upon a famous quote by William James an early influence in Psychology who said that our normal waking consciousness was but one special type of consciousness, while all around it there lay potential forms of consciousness entirely different. After reading that, I was convinced that this was the real Psychology, and I knew that these dimensions of consciousness were what I really wanted to study.

Then I picked up a book by Timothy Leary and Richard Alpert (later to be known as Baba Ram Dass). They were Psychologists at Harvard who began experimenting with Psychedelics. Eventually, they were fired from Harvard for their unconventional approach to science. That's when Alpert made the statement that he no longer wanted to be the experimenter. From then on he would be the experiment! The book was called *The Psychedelic Experience*, and in it Leary and Alpert charted the outer territories of the mind, worlds beyond this everyday reality, and the journeys that could be taken into the miraculous and the divine. It was in that book that Tim made this famous decree: "Turn on, tune in, and drop out." To *turn on*, he said, is to realize that we are not isolated, separate social egos, but part of the energy dance of the universe. To *tune in* is to arrange our environment to reflect that realization, and to *drop out* is to let go of the social commitments that no longer serve the new paradigm.

After considering these ideas of Dr. Leary, I could feel that I was ready for the journey. I was tired of living in a strictly rational universe and I was beginning to suspect that there was more to life than what I was experiencing. Now, having dropped out already, I was free to make the trip. In fact, I was in a prime position to *turn on* and *tune in*, and I was convinced that Psychedelic drugs were my gateway to this new consciousness. Leary gave one final precaution to the would be inner explorer by stressing the importance of what he called "set and setting" in taking the drug. What he said was that a would-be-explorer needed to set the right intention for him or her self, and then take L.S.D. in a safe and nurturing environment.

It was the summer of 1973, and I had the rest of my life before me. With no plans and no commitments, I was ready to explore consciousness from the inside, navigating the many layers of my own mind. In contemplating this journey, I sincerely believed that these deeper reaches of subjective experience held the key to life's true meaning, and that the pursuit of this meaning was the true education.

To *turn on*, I began taking L.S.D. once a week. I took it in nature and lost myself in the variety of life forms: trees, flowers, insects. I saw everything as intensely beautiful and mystically significant. All that I encountered had lessons to teach, about pattern, form, and harmony. On one journey into the woods, I saw the mysterious Luna moth of my childhood, and it led me to eat some berries.

"The moth led me to them," I told my friends and fellow travelers. "There is a secret in these berries."

Remember, under L.S.D. everything is pregnant with significance, and there seem to be no random events. I was convinced that I was being told to eat these berries, and I ate them without hesitation. My body, however, had its own wisdom, and an hour or so after eating the berries I vomited. What was the secret that was revealed on that trip? It was simply that there is body intelligence that operates completely on its own. I saw how I was protected from within, and my conscious mind was overwhelmed by the mystery and wisdom of this biological intelligence.

Other trips were more *inner*. One trip was spent in total darkness, in my basement. Actually, I should say total outward darkness, because there was plenty of light and color, cartoon Technicolor all around me mostly in paisley patterns.

"Hmmm. What is it about paisley? Looks a lot like Paramecia, those little one-celled creatures that we studied in high school. Yes... that's right!"

As I watched these cartoons on everything, my consciousness began to zoom in... in... in... into the very fabric of everything, and at that moment all of life was reduced into their component cells. Then I saw my own body as a giant city. From where I stood, high above but at the same time inside myself, in a kind of control tower, I looked out over the whole operation and was overwhelmed by the enormity and complexity of it all. From my vantage point I saw millions of beings all living in harmony, each going about its work, each one a specialist. There were carpenters, building and maintaining the walls of the city. There were boiler room workers keeping the furnaces running, while many workers were dedicated to gathering and transporting the fuel. There were specialists in ventilation and others working in waste management, and there were vast and sophisticated transportation and communication networks connecting everyone. As I watched all this in fascination, I was suddenly struck as if by a bolt of lightning with this burning question:

"Who's in charge of this operation? Certainly not *me*. This is far too complex! Besides, I'm out here watching it all. So, who's running the show?"

With this realization came a rush of fear that soon subsided into shear, benevolent wonder as I settled into watching the absolute perfection of it all.

"Life is a miracle!" I spoke out loud and realized the truth of these words.

I can still see myself in this way today, and I realize that life is truly amazing. This body is incredible. How was it possible for me to overlook this fact while searching so long and hard for the miraculous out in the world somewhere?

Another, less inspiring, but never-the-less equally revelatory trip found me sitting on the toilet, afraid to let go. The whole experience was so textbook, classically Freudian. Then and there, sitting in my bathroom, I really deeply understood what Freud meant by *anal-retentive*. As I sat there with the natural urges pressing upon me, I was overcome with intense fear of emptying my bowels. It seemed clear to me in that moment that I was at risk of losing my entire self down that toilet, that if I pressed too hard I would certainly turn inside out, and all of me would plunge down that drain. Wow! It's amazing what we can become attached to!

In another trip, I was with my girlfriend, Kimberly who was also tripping. As I mentioned before, Kimberly was the queen of showing her feelings, and she had a rubber face that displayed them with graphic honesty. I was both attracted and repulsed by this quality of letting it all hang out. It was something my breeding prevented me from doing easily, despite all the group therapy I had explored.

Kimberly was a Scorpio and was not only comfortable with emotions, she loved sex, something I could go along with breeding or not (Hmmm, there's a bit of a pun there!). So, even though we were tripping, a state where my awareness was not exactly centered on physicality, she was feeling horny and wanted to make love. As we undressed and I saw her there naked beside me, I was struck by how beautiful her feminine form was. She had a petite frame, but large breasts, and as I caressed her I felt a primitive force stirring deep down in my being. Then as I gazed at her lying in the bed with the bed-sheets softly draped over her, I was overwhelmed by the beauty... of the bed coverings.

"Wow, look at the pattern in these sheets! Amazing!"

So much for the primitive urges. I was definitely having trouble staying focused on the task at hand. But with renewed determination, Kimberly caressed me and encouraged me to caress her. She had to work really hard to get me aroused and keep me that way, and I really had to stay focused. At last, I was inside her, and as we moved together the energy began to rise. The primitive urges were back and getting stronger and stronger, beginning to take me over, filling my whole body with focused passion. Next came deep rushes of feeling accompanied by stroboscopic patterns of light that were centered around my third eye.

"My God! My God! It's so intense... so beautiful... so incredibly beautiful."

I was journeying down a long tunnel of psychedelic colors, and just as all that energy seemed to be coming to a peak, I was suddenly overwhelmed by a deep, deep primal feeling.

"What is this feeling? It's so familiar but I just can't quite identify it? If I could just find the name for it, I'd know what it is. But God, it's so deep."

I searched and searched through my databank brain, all in a nano-second, all while the primitive urges were still strong, and then suddenly a word came floating into my consciousness.

"Mummy."

It was the name I called my mother when I was really little. As the word formed in my brain, I was immediately flooded with a deep, deep feeling, like an infant longing, and then I had the distinct impression that I was climbing back into the womb... safe, loved and totally enveloped by something universally feminine. Everything else disappeared. Needless to say I lost all interest in the *climax*.

I can see Freud observing all this and saying, "Hmmmm. Very interesting. I shall have to have a name for this."

Chapter 16

A Glimpse of Paradise

Somewhere in the middle of that timeless summer, Kimberly and I took a trip to Florida. I remember nothing of the trip except this one experience with L.S.D., an encounter with both heaven and hell. We had gone to a beautiful wild area of oceanfront called DeSoto National Monument. I decided to go to the beach and drop some acid.

"Acid in paradise", I wondered. "What would that be like?" I would soon get my answer... one of the peak moments of my life.

I set my shoes and towel down on the sand and began walking among the dunes. I climbed a little hill, and just as the L.S.D. started to take effect, I came upon a scene that was the epitome of what I would call paradise. The sun was shining in a vibrant blue sky, the waves of the Gulf of Mexico were gently caressing the shore, and there before me was a heavenly lagoon, complete with palm trees, emerald blue water and one large, majestic Great Blue Heron. The palms were gently swaying in the breeze, and the heron was standing statue-like before me. It was a picture perfect moment, and as I stood transfixed by the beauty time somehow unwound itself and quietly came to a standstill. In that moment the vastness of eternity descended upon me, and I became pure, limitless presence.

"This is it!" Something deep inside me reported. "This is the promised Shangri-la that all the mystics and poets have written about."

It was Heaven... here in this very moment. I had arrived... and yet "I" wasn't. By the grace of something vast, I was given an opportunity to be a witness to this magnificence, and now it all just was... there... complete in every way... just bathing in this ever-present moment. As I stood in the enormity of this forever-timeless presence, through the accumulated history of all life on earth, there came a sound... first quiet and then stronger, louder... and then all around me and within me... a most beautiful song... from a most exalted choir of angels... breaking my heart with its otherworldly sweetness. As the moment unfolded and I was swimming in song, a whole succession of births and deaths passed through this timeless space... God taking one great breath after another....

And then at some point, after an eternity of bliss, and seemingly out of nowhere, came a thought.

"Will this last?"

Just then I descended from Heaven, the world came crashing in around me, and time started moving again. I took a step, and the next thing I noticed was a strong sensation in my feet and legs that rapidly intensified to become pain.

"What's going on?" I yelled.

I looked around me and discovered that I was standing in a gigantic patch of thorny bushes that were piercing my skin in a hundred places. Barbs were stuck in my feet and legs, and blood was running down onto the sand.

"Welcome back to life," the thorns seemed to be saying.

Many years later, I would move to a Costa Rican paradise and discover once again that paradise had a shadow side. Spiritual teacher Satyam Nadeen has a truism about what he calls "life in the third dimension". He calls it the freedom/limitation equation and says that what he calls "source" always keeps these two aspects of the divine in balance. Another similar idea that's part of our folk wisdom goes something like this: "The higher you go, the harder you fall." Whatever the spiritual principle may be, I was experiencing shear hell.

At last, after a very painful process of extracting myself from the burs and the burs from me, I walked back to the beach to where

I had left my shoes, towel and other things... or at least where I thought I had left them. The wind was picking up now, and the sun was noticeably lower in the sky.

"It's getting late. How long was I there... in paradise?" I wondered to myself. "And where is my stuff?"

I walked on and on in one direction down the beach. There was still no sign of my things. Then, I felt an adrenalin rush at the thought that I didn't know where I was.

"Okay. Get a hold of yourself," my rational side mumbled. "My stuff has to be here somewhere. There's only one ocean around, and it's right here."

That's when I had the mental experience I call the gambler's dilemma. At some point, after walking a long way, I was struck with the thought.

"My stuff is either just a little bit further down the beach, in which case I need to keep going, or it's way down the other way."

There's a mental trap in this perception, which is why I call it the gambler's dilemma. It's this: If what I'm looking for really is just a little further this way and I give up now, I'll never find it. On the other hand, if I keep going and it's really way down the other way, I'll keep walking forever and never find it either. At what point do I know I've gone too far?

With my warped sense of time and a distorted sense of space, I really didn't know if I'd gone too far, so I kept walking in the direction I had been going. But, as the sun started to go down, I finally had to conclude that my things were miles away in the opposite direction. At last, I turned, ran back the other way, and in the dim twilight, came across my stuff. At the same time the effects of the acid started wearing off, and reality reassembled itself.

"Whew. Everything's back in its place." I sighed.

I loved the altered states, but was always glad to return to normalcy. We drove back to Ohio the next day.

Now it was time for me to *tune in*. The old identity was crumbling. I was no longer an academic. So was I something else besides an inner explorer? Through the psychedelic explorations, I had seen so much beauty, that I felt compelled toward artistic expression...

so that I could share that beauty with the world. That's when I began constructing mobiles and making designs in string. I loved working with my hands and spent hours in the construction of the mobiles, finding that perfect balance point, and drilling holes in wood and threading string to make mandalas of color. I also took up embroidery and began decorating my clothes with bursts of color and pattern. This was a period of my life when I dropped my preconceived notions of identity and let go of my assumptions about what was possible. In short, I was recreating myself.

It was easy and natural for me to *drop out*. I no longer had to please anyone but myself, and I had nothing to prove. I wasn't accountable to anyone, and I had endless amounts of time on my hands. I was free. In retrospect, I'm not sure Kimberly felt this way. I think she may have wanted me to be more accountable. There was definitely some tension building in that relationship as I continued what society would view as an *irresponsible lifestyle*.

Despite hidden pressures, though, I continued to explore those inner spaces that summer. I was really fascinated by the layers of the mind that I had seen on L.S.D., and I was convinced that the drug was helping me break down my assumptions and projections of reality and my rigid, biased interpretations of what the world was. I was hoping to tear down my worldview and then build it all over again for myself, piece by piece, through personal choice and experience rather than through indoctrination and belief. It took a lot of L.S.D. for me to even see the possibility of other worlds. Raised, as I said, by scientific pragmatic parents, I had a thick veil of "I only believe what I see" to blast away, and the psychedelic drug sessions did give me glimpses of a radically different perspective on what life is. It helped me look into the inner workings of my body and my mind, and it filled everything with mystical significance and luminosity that I perceived as divine. But after many psychedelic sessions, I began to feel a sort of frustration. Although I had many glorious experiences, saw the world with expanded vision, and had many creative ideas, I couldn't manifest much while under the influence of the drug. It just didn't lend itself to practical application. And when I came down from the drug, I would be a bit hung over and in a less-than-inspired state. I was growing tired of the ups and downs, tired of being given a taste of paradise only to have it continually taken away. The cycle of repeated highs and lows was taking its toll.

"Have you seen the new book, *Be Here Now*?" Fran asked me one day while I was over visiting.

She and I seemed to share this search for mystical meaning, as well as an increasing disillusionment with drugs, whereas her husband Jerry and the others in our crowd showed no interest in quitting. Of course, for Jerry there was an added dimension. He was in the business and seemed to thrive on the danger of drug dealing. Perhaps it had something to do with the fact that his father had been in the mafia.

"Be Here Now? I haven't seen it," I answered. "Who's it by?"

"Baba Ram Dass," said Fran. "It's a name Richard Alpert took after he went to India. Here. I've got a copy. Take a look."

She pulled the book off the shelf and handed to me, and I started turning the pages. I could immediately see that it was written from an acid trip perspective with psychedelic drawings and bold print. The words and images jumped out of the pages and went directly in to the *turned on* part of my mind. The book seemed to be a roadmap to altered states of consciousness. In the book, Ram Dass talked about how yogis of India were experiencing the same states we were having on L.S.D., but they were experiencing them without drugs. He went on to say that there was an illuminated state of consciousness that lasted beyond a twelve-hour drug induced experience, and that there were people, spiritually enlightened ones, who lived in these spaces... permanently... beyond time, beyond mind.

I bought my own copy of this remarkable book, took a deep dive into its contents, and here is what I heard Ram Dass say:

First he gave us L.S.D. wisdom by telling us that consciousness, energy, love, awareness, light, wisdom, beauty, truth, and purity were all the same trip... and that any journey we wanted to take would lead us to the same place. He invited us to embrace all the beautiful visions and become one with the universe. He said that all the energy passes through us. In fact, we are all the energy.

Next he began describing the meditational state by saying that if we go deep enough inside we can see patterns unfolding of which this life is only a part. But, in order to do that, he said, we have to step out of time and space and get out of our thoughts.

Then he addressed the longing that's inside us to begin the spiritual journey. He said that there's something that pulls a person toward this journey, that there's something inside each of us that comes from behind the place of our own birth. It was as if we have tasted of something somewhere in our past that had so much light and so much energy, that nothing we could experience through any of our senses or our thoughts could be enough.

And finally he began describing the Bhakti, or devotional path in yoga. He said that the way Bhakti works is that we just love until we and the beloved become one. He told us about the profound love that he felt around his guru, Maharaj-Ji, a love that seemed to emanate from this little man wrapped in a blanket, and then he pointed the way and gave us a glimpse of what was possible by telling us that when we clear away all the underbrush, when we go back to being who we really are, who we are turns out to be spirit, turns out not to be matter at all.

"Wow", I thought as I read this last part. Could that really be true?

The path he was bringing us to was the path of yoga, the ancient spiritual practice of India, which included postures, breathing, chanting and other devotional practices designed to help us experience the exalted states that we had glimpsed under the influence of psychedelics. By reading this book, a seed had been planted in me, and only time would tell how this seed would grow.

***

"Hey, Ram Dass is going to be in Columbus. Do you want to drive down and see him with us?" Fran said to Kimberly and me one day a few weeks later.

"Absolutely!" Was my immediate response.

After the drive we found ourselves in a large auditorium packed full of people.

"Wow! We're not the only ones who have turned in this direction!" I exclaimed in amazement.

Ram Dass was a great storyteller and he was in the midst of a great one about meeting his Indian Guru.

"Maharaj-Ji told me I was thinking of my mother," Ram Dass told us. "It just blew my mind. He knew what I was thinking. He saw all my doubts and selfish thoughts, all the crap inside me, and still he loved me."

Then Ram Dass stopped, looked out at us and said, "You know, I'm just telling you these stories to keep your minds busy, while what's really happening is going on underneath the words."

Yes, there was something else going on, something beyond what was being said, and my consciousness was just beginning to open up to it.

Next, Ram Dass told us the story of giving his Guru mega doses of L.S.D. and nothing happening. It seems that the guy was already in that state without the drug. In fact the yogis of India had a whole system for getting to the rarified states of consciousness I was exploring with L.S.D., and they were achieving these states without taking substances. The message was clear. Meditation and yoga could take a person to the same spaces as L.S.D. I left the auditorium inspired to dive deeper into this exploration of consciousness.

It was in this same time period that I began exploring the works of John Lilly and experiencing an invention of his called the isolation tank. This tank was an amazing meditation chamber. It was completely sound and light proof, and it contained a saltwater solution at close to body temperature that was kept at the perfect saline level to allow a person to float. The result was an environment that was almost completely sensation free. Jerry and Fran had a tank in their basement and let me try it. I remember the first time I climbed in and pulled the lid shut over me. Suddenly all the light and sound were cut off. I settled down into the saline solution and soon I had no tactile sensation either. At first my mind was racing and there was a period of disorientation, but as I relaxed into it, all awareness of my body began to disappear.

Before long, I had the distinct impression of flying, or more like soaring in an infinite void. Then I began to expand to the point where I felt totally uncontained, and the sense of time disappeared. I was reminded of the L.S.D. trip with the Great Blue Heron. I was feeling so expanded and so free as I floated out into the infinite for what seemed like forever....

And then, at last, I began to notice a light tapping. It took me a while to orient to it, like coming out of a deep sleep, and then I finally realized it was Jerry signaling to me that the hour was up, and that it was time to come out. The reentry gave me an inkling of what it must have been like to be born. What a shock it was, as the world came rushing into my heightened senses.

Now I had glimpsed what was possible in meditation, and although I would continue to take psychedelics now and then, I had seen another path.

As summer rolled endlessly on, Kimberly and I befriended a young man named Doug. He was one of Kimberly's clients at the counseling center, and he started coming over to our house and just hanging around. At first I thought he was just trying to *hit on* Kimberly, but then as I got to know him better, I could see that he just wanted some company and a little guidance in his life. He was a strange guy, kind of kept to himself, and didn't seem to have any friends. He'd come around just about every day for awhile, hang out and ask a lot of questions, life questions like "What is this world we're living in?" and "Why are we here?" I shared my experiences with him, showed him Be Here Now, and after a while, I'd say we became friends. Little did I know that he would come to be in just the right place at the right time to help me along in my journey... when I needed it the most.

Chapter 17

Personal Floundering

My girl friend Kimberly received her master's degree in Counseling in the spring of 1973 and was to start a job at a Psychiatric clinic in Tiffin, Ohio in the fall. She invited me to come along as a sort of househusband, and so as summer came to an end, we packed up our things and moved to this sleepy little northern Ohio town. Each morning, she went off to work, and each day I was left alone in the house. I did the cooking and the cleaning and had dinner ready for her when she came home. I felt like June Cleaver from a popular TV show I grew up with, *Leave it To Beaver*. June was the perfect wife and mother. It was a real role reversal for me, but I was a liberated male and had feminine tendencies, so it was okay... for a while.

In the time left over from my househusband duties, I continued to make my mobiles and string designs. We had an attic as part of our apartment that had a separate entrance, perfect for opening a small shop, and as the months passed, I filled that attic with more and more mobiles. I was fascinated with balance and motion, and discovered that the more precariously balanced the mobile was, the more motion it would produce. I was really absorbed in this little shop, but being in this small, conservative town in Ohio, I rarely had any visitors; in fact, I can't remember a single one.

And then... over time... I began to have a nagging feeling of being trapped in Tiffin and that house. I really needed to do something, to get out in the world, and make something of myself. It was a male impulse I guess, to be someone and to do something in the world. As the frustration and feeling of being trapped increased, my relationship with Kimberly started deteriorating. The real problem was that I wasn't feeling good about myself, and, as a result, I could no longer be there for Kimberly. Finally the whole situation came to a head and we had a big fight, which resulted in me loading all my stuff into my old dodge van and heading for the closest *hip* place I could find. That place was Ann Arbor, the place coincidently where I was born.

I landed in town and somehow found this house... a sort of hippie boarding house.

"We don't have any rooms right now, but the living room couch is available."

"Perfect!" I told the young longhaired guy standing at the door.

I took the couch and began a hippie life in Ann Arbor. I delivered pizzas in the evening to pay the rent, slept on the couch at night, and met dozens of young hipsters as they came through town. This house seemed to be the first stop on the hippie trail through Ann Arbor, and I was in the middle of *where it was happening*. Eventually, I moved to a room upstairs when it was vacated and I became a real house member. Every evening there was a music jam and every night a new person would end up staying on the couch. Sometimes it was a beautiful young woman, and sometimes she'd end up in my bed. [3]

At that time I began studying the guitar with a guy who was a musical genius and a builder of guitars. In fact he had just invented a fretless, nylon stringed electric guitar. He helped me break into the world of bar chords, and thanks to him, I was playing and writing songs again. [4]

Life was good... and of course, as it always does, life continued to present opportunities. Somewhere in my movements about town, I came across a small announcement on a bulletin board.

It said, "Wanted: earnest spiritual seekers to share a house and a life. The right person will be a vegetarian, into meditation and conscious living." I called them immediately and moved in the next month.

In the commune, we ate our meals around a low table sitting cross-legged and eating with chopsticks. We had a Native American sweat lodge in the back yard that we'd use even in the dead of winter. First, we'd make a small fire in the back yard in which we heated large stones. Then, we'd bring the stones ceremoniously into the lodge and pour water on them to make steam as we sang sacred songs. Participating in the sweat lodge ceremony was a very bonding experience and also quite cleansing to the body, mind and spirit, but it always was a shock to come out of that lodge barefoot and walk through the snow back into the house.

There were five of us in the commune, and every morning we gathered together for sitting meditation. It was there, in that house, that I became a vegetarian after going on a forty-day brown rice fast. I never desired meat after that. It just seemed too heavy in more ways than one. During that time I also developed a daily yoga practice. One of my housemates showed me some yoga postures and taught me diaphragmatic breathing. This technique of breathing from the belly was very helpful for deepening and lengthening the breath for both yoga and meditation.

As I mentioned, we meditated every morning. What I didn't mention was that one of our roommates was a jazz saxophone player in training. He lived in the room next to mine and he practiced his scales for many hours a day. From him I learned perseverance and also how to tune out sounds.

It was about that time that I participated in my first Sufi dance. Also known as the dances of Universal Peace, these dances are a kind of spiritual folk dancing. It happened at a spring festival in one of the local parks, and about a hundred of us hippies gathered around a dance leader and some musicians. The leader arranged us into four concentric circles in the middle of a field. We held hands and walked slowly around, each successive circle rotating in the opposite direction from the one inside it. All the while we chanted a Buddhist mantra, Om Mani Padme Hum. The people in the inner circle were chanting "Om". Those in the next circle out were chanting "Mani", those in the third circle chanted "Padme" and those in the fourth, "Hum". I was in the third circle busily chanting, "Padme, Padme, Padme, Padme", and we stepped around to the right as we chanted. We kept at this for quite a while, and then, even while the words continued to tumble out of my mouth, "Padme, Padme, Padme," my consciousness began expanding out to the neighboring circle and I was filled with "Mani, Mani, Mani." Then I was with the outer circle, "Hum, Hum, Hum." As this was happening I was still chanting "Padme" over and over... and then, suddenly... something snapped. I was no longer "Padme." I wasn't "Mani," "Om" or "Hum." Instead, I was the whole thing: "Om Mani Padme Hum." My *self* dissolved into the entirety of the chant and "I" disappeared. It was just "Om Mani Padme Hum," and there was no one doing it.

At some point, the mind kicked in again and said, "Wait a minute. What happened?" And then of course, I was back to being the one chanting "Padme." But for a little while there... well for an eternity really, I was gone! It was my second transcendental experience without drugs, and now I was convinced of what Ram Dass was talking about in Be Here Now! I didn't need Psychedelic substances to expand my consciousness.

***

"Hey everybody! I hear Ram Dass is going to be in Boulder this summer!" a young woman housemate of mine announced at the dinner table one night.

I put down my chopsticks.

"What's he going to be doing in Boulder?" I asked, my curiosity piqued.

"He's helping to open Naropa Institute!" She told us. "It's a new Buddhist University being started by Chögyam Trungpa Rinpoche. Ram Dass will be there for the whole summer session teaching a class of some kind, and everyone is welcome."

I was filled to overflowing with excitement.

"I'm going!" I blurted out.

I didn't know how, but I knew I couldn't miss an opportunity like that. I was ripe for it in so many ways. Besides, there was nothing to hold me in Ann Arbor. The commune was dissolving over some problems with the landlord and everyone seemed ready to go their own way.

Near the end of May, I loaded everything I owned in my van. It really wasn't that much. The van had a bed and curtains (hippie fashion), and I had a backpack, my guitar, some clothes, and a little bit of money to pay for gas to get out there. The young woman who had first told us about Naropa was going with me, just the two of us. Hmmm! I really can't remember her name. That's kind of strange. She must not have been my type, or maybe it was that I was a Yogi and on a spiritual path. Well, for whatever reason we were just to be friends on the trip and eventually go our own way in Boulder. And so we said goodbye to our other housemates, and we were off.

The trip is a blur until we got all the way out to Colorado. Then I remember driving the van up the first mountain we came to outside of Denver. It was called Lookout Mountain. I blew out the transmission in the van on the way down, and then managed to get the van the rest of the way down the hill and in to the first gas station we found. We put a "for sale" sign in the window, told the guy we'd check back with him, grabbed our backpacks and my guitar and left the rest. [5]

Eventually the van was sold, and I got some money (I don't remember any of the details... title, etc.). I do remember that from that gas station we began walking, we stuck out our thumbs, and soon got picked up by a young hippie from Boulder.

"I've got just the place for you," he said, "a place where you can camp out for free. You're gonna love it. It's called Gold Hill."

He told us all this as we were driving through Boulder and began climbing a winding, dirt road into the mountains. He dropped us off on a curve in the road.

"Just follow that path there and find yourselves' a spot," he told us pointing up the hill.

"Hey thanks, man!" I said with much gratitude.

We got out and started hiking up the trail, and soon my feet felt like lead pipes, and my lungs began burning. My body was not used to 7000 feet of altitude. My companion was feeling it too, but we finally made it up to a nice, relatively level spot, set up our tents, and settled in. We had a few days before the start of Naropa's summer session. That's when I met Crazy Larry.

I was sitting on a rock perched on the mountainside just a few yards from my tent. I was gazing out at the vast expanse of the Great Plains that stretched out from the Rockies, clear across Kansas and on to the mighty Mississippi. I was contemplating my life, how I had gotten to this spot on a mountain in Colorado, and wondering what lay ahead at Naropa. This is what always happens to me when sitting on a mountaintop. The mountains contain an eternal, solid stillness that encourages my mind to reflect on my place in the cosmos. There was a gentle breeze playing the Aspen trees, and there was the sound of bees and the cheerful colors of wildflowers everywhere. Just then, a man appeared in ragged clothes and long black beard.

"Hey!" he said as he approached. He had a sort of distant look in his eyes, and he avoided eye contact.

"How's it going?" I answered back and stood to greet him.

"I've got some fish. Today I get my check."

"You went fishing?"

"You can see my place, if you want."

Although, the man wasn't making much sense, he seemed genuinely friendly, so I went with him on up the mountain. We came upon a rocky area, and then suddenly there, almost invisible in the rocks, was a small rock hut. He pulled back the door and invited me in. There were a couple of rocks to sit on, some bedding at one end, and an old oil drum with a pipe coming out of the top.

"She burns wood," he blurted, noticing my eyes. "Made it myself," he added.

Then he pulled out a small can of sardines and offered it to me. It was clearly all he had and I was touched that he wanted to share it. I nibbled a small bite.

"Got some marijuana under a rock outside. Wanna smoke?"

He was already out the door and down a little path before I had a chance to respond. When he returned, we smoked and talked for quite a while, although the conversation was always a bit disjointed. The whole time, his mind jumped about from topic to topic, and I was constantly trying to play catch up to what he was talking about. Despite the disjointedness, I did piece together some of his story. Apparently, as a teenager, he had been diagnosed with a mental condition and was given shock therapy. If he wasn't crazy before that, he certainly was afterwards. From then on his thoughts became very disjointed. His parents didn't seem to want him around any more, so they gave him money every month and told him to stay away. That's when he moved up to Gold Hill where he'd been living in this rock hut for three years, summer and winter. He fished when he could and communed with the trees and the wildlife. I could see that his thinking was distorted, but I was struck by the warmth and generosity of his heart. Here was a man who had practically nothing, and yet he was offering me half of everything he had. This touched me very deeply. At last I said goodbye to the man and headed back down the hill to my tent. I could hear him still talking as I walked away. When I got back to the tent, the young woman who was camping with me was sitting on a rock, bare-breasted, soaking up the afternoon sun. She liked to do that, as I recall. She turned toward me as I approached.

"Where did you go?" she asked.

"Oh, I met this really nice guy, and he invited me up to his rock hut."

"Oh yea, that must be Crazy Larry," she said. "My friend was talking about him. Nutty as a loon he told me." By then she had a boyfriend.

That night, there was a cold wind blowing, so I retired to my sleeping bag shortly after dark. When I awoke the next morning, it was June fourth I believe, I felt this intense chill penetrating my body. I also noticed the tent was sagging in the middle. I reached out of my sleeping bag and unzipped the tent to see what was happening, and to my utter surprise, I discovered that I was buried in two feet of snow!

"Shit! Snow in June?"

This was more than I could take. I had been feeling vulnerable up there on the mountain, and the snow and the cold were just too much for me. I shook the snow off my tent and loaded everything in my pack.

"I'm out of here!" I yelled back to the young woman who was just climbing out of her own tent with her boyfriend coming out behind her. "See you around!" And with that I tossed the heavy pack onto my back and headed down the mountain to civilization. I ended up renting a small room in the basement of a house in Boulder owned by a young Christian family. The place was a hole, really, but somehow it suited me. I saw the young woman from time to time around Naropa, but never really talked with her after that. I felt a little like I had abandoned her, but then reminded myself that she wasn't alone. Later I heard that she had gotten pregnant and had an abortion. For some reason, I felt somewhat responsible, as if I had some sort of fatherly or big-brotherly obligation to her. She was a few years younger than me, but I reminded myself that she was old enough to take care of herself. Incidentally, that was the last snowfall of the year. Out of fear, I had over-reacted, and as a result I would spend the next three months in this dark dungeon.

After getting settled in to my basement room, I walked down town and registered for the summer session of Naropa. At the registration desk, there were some job postings, and I ended up getting a job as a cook's assistant in the Naropa kitchen. I was the prep cook, which meant I mostly chopped onions, lots of them, every day.

"What are we cooking today?" I would ask.

"I haven't decided yet", the head cook would say, "but you can get started by chopping some onions, about fifteen big juicy ones. Whatever we're having, I know we'll need onions."

That's when I developed my theory of the correlation between onions, tears and barometric pressure. I never published it, so it never entered the general body of scientific knowledge. But I wasn't in Boulder just to discover something about onions. I had a higher purpose, and at last the time had come to fulfill it. It was the first day of classes at Naropa, and I was ready to dive in.

Chapter 18

The Pathless Path

The detailed content of the summer course on the *Bhagavad Gita* taught by Ram Dass in 1974 is contained in the book, *Paths to God, Living the Bhagavad Gita*, by Harmony Press. What follows are the memories of my experiences that summer, some of the core teachings I received, and where life took me from there.

We gathered in an old warehouse near downtown Boulder. Years later that building would become, to my knowledge, the first natural foods supermarket in America. There were about a thousand of us there that first day, and we came from all over the country with one objective, to hang out with Ram Dass. I grabbed a spot of floor somewhat near the elevated stage and then looked around to see who had come. There were mostly longhairs like myself in the crowd, and most were dressed in jeans or hippie garb. There were an equal number of men and women, and most were in their early twenties. After much anticipation, the crowd broke into an enthusiastic applause as Ram Dass came up on stage with two or three others. He was dressed in a simple t-shirt and white drawstring pants. Bald on top, he had shoulder-length curly hair, a bushy beard, intense eyes, and a beautiful smile. Ram Dass sat on a high chair in front of a tall podium and leaned forward into the microphone.

"Good morning and welcome to Naropa." He began and then outlined his course on the *Bhagavad Gita*, one of the pivotal texts of Hinduism. As he spoke, some of his assistants walked among us passing out the syllabus. When I received mine, I looked it over and could immediately see that we were going to take quite a journey!

Here is the course syllabus for the *Yogas of the Bhagavad Gita*:

In addition to the lectures, this course includes a number of exercises designed to provide experiences, which can evolve into a complete Sadhana (a program for spiritual practice.)

A. Keeping a Journal
B. Contemplation (on various topics including time and death)
C. Meditation
D. The Witness
E. Giving and Receiving
F. Silence
G. Tapasya (austerities, e.g. fasting and working with desires)
H. Hatha Yoga Asanas and Pranayam
I. Japa Yoga
J. Going to Church or Temple
K. Kirtan
L. Satsang Collaboration
M. Puja Table
N. Karma Yoga

Every day, Ram Dass would speak... telling his mind-blowing tales, mostly. He would weave these intricate stories, parables and jokes into a seamless whole. He'd go off on long tangents, and then when we'd all completely forgotten where the conversation was going, he would suddenly confront us with some obvious fact of spiritual life.

The Gita is Krishna, Ram Dass told us, and Krishna is a manifestation of our own inner being, so opening to the study of the *Gita* will open us, in a profound way, to our deeper selves.

I'd heard of Krishna, of course. I'd seen pictures of him as a young cowherd and as a flute player in those books that the *Krishna Consciousness* folks with their shaved heads, ponytails and long robes were always handing out in airports. In Hindu mythology he was the eighth incarnation of Vishnu, the aspect of God that preserves and sustains the universe (Ram was the seventh incarnation). The other two aspects of the "Supreme Reality" in Hinduism are Brahma, the aspect that brings forth the creation of the universe and Shiva, the one who dissolves it so it may be recreated again. At the time of the *Bhagavad Gita*, Krishna is an adult and plays the role of a spiritual advisor to his friend Arjuna. So what did Ram Dass mean when he said that Krishna is a manifestation of our own inner being?

Ram Dass suggested that we read the *Gita* the first time just as an interesting story, and so I read it, because he asked us to, but I didn't really care for it. For one thing, it takes place on a battlefield on the brink of war. The prince, Arjuna, is having second thoughts about leading his troupes into combat. He really doesn't want to kill anyone or put his friends and family in danger, but Krishna, his charioteer and confident is telling him that it is his duty and his karma to fight. All I could think of when reading the story was how much I hated war. In this way, I empathized with Arjuna. But Krishna was supposed to be a manifestation of God, so why was he urging Arjuna to fight?

Then Ram Dass suggested that we read the text again after we had finished our discussion about the basic conflict in which Arjuna finds himself. This time he wanted us to read it identifying with Arjuna; that is once we had figured out what our own conflicts, our spiritual struggles were. Then we could use them as our frames of reference and listen to Krishna tell us how to proceed on our own battlegrounds.

Ah... so from this I gathered that the *Gita* was really a story of a master and his disciple and that the battlefield represented our spiritual struggles here on earth. But what was my spiritual struggle? Let's see, I had taken Psychedelics because I wanted to experience something beyond my limited view of reality. I wanted to experience the so-called *higher* realms. Through my experimentation I had caught a glimpse of something divine, and now I wanted a more sustained experience. Ram Dass had found a better way, a better experience, and I wanted that. But why? Well I think back on my life, I can see that I spent a lot of it trying to get beyond my basic disappointment with everything. I was looking for the juice, the passion and the inspiration, and I was also struggling to find love and acceptance. I'd keep all this in mind as we got deeper into course.

In the afternoon talks, Ram Dass continued to tell us about the *Gita* and how to apply it to our spiritual work, sewing the subject in among his wonderful stories. Then he began telling about cultural conditioning and how society socializes its children by teaching them to rely primarily on judgments from outside themselves. He said that there were three basic principles a child must learn in most cultures: to accept his information from the outside, to look outside for his rewards, and to ignore his inner voice if it conflicts with what comes from outside authority.

Then he said that when we're asked to "trust our intuition" we are reversing the conditioning process, and that as we awaken, we begin to act from the inside out rather than from the outside in – and that that's the transformation we're really looking for.

As he said this, I could see how I had always listened to external voices, those of my parents to be responsible, get a good education and be someone important, and those of my peers to be *cool* and act a certain way to be accepted. I even followed others in my acts of nonconformity. After all, being a longhaired hippie was fashionable in 1974. Of course, even there at Naropa in that great hall, I was still listening to outside voices. This time it was the voice of Ram Dass telling me to listen to my inside voices, but at least I was beginning to see that. And wasn't it my inner voice that brought me, unquestioningly to Boulder to be with him in the first place?

Then Ram Dass arrived at what I would consider to be the essence of the spiritual journey when he suggested that following the inner voice leads to behavior that is not based on self-interest, but on the workings of an awakened heart. He told us that that's where the work of the spiritual journey comes in. We look for practices that will take us outside of our thinking minds, and set us free. When I heard him say that I could suddenly see what my true spiritual struggle really was: to get free of my thinking mind and my cultural conditioning, the very source of my disappointment, so that I could live in the space of love.

Then Ram Dass put us all on the spot when he said that we have come to recognize that the choices facing Arjuna are the same choices facing us. Then the question becomes: How ripe are we to let go? How free of our egos are we ready to be? How willing are we to surrender to the mystery of God's plan? He told us that those were the questions that confronted Arjuna and that that's the battle we also faced.

In the *Gita*, Krishna was telling us that we needed to engage in certain practices to help us let go, and this would in turn allow our hearts to awaken. With an awakened heart, would I find the passion and inspiration I was looking for? I would just have to do the practices and see what happened.

The days went by, and we all started dropping into a sort of routine at Naropa. Every morning someone would lead us in Hatha yoga. I enjoyed the yoga practice, although there were postures that were difficult for me. My hamstrings were tight from my years of running track, and so I found forward bends challenging. I also had very little backward bending flexibility, a sign of stubbornness someone once told me, and I found the bow pose oddly sexually arousing, which I didn't think was an appropriate response. I don't know what that was about. But despite these limitations, I noticed that, over time, I was able to relax into the practice more and more.

Twice a day we practiced sitting meditation, once in the morning before yoga and again before the afternoon talks. A thousand people just sitting, watching their breath created a powerful field of energy, and one could hear a pin drop there was such profound silence. Well... at least there was silence on the outside. Inside my head was another matter. In there was constant chatter, and then after sitting cross-legged for twenty minutes or so, I seemed to be primarily meditating on my physical discomfort. But gradually some quiet found its way inside, and as the silence settled there, I was able to reflect more and more on the message of the *Gita*. Here is what I was beginning to see as the core teachings:

First, we are born again and again into bodies. We needn'i _ so attached to the form. We are immortal.

Second, all of life is action. Our predicaments are the result of our past karma. But if we act from a place of nonattachment, surrendering to our *dharma*, our calling in this life, our actions will no longer create karma and we can step off the wheel of birth and death.

Third, we listen to hear what our *dharma* is, and we try to become harmonious with that in our actions. Then, we perform each act as purely as we can, without thinking about any rewards and without thinking of ourselves as being the actor. If we do that, we will turn our lives around and make them our spiritual practices. Then, at some point in our practices, "we" disappear and then there is only Brahma, there is only God.

***

One day, we were given mala beads, each with a little square piece of cloth attached.

"The little piece of cloth is a piece of Maharaj-Ji's blanket," Ram Dass told us, and then he personally handed each of us a set of beads.

When I received this sacred gift, I felt the strong presence of his Guru and felt an overwhelming sense of gratitude for the gift he had given each of us.

"These mala beads are used to do Japa," Ram Dass told us. "You can use them any time: on the bus, while watching a movie, while meditating. There are a hundred and eight beads and then the big one at the end, the Guru bead," he went on to say. "Count each breath by passing a bead through your fingers as you silently recite one of the holy names. I use Ram. You can use Ram or Shiva, or Krishna, whichever name resonates with you."

Here's a little background into reciting the holy names. Repeating the name of Ram puts one in the place of a servant to the one who is brave, wise and dutiful. Together with Sita who is beautiful, generous, loyal and saintly, they are the perfect divine couple. Repeating the name of Shiva is calling on the lord of yoga and transformation to help destroy the illusion of the separate egoic self. Repeating the name of Krishna, one forgets his worldly activities and merges with the Supreme Being in divine love. As one dissolves in this love, he becomes Krishna's consort Radha, the passionate lover.

So we all did Japa. This seemed to help with the "monkey mind." I decided to use the mantra "Ram" in honor of Ram Dass. The beads were an outlet for nervous energy, and the recitation of the mantra "Ram" gave my mind something to focus on. Every time the mind would wonder off on some train of thought, I could gently bring it back to "Ram, Ram, Ram". And then, after doing Japa for long periods of time... I noticed that Japa became what Ram Dass told us was called "ajapa-japa." The repetition of the name became automatic, and then I wasn't doing the mantra any more - the mantra was doing me.

"It's a great moment when you notice that beginning to happen," Ram Dass told us. "That's the point where you're approaching the merging into Brahma."

Chapter 19

Heart Cracked Open

As part of our daily routine at Naropa that summer, we were practicing some breathing techniques, which the yogis call Pranayama.

"Inhale for the count of ten. Hold for a count of ten. Exhale for a count of ten. Hold again for a count of ten. Do this cycle one hundred and eight times."

I really liked this practice because it was quite physical and it created an altered state of consciousness right away. Let's face it, at this stage of my spiritual journey, I was very much in search of the *high* I was used to having with L.S.D. For me it was all about the states I was achieving. I suppose you'd have to say I was an experience junky. After all, that's why I had come to Naropa, and that's why I was hanging out with Ram Dass. I wanted more experiences, but I also wanted to feel the love he was radiating.

I guess that's why my favorite of all the spiritual practices we were doing was Kirtana, a form of Indian devotional singing. Every evening we would gather to chant the names of God in call-and-response. This was the practice I loved the most because it involved music and it immediately took me to ecstatic states beyond the mind. A longhaired guy named Krishna Das, who had gone to India with Ram Dass and spent a lot of time with Maharaj-Ji, led the chanting. He was accompanied by a young guy named Ganga on the Indian drums, which are called Tablas, and another guy on the harmonium, a small pump organ that was brought to India from

Europe and very quickly adopted for devotional singing due to its ability to sustain notes in support of the voice. Singing Kirtana was always a highly charged experience, all of us gathering together to chant the names of God, and it often resulted in many of us jumping to our feet in spontaneous ecstatic dance.

Years later Krishna Das would write a book called, *Chants of a Lifetime* in which we would describe how chanting the divine names could help us let go of our stories and bring us into the present moment. He said that if we go deep enough, we will all arrive at the same place, the place of our deepest being.

The highlight of the practice of Kirtana at Naropa was the July third all-night, chant that was held outside around a big bonfire in celebration of Guru Purnima, loosely translated as "All Gurus Day." It was a beautiful full moon night, and after chanting for hours to Ram and Sita the divine couple, and Krishna the playful mischievous one, the energy around us began to intensify and we began chanting to the wrathful ones, Kali and Shiva, the ones known as the destroyers of the ego.

Ram Dass had told us about the importance of honoring Shiva. "'Unless you honor Shiva, you cannot come to me,' said Ram in the *Ramayana*."

Over the long night I passed through excitement to boredom and fatigue, and back to excitement, and then as the energy rose to an exalted frenzy in honor of Shiva, something snapped inside me. Yes, it happened to me again, that state I had experienced with the Sufi dancing back in Ann Arbor. The "I" disappeared and only the chant and endless waves of bliss remained....

... and then slowly, ever so gradually the sky lightened, the music came to an end, the energy ebbed, and I came back to myself and eventually back into the things of the world. But still, a spaciousness remained.

The next day Ram Dass told us that when we were ready we should read the *Gita* a third time, this time identifying with Krishna, "...because", he said, "that, in fact, is also who you truly are."

***

Along with Ram Dass, we had many other presenters at Naropa. Trungpa, the founder of the University spoke to us regularly and he and Ram Dass would hold colloquia in the afternoons and debate the fine points of devotional practice versus Tibetan Mahayana Buddhism. It was obvious in the playful banter that each shared a deep appreciation of the other's spiritual path, and yet it was clear that there wasn't just one path to follow to enlightenment. Trungpa had just published his book on spiritual materialism and in his talks cautioned us not to be so attached to what our spiritual practice looked like: the proper lotus position, beads, clothes, mantras, etc. It was a good caution. As newcomers to the path, many of us were attached to being and looking holy.

One morning, after Trungpa's warning about spiritual materialism, Ram Dass told us about how Arjuna had been used to the security of always knowing what was right, and of having a fixed set of social rules to live by, but that at this moment in his life he was faced with the discipline of not being attached to any patterns whatsoever, the discipline of standing nowhere, of having no definitions to cling to, no reference groups, no identifications, no self-concepts, and no models. Then Ram Dass looked at us all sitting in the hall and asked us if we were willing to embrace that kind of discipline?

Frankly, willing or not, I knew I wasn't ready for that level of spiritual practice. At the time, I was in the phase of my spiritual journey that Gabriel Roth, the founder of the five-rhythms ecstatic dance movement, would call "imitation." It's a time when the student pulls himself out of the inertia of the way things have always been and begins modeling himself and his behavior after his teacher. It would take many years for me to let go of all that, despite what was being said by these teachers.

Ram Dass and Trungpa were not the only teachers around that summer who encouraged us to let go of definitions. The most infamous one was Allen Ginsberg, the beat poet. He was a regular speaker at Naropa, and he would often come to meditate with us as well. It's hard to describe Allen to someone who has never seen him, but here's an attempt: He was a scruffy looking, balding little man with a bit of a paunch whose words were often crass, vulgar and seemingly very unspiritual. In short, he just let everything hang out... in his poetry and also in his everyday speech. He reminded me of Fritz Perls in that way, and like the standup comedian Lenny Bruce, Allen was devoted to shock value. And yet he was also a devout Buddhist and a longtime meditator. No doubt, he was a living example of Trungpa's message, and his manner made it virtually impossible for anyone to follow in his footsteps.

But other teachers were easier to emulate as they shared their many gifts with us. We took Tabla lessons from Ganga, who taught us the intricate North Indian rhythms, and many of us studied Japanese painting. We even tried our hands at beat poetry. It was a real eclectic happening. We also had special guests come and perform from time to time. Louden Wainwright III gave a concert one evening, which had us all in stitches of laughter, and on another occasion the great Indian flautist G.S. Sachdev performed for us.

As I sat there in the front row for Sachdev, he placed his classical Indian bamboo flute to his lips and start playing a traditional evening romantic raga. Maybe it was all the chanting and breathing and meditating I'd been doing, or maybe it was just his open hearted playing. Whatever it was, when I heard his sweet sounds emanating from the stage, something cracked open inside me. It was my heart, filled to overflowing with gentle joy, and the tones being formed through his instrument were like liquid love, each nuance bathing me in bliss.

As I sat there dissolving in this heavenly aroma, a beautiful young woman named Sandy, whom I had recently met, came over and sat down beside me. Sandy was originally from Alabama but was now living in Berkeley. As she sat down beside me, I gazed in her eyes, and suddenly all that love and joy that was building up inside me rushed out toward her. It was absolutely uncontainable. I had never felt so hopelessly, head-over-heals in love in my whole life. Maybe it was the long brown hair that tumbled down her back or the shade of deep brown of her eyes. Perhaps it was her cute figure or the way her soft voice poured forth in a deep Southern drawl, or as I said before, maybe it was just the result of all the heart opening devotional practices we were doing there at Naropa. Whatever the cause, in my eyes, the young woman beside me became Radha, the divine consort of Krishna, the goddess personified, and my heart fell at her feet.

After the concert, Sandy and I went up to Bluebell Meadow, a nearby park on the edge of the foothills, and found a secluded spot to melt into oneness. There, sitting beside her beneath Boulder's famous Flatirons, I confessed my undying love, and much to my own surprise, told her I wanted to marry her and have her with me always. She said "no" to the marriage proposal, but suggested we make love instead, as if to say, "Never mind eternity. Let's be with right now." I acquiesced, and so we spread out a blanket under the stars, gazed into each other's eyes, and dove into each other souls.

Somewhere in the process, I completely disappeared... dissolved into oneness. Wow! I was doing a lot of that back then, wasn't I? But to me, right then and right there was the only time and place and I was lost in bliss. The only thing was, and I see this now clearly in retrospect, I thought Sandy was the cause of my bliss, and so I felt like I had to have her. In fact, I was desperate for her... and she was so open to me... like a flower to a bee, and I was drunk on the nectar.

But around the next turn was the heartbreak. You see Sandy was leaving in a few days, heading back to Berkeley, and to make matters worse, she was going home to her boyfriend with whom she lived. I was devastated.

"If you want to be a preserver of love and beauty, you've got to be able to look at the destruction of love and beauty with wide-open eyes and say, 'Yeah, right, and that too!'" encouraged Ram Dass the next morning, as if he knew just what I was going through.

I retreated into my basement room, meditated, fasted, slept, and dreamed. At that time I was recording my dreams in my journal, and as a result I was remembering three or four dreams a night. Then the dreams began reoccurring. I wasn't really interested in the content of these dreams. What I was trying to do was to remember to look at my hands. Carlos Castaneda, the writer of the Don Juan books, had said that if you can remember to look at your hands in your dreams, then you will remember yourself, thus allowing for the possibility of lucid dreaming, taking conscious control. Why did I want that? Perhaps I thought that if I could take control of the dream process, I could go visit my beloved one in Berkeley, unencumbered by such things as boyfriends.

I never did remember to look at my hands in those dreams, but the days went by and at last the summer was over, and it was time for me to come out of dreaming and back into reality. The first snow could be seen in the high mountains, and with the end of summer also came the end of Ram Dass' class.

Over the course of the last three months, I had been exposed to a lot. I'd developed a Hatha yoga and meditation practice and I'd reached some transcendental states, particularly in the practices of Japa and Kirtana, and through my time at Naropa, the ideas that I had been exposed to in *Be Here Now* had become much more alive and vivid to me: the notions of karma and following our dharma, and listening to my inner voice. There was also the lesson of Trungpa not to be too attached to how my particular spiritual path looked. But the most esoteric message of all was that ultimately, we aren't who we think we are. We are actually just the play, the *lila*, of God. I don't think I was ready to fully grasp that one, but seeds had been planted, and they would eventually sprout. But the most immediate result of my time at Naropa was that I had opened my heart and learned to let go of a certain level of control.

"It's all a totally preprogrammed journey we are on," said Ram Dass, "a journey that is taking us through this dance of incarnations, through all the roles and forms, all to bring us back to God, back to the One."

But at that stage in my spiritual journey, I was still strongly identified with my predicament and still thought I was the one running my life. And so, from that vantage point, time was running out, and "I" had to take action, but all I could think about was that girl, Sandy. I only had a little money left and no real plans, but I had an old one-speed bicycle I'd bought at a garage sale for two dollars. Then the idea came to me.

"I know! I'll ride my bike to California."

I was definitely love crazed! I was planning to ride a one-speed bicycle across thirteen hundred miles of mountains and desert in early September when the snows of winter were already blanketing the great Rocky Mountains! If the mountains didn't kill me, that thousand miles of desert surely would, but I didn't have a better plan. I had virtually no money, but I had a bicycle and I had an open heart. What more could anyone need? And if the whole life journey really were preprogrammed, if this were just the dance of this incarnation and the following of my dharma, then I'd just have to let go and discover where it would take me.

Chapter 20

The Universe Provides

The night before leaving on my bicycle trip to California, I packed my things and was preparing for bed. Suddenly I was startled by a knock on the door.

"Who could that be?" I wondered as I walked over and pulled open the door. I couldn't believe my eyes. There standing at the door was.....

"Doug! What are you doing here?"

It was my old friend from Bowling Green.

"I'm driving a car from Ohio to Portland for an elderly couple," he told me. "I've got my bicycle on the back so I can ride it down the coast for a few days before flying back to Ohio. Wanna come along?"

What did I say about an open heart and the Universe providing? I'm still amazed at the synchronicity of this event: that my friend Doug should appear out of nowhere the night before I was to begin a suicidal journey and have a bicycle rack on a car heading West.

"You bet I wanna come along!" I told him, bubbling with excitement. "You won't believe what I was about to do!"

I told him the story, and now we were both amazed. The next day, I tossed my things in his car, put my bike on the rack next to his beautiful new ten-speed, and we headed across the western United States. We took the northern route up to Wyoming, through Idaho and Western Oregon, and at last arrived in Portland. All the while we traveled at seventy-five miles an hour along those freeways I thought about my one-speed bicycle and what might have been. At last we arrived in Portland, dropped off the car, and began loading our bikes for the journey south. I was heading for San Francisco. Doug would accompany me for a few days and then head east, eventually catching an airplane, from where I frankly do not remember.

Getting all my stuff on the bicycle was a real challenge. I was carrying everything I owned with me: books, clothes, mala beads, and even my guitar. I had some bungee chords and finally managed to get the whole pile fastened on. I climbed on the bicycle and immediately noticed that I was having trouble steering. I could tell that I had more weight behind the back wheel than I had on the saddle, but what else to do. We started on our way.

To get to the coast from Portland one must climb a few small mountains. Well this proved to be too much for me and my poor bike. I just couldn't keep it on the road. It was obvious I was just carrying too much stuff. Something would have to go. First, I let go of some of the books. That helped, but I was still struggling. Then, on the biggest mountain in the middle of Tillamook State Forest, I had to let go of my guitar. I set it by the side of the road with a note attached. The note read, "For whoever finds this guitar, may it be your inspiration to become a great player and to always have music in your life." I wonder who found it.

Now that I had let go of the guitar the bicycle was more manageable, and I made it over those mountains. As I was coming down the other side, I learned an interesting lesson in bicycling. Mountains are not as bad as wind. With mountains you can get to the top and get a free ride down. With wind there is no escape, and that day there was a relentless wind blowing directly into our faces from the ocean to the west making each mile a struggle. I have to say that Doug was extremely patient to stay with me during this time. I was making very slow progress.

But, at last our perseverance paid off, and we arrived at the majestic Pacific Ocean with its waves crashing into the great cliffs of Oregon. From here we turned south and traveled along the magnificent Highway 101 along those cliffs. Each night we bedded down on a deserted beach or under a cluster of redwoods.

Each morning we'd wake up in dense fog, teeth chattering and our bedding damp. By midmorning the fog would break, and we'd have glorious views of the ocean. One night we shared a beach with Hell's Angels. They were nice enough. After a few breathtaking days travel along the ocean, Doug, deciding that I was going to be okay, said goodbye and rode on ahead. He had a plane to catch and a life to return to. For me, the lonely road south, an idea about stopping in to see my brother in San Francisco, and a vague hope about connecting with a woman in Berkeley were my only "commitments". But I was on no schedule. No one even knew I was coming.

Riding a one-speed bicycle upon the mountain terrain of that coastal highway made progress slow. There were many times when I just got off the bike and walked, but there was exquisite beauty all around me: the magnificent trees and the ocean's constant luring appeal keeping me inspired to continue ever onward around each successive bend in the road.

I had been on that bicycle for over a week now. I hadn't had a shower, combed my hair, or even looked in a mirror in all that time. I was just sleeping and riding and eating... mostly fresh fruits and vegetables. I didn't have any cooking gear. Eventually, I crossed the California border, went through the small town of Crescent City, and then entered Redwood National Park. This park is dedicated to the coastal Redwoods that grow some 100 feet or more high, and riding through them I felt dwarfed by their magnificence.

Onward I traveled... through Eureka, a big logging town and finally as highway 101 turned away from the ocean, I followed the coastal route, Highway 1, a road with some of the most beautiful scenery in the world. The highway wandered down through Fort Bragg and then down past Mendocino, a very beautiful little town stuck out on rocky cliffs. Each night when it was time to sleep, I would hide my bicycle in some bushes along the asphalt and then climb down the cliffs to a hidden beach. Of course, I had to pay attention to the movement of the tides. Fortunately, I never got washed away. As I got closer and closer to San Francisco, it became more difficult to find a secluded place to sleep. One night I had to settle for the bushes along the highway.

After another couple of days I was at last in Marin County. That night, I camped at a real campground in Point Reyes National Seashore, but still with no shower. The next day I went by Bolinas, a town years later I would grow to love for its hippie vibe and wonderful Fourth of July celebration. From there I rode along some cliffs up behind Mount Tamalpais, an old volcano that is a Marin county landmark, and through the quaint little village of Mill Valley. At that point the road merges back with highway 101 in preparation for crossing one of the most famous bridges in the world, The Golden Gate Bridge.

After almost two weeks of calm and quiet, I was coming into civilization, and I was filled with excitement as well as some fear. My plan was to go find my brother, and although I hadn't even talked to him in more than five years, I hoped he would be willing to take me in for a few days. But first I had to get across the bridge. The road was now a four-lane freeway with very fast moving cars, but there was a bike lane that actually became the sidewalk as I climbed onto the bridge, and so after almost two weeks on the road, I had to dismount my bike and walk the last one point seven miles across the glorious San Francisco Bay. There's something about the view of the "city by the bay" from that bridge that always reminds me of that scene in the wizard of Oz when Dorothy sees the emerald city for the first time. San Francisco is certainly one of the most beautiful cities in the world.

At the end of the bridge, I walked my bike down the last few steps and climbed back on. I had a vague sense of where I was going. My brother lived on California Street so all I had to do was find its starting point near Golden Gate Park and ride toward downtown until I came to his house. The going was not easy, as the city is very hilly, but I found the street and at last I arrived at a small house next to a fire station. The address was right. I parked my bike and walked up to the door. My stringy long hair hung in my face and flowed into my long scraggly beard. My clothes were dirty and I hadn't bathed in weeks. That's what's great about family. They'll always take you in. At least I hoped so. I knocked. There was a bit of a delay. Then I heard some movement inside the house. At last the door opened ajar.

"Yes? Can I help you?" Came the hesitant voice from the other side of the doorway.

"Umm... I'm your brother," I said with a hesitancy that matched his.

There was a long silence and then a slow recognition, and at last a joyous welcome. Then I entered and began to share my adventure.

"Fourteen days... down the coast from Portland... got a ride from Boulder... etc, etc." I was very grateful for relatives in that moment.

My brother's place was very small, and it was clear that I couldn't stay there indefinitely. Besides, what I really wanted to do was visit Sandy, the young woman I had met in Boulder. Of course, she lived in Berkeley with her boyfriend, so I knew I couldn't just knock on the door hoping to be invited in with open arms. What I decided to do, instead, was to see if I could find a place to live and some work in Berkeley first, and then I could visit her more casually and from more of a rootedness.

With this in mind, I left my bike, took the trolley downtown, and then took the Bay Area Rapid Transit, known as BART, through the newly completed tunnel under San Francisco bay to Berkeley. Then from the BART station in Berkeley I walked up Ashby Street toward U.C. Berkeley, the hotbed of radical politics. On that day, there was some sort of demonstration going on, the norm for that University. It was as if there were a school of radical politics there. From the University, I wandered down Telegraph Avenue. There were lots of hippies out selling their wares along the sidewalks, and someone was playing the guitar for spare change. It was an old Bob Dylan song.

I crossed the street and came to the next block. There were lots of people hanging out in front of a music store and a Jefferson Airplane song was playing through some loudspeakers. "... you've gotta find somebody to love...."

I kept walking and in the third block I was captivated by a big airbrush sign with the words "The One Love Family." On the walls of the building were airbrush paintings of happy people surrounded by flying saucers. The place appeared to be a buffet-style vegetarian restaurant. I was getting hungry and the prices posted on the door seemed reasonable, so I went in. At the buffet counter I was greeted by some happy, smiling faces, and the food looked wonderful.

"Everything is prepared with love and natural ingredients right here in our own kitchens," said a lovely blonde haired young woman in an airbrush t-shirt.

There was a picture on the wall of people with guitars, and they were wearing colorful airbrush t-shirts like the one my server was wearing. I decided to ask her about them.

"Yes. They're our family band. They'll be playing tonight, if you want to come hear them."

Then I noticed a sign, something about the One Love Family looking for more members to live and work at the restaurant. I started getting excited. Maybe this was what I was looking for, a place to live and work. There were even some musicians here, and it was a real Berkeley commune! I spoke to the young woman again.

"Hey, this poster says you are looking for more people to work at the restaurant. I might be interested. I'm looking for work."

"I'll be off duty here in a few minutes," she said sweetly. "Why don't you have a seat and have some food, and I'll come talk to you in a little while."

I sat at a simple wooden table with an airbrush tablecloth in colors of white and blue and had a wonderful meal of brown rice, cooked vegetables and some kind of nut loaf. After a few minutes the very friendly young woman came over to talk to me.

"We'd be glad to have you join us. We can always use more people to help in our work. Everyone works about five hours a day, mostly in the kitchen, but there are other jobs as well. We have no personal possessions and don't use money. Instead, we pool all our resources and share everything. If you want, I can show you where you can sleep and we'll get you signed up for a work shift. Tonight, our fantastic One Love Family Band is going to play and you can hear our leader Aaron Michael speak. He's an amazing speaker and has a very inspiring message about the new world order."

That was it. I was in! I was shown a dorm room where I could sleep and given a work shift washing dishes in the restaurant. I put on a big black rubber apron and started that very afternoon. That evening after a very upbeat concert by some wonderful musicians and singers all dressed in airbrush t-shirts with flying saucers on them, Aaron Michael, whom they called the One World Comforter, got up to speak.

"Wait 'til you hear him," someone said to me. "He's in communication with extra terrestrials!"

"Greetings friends. I am here to give you channeled communications about world transformation and planetary enlightenment. Galactica is our civilization of eternal beings inhabiting the entire Universe that have their headquarters in this galaxy at the Great Central Sun. We are currently assisting humanity to awaken and in the process bring a whole new world into being, a space age paradise of absolute freedom, security and abundance for all people."

I looked around at the attentive faces in the crowd. "He's serious!" I thought to myself. "What have I gotten myself into?" He continued with his talk.

"We also know that most of man's laws are not made for spiritual progress, but have been blindly made to promote and protect the many commercial things that are more or less filthy rags when compared to God's New World in which beautiful cities gleam forth in the sun by day and sparkle under the stars at night. These are the Cities of God: wherein all the people dwell in comfort and safety - all having absolute freedom, security and abundance."

As he finished his speech, I sat transfixed. This guy seemed crazy, but there was also something beautiful about his vision. All that stuff about the Galactic Command seemed absolutely nuts, but what he said about the greed of Capitalism seemed right on... and his vision of love and universal brotherhood was absolutely beautiful, utopian. It's what we all want. And then there's this place, the food and the people, all so beautiful and open and loving. Surely it had to be a reflection of the goodness of Aaron.

Having considered these things, I vowed to keep an open mind. After all, I had been welcomed with open arms, and so I stayed, worked at the restaurant, slept in the dormitory with about five other people and gave everything I owned, which was very little, to the commune. In exchange, they gave me three wonderful meals a day, a place to lay my head at night and camaraderie. Life was simple, but life was good, and I was surrounded by dedicated and loving people who all acted pretty normal... well almost. The main evening activity, when there was no musical evening and Aaron wasn't speaking, was U.F.O. gazing.

"Hey, we're going up on the roof. Wanna come up?" A pretty young woman asked me.

"Sure," I said not one to turn down an invitation from an attractive woman.

Several of us climbed up a ladder behind the kitchen, pushed open the hatch and pulled ourselves up onto the wide flat roof of the restaurant.

"It's beautiful up here," I said, looking out at the Berkeley hills to the East.

"You haven't seen anything yet," the woman said looking me deep in the eyes.

We joined some other people who were lying on their backs looking up into the sky.

"They're just starting to appear," said a big guy with a long beard.

He turned to me and for my benefit he said, "They use the clouds to manifest in the physical realm. Look for them there."

I gazed up into the late afternoon sky, blue dotted with white puffy clouds.

"What are we looking for," I asked naively.

"The Galactic command, of course. They're hovering over Berkeley all the time. There. See that cloud? It's uncloaking now! Look. There, now it's moving!"

I did look and so did everyone else. People were all pointing and looking and agreeing. Did I see them too? Well, this is what I ask myself, thirty-seven years later.

"Did I really see them?"

The answer? Yes! I did see them, and not just once but many times over the course of the next few months. But did I really see them, or was it just a strong case of collective insanity? I guess I'll never know the answer to that question, but I certainly knew why there were airbrush flying saucers on everything.

"Hey. You're new here, aren't you?" A tall man with a well-trimmed beard, assertive manner and not a stitch of clothing on said as he approached me in the hallway of the commune one morning a few days later. "People call me Rex. I have a room just down the hall there."

"Nice to meet you," I said shaking his hand. "Been here long?"

"Long enough," he answered. "We'll talk later. Right now I'm going to go catch some more sun."

Then he slipped out the window at the end of the hall onto a towel laid out on a bit of roof. I was immediately impressed by his confident manner and lack of self-consciousness. A little while later I met another person, Candy, and her two young children out by the community pool. She told me how the people in the One Love Family had taken her in when she had no place to go. And so the weeks passed I began to feel more at home and increasingly more comfortable with this strange group of intergalactic explorers.

Chapter 21

Down the Rabbit Hole and Back Out

At last I decided that it was time to call Sandy. She had given me her address back in Boulder, and I had walked by her house once. It was just a few blocks away from where I was living, but I hadn't talked to her yet. In fact she didn't even know I was in town. I called directory assistance, got her phone number, and finally mustered the courage to call.

"Hello," said a soft voice with a southern accent.

It was she! I thought my heart was going to beat right out of my chest.

"It's me, Bryan. Remember? We met at Naropa."

"Of course I remember. Where are you?"

When I told Sandy where I was staying, I could tell she was surprised, but glad to hear from me. She immediately agreed to come over for a visit the next day. The whole rest of the day, I was beside myself... scared... excited. I could hardly concentrate on my dish washing at the restaurant, and when people talked to me it was all I could do to respond.

The next day finally came, and so did she. It was a bit awkward. I showed her around the One Love Family and introduced her to a few people, but everything was kind of dead-ending. Then Sandy told me that her relationship with her boyfriend had gotten stronger since she had been back, and that they were making a more serious commitment. When she left the commune to go back home, I suddenly felt lost and alone. I went into my room, threw myself on the bed, and cried.

***

I was working with a blonde haired guy with warm blue eyes in the kitchen the next morning.

"You see, there were these two spaceships that arrived and parked at opposite poles of the planet," he explained as we were scrubbing the pans that were used for baking the macroburgers.

"Then they used the energy of supernovas from other galaxies to shift the planetary vibration," he continued with enthusiasm, "and this is what brought about the birth of the hippie movement."

Another evening, it was Aaron speaking:

"I came down in my spaceship clothed in a cloud. I came to bring harmony and blissfulness. I am the One World Comforter... the one prophesied in the bible."

Then he looked us all in the eyes and continued. "Two million souls came to create a space age utopian paradise here on earth. These are all-knowing telepathic entities in communication with spirit God who have been sent here to come in to these new psychedelic, clairvoyant bodies that have been transformed by free love."

Wow, what an idea... that the hippies by taking L.S.D. had prepared themselves for aliens to inhabit their bodies. Maybe this is just a way of looking at the awakening process, the attunement to the divine, and the attaining of higher consciousness. Who's to say? The world is a mysterious place, and I know that I don't have all the answers. But whether I believed in telepathic entities or not, what was important to me back then was that I was making more and more friends, and this commune continued to be a great place to be.

A week later, I was approached by one of the men of the *Inner Circle*.

"Say listen Bryan... it is Bryan right?"

"Yes," I said.

"Well, Bryan, we need to have you go down to Social Security and apply for SSI money. We need more capital to keep our operation going. We're asking everyone to do this."

"I thought SSI was for people with disabilities," I said.

"That's right. What we want you to do is tell them that you believe in the Intergalactic Command and that you know they are here to usher us into a new age, and then tell them you can't work, because you can't support the capitalistic model. They'll realize you're unfit to work and put you on social security. Some of us are already getting SSI money."

When I looked hesitant, he added, "Listen, the commune is counting on you."

I went as far as making the appointment, but then realized that I just couldn't go through with it. It was one thing to be in a hippie flying saucer commune, but it was something else to get involved with the U.S. government, and to try to convince them that I was crazy. Somehow I just couldn't go that far.

That night Rex came in to the dormitory.

"Listen. We've gotta talk," he said. "The powers that be in this place have gotten out of hand and are misusing their power. We've got to overthrow them and take over this commune, bring the power back to the people."

"We have to do what?" I questioned.

At this point, I was really confused. I had what I thought were friends in the *inner circle* and they had been good to me, but I had a lot of respect for Rex as well. Was there really corruption in the ranks? I began to really lose my sense of foundation. Had I more perspective I would have seen that this whole *them-and-us* drama was quite normal for Berkeley. It's always been a very radical political place and it seems like there are always radical factions making claims about those in power. You see it in local politics, and you see it at the University level, and now that same "power to the people" cry was being reflected here in this commune. Who was right? What was true? I really didn't know whom to believe, and my sense of security was definitely on shaky ground. I had nothing except this commune.

About that time, someone offered me some L.S.D. Why in the world would I take L.S.D. in this situation? Looking back on it, I can see that it was crazy, but the truth is that all my life I've been impulsive, but not in a proactive way, really. My impulsiveness is more like going with the flow, taking what the universe offers, embracing what comes fully and finding out where it takes me. Well this L.S.D. took me places, I can tell you that! This is what I remember of the next couple of days:

As I first began to *get off* on the acid, I was sitting in one of the One Love Family lounges. There was a *community guitar* sitting in the corner and so I picked it up and began to play. It was an electric guitar and my fingers flew over the fret board effortlessly. Then I started experimenting with a new way of playing, more improvising, less formula and really lost myself in this experimentation. For a time, all that existed was the guitar, my fingers, and the sound. Then I noticed that if I pointed the guitar in a certain direction, a focus of energy would come out of the guitar and into the room, almost like some kind of ray gun. I zapped this energy at several objects in my sight and then for some reason set down the guitar. That's when I noticed that I didn't even need the guitar to do this. If I put my hands together in prayer position and then just pointed my hands at something, I could send that same energy beam out into the room.

"Hmmm. I wonder how far this beam will go?" I asked myself.

I decided to climb the ladder up to the roof, and I sat there looking out into the night sky and the stars. Then I placed my hands in prayer position again and began shooting energy out into space. When I did this, some of the distant stars began to come alive and dance around in the sky! U.F.O.'s? Yes, I was manifesting U.F.O.'s! And then at that moment, the lights began to make a pattern and move in unison. I got very excited, but also very scared. I could hardly believe it was really happening. There were U.F.O.'s everywhere in the sky. Then this idea came to me. What if I took my palms and turned them inward toward my own heart? What would happen then? I slowly began to turn my palms, and immediately I began to feel intense heat in my heart center. Then I started moving my joined palms up my spine, illuminating the various energy centers (chakras as they are called in the Yogic tradition). I started with the lower chakras. I immediately felt revitalized and noticed an energy moving up my spine. Then my hands moved up to the power chakra, and I suddenly felt invincible. I continued with the movement, up the spine to the higher centers: heart, throat and third eye, and I began to see blue light pouring out of these centers.

"Wow. It's really happening!"

The next thing I knew, I was soaring out of my body, zooming out into space to join the light beings who were dancing out there... and then....

I don't know what happened exactly, but suddenly I got very afraid. It was all too much. I was losing my body, my mind, my identity, my very self. I had nothing to hold on to, and there was nowhere safe. I freaked out, rushed back into my body and then quickly climbed down off the roof.

"Where can I go?" I cried.

The next thing I knew I was in my friend Rex's room huddled in a corner on the floor. He was in the bed with his woman, and they were both sound asleep. I started crying out softly.

"Oh God! Help me. Help me. I'm really freaking out here," and then I began sobbing. I'd never felt so desperate in my life, and although I never believed in a God that I could pray to, there I was praying with all my mind and heart to be saved from this hell realm I was in.

At that moment, Rex rose up out of bed and spoke. "Everything is all right my son. I am here and I am always with you."

The words entered me as the words of a loving God and I felt their truth. I wasn't alone and I was all right. God was there with me. And so I went back to my room and dosed off to sleep. The next morning I told Rex how much his words meant to me.

"What words?" he asked. "I never spoke to you. Were you in my room?"

That day, although no longer under the physical effects of the acid, I was not normal. In fact, nothing was normal. Later in the morning, I went into the restaurant to work. I was no longer doing dishes, I was now helping out on the buffet line, so I put on an apron and walked out to the food line. Nothing there was right. The nice silverware had been replaced with plastic, and all the food was greasy and spoiled.

"I can't serve this to people," I thought. "What's happened?"

Then a young man walked into the restaurant, a customer. I looked up at him and immediately thought to myself, "I don't like this person. He's evil."

Just then a two-inch scar appeared on the man's cheek! I stared in horror!

"Oh my God! I created that! My negative thoughts just put that nasty scar on that guy's face! It's instant karma!"

I suddenly saw in a very graphic way the power of my thoughts, and this really scared me because I knew I had no control over these thoughts. They just came into my head unsolicited.

"I've gotta get out of here, get away from the restaurant before I do more damage," I thought.

I pulled off my apron, told a fellow worker that I had to go and took off running. I headed back toward my room, and there coming the other way was Candy and her two children.

"Come to the pool with us," she invited innocently.

"Okay." I said hesitantly. Maybe it would help to be with loving people.

We got to the pool and the little girl was asking me to help her into the water. I was really out of touch with what the little girl needed from me. I just threw her in and she began crying.

"I'm a danger to everyone," I thought. I turned and just started walking away as fast as I could. As I walked I started feeling more and more alienated from the world and from the commune and all the people around me. It was as if I was inside a bubble... like in my very first acid trip... and I felt completely cut off from everything and everyone. Only this time it really scared me.

"Where can I go? Where is it safe?" I asked myself.

Then, I thought of Sandy. I imagined her loving, grounded presence and thought, "She can help me." I felt desperate as I walked the several blocks to her house, walked up the steps and knocked on the door. The boy friend opened the door and looked at me a bit disdainfully.

"I'll get her," he said and left me on the steps.

When Sandy came out I melted in her arms and began sobbing.

"There, there. It's all right," she said as she held me in her embrace. "Come in and we can talk."

I walked into her kitchen and sat down. She offered me some mango juice freshly made from her tree. I took the glass and held it up to my lips. Immediately the juice turned rancid.

"I'm poison!" I exclaimed holding up the juice. "I've corrupted this juice and I will corrupt you. You better stay away from me."

She didn't listen to me, but came and held me, soothed me, caressed me and eventually I began to settle down.

The next couple of days were a bit of a blur. What I recall is that I found a ride back east from a University ride-board and stayed at my brother's while I waited for the ride. Then, in late November, with only sandals, a pair of jeans and a t-shirt, I headed across the country back *home* to my parents in Ohio. I had glimpsed the farther reaches of consciousness and what I saw really scared me. I needed some solid ground.

After some days of seeing me wandering around the house aimlessly, my father thought that getting me back in graduate school was what I needed, and so once again he used his influence, and I found myself in a Graduate program in his department, Biophysics. He also got me a job in his institute, and I began helping my dad develop a mathematical model to predict results from his research. I was taking graduate level classes in things like membrane transfer, a whole semester studying how substances pass through cell membranes, and I was studying the theoretical side of computer science, focusing particularly on artificial intelligence.

My idea was to build a computer model to simulate the functioning of the human brain. It all seems crazy, when I think about it now, so grandiose. But it was my father's belief that academia would save me, and I was just lost enough to go along with it. Well, it only took a few months for me to realize that the whole endeavor was really beyond me. I didn't have the background in biology and the work required was far too much for me. I did make headway with the mathematical model of my Dad's research, though. He eventually hired a computer programmer to take my model and computerize it.

After leaving the graduate program in Biophysics, I went back to something I did have some background for. I landed a job working with "juvenile delinquents" to help them readjust to society after being incarcerated. This was a bit like the blind leading the blind, but somehow it was just what I needed to get my own *shit* together.

As I was *guiding* troubled teens, my friend Lori fixed me up with a young woman she knew named Jill. Jill was also a social worker and was the director of an afterschool program for teens. She was strong, confident, self-assured and grounded, just what I needed after my experience in Berkeley, and the chemistry between us was good. Let's face it, I was ready for some stability in my life, so we soon went from dating to living together.

There was a Kundalini yoga center in Columbus and I began attending regularly when I wasn't with Jill. One weekend, Yogi Bhajan, the founder of the movement, came and led an intensive. Wow! He was a real character, strong willed and wild. He really encouraged us to push beyond our limits by holding postures for long periods of time and doing intense breathing. I felt so alive doing this yoga, but I wasn't ready to wear white, wrap my head in a turban, and get up at 3:30 every morning, which was their practice, so I just attended a couple of classes a week. The truth was, I was still *jet-lagged* from my last intergalactic journey.

I met Riita at one of the Kundalini classes. Riita was from Finland and didn't speak much English, but she had a very sweet and sensitive demeanor and she was very cute. We quickly became good friends and spent time together. One of Riita's unique attributes was that she lived her life and made all of her decisions, by listening to voices in her head... spirit guides, she called them. She wouldn't do anything until they had spoken. At one point, I had made arrangements to do something with Riita, and Jill confronted me about it.

"I don't want you to see Riita anymore," she said to me firmly.

"Why not?" I pleaded. "We're just friends."

Jill dug in her heals. "Yea, I know about friends," she said accusingly. "Listen, I'll make it easy for you," she continued. "It's either her or me. If you see her again, I'm leaving you."

I couldn't believe it. "It's so unfair," I yelled out.

"While you're thinking about, I'll be staying with Nick and Lori," she said sternly, and then she grabbed a few of her things and was gone.

I thought long and hard that night. On the one hand I felt unjustly accused and resented the ultimatum, but on the other hand I felt like Jill and I had something special that I didn't want to lose. The question was, how much was I willing to sacrifice for a mere friendship? I called Nick and after talking it over with him, he handed the phone to Jill and I acquiesced.

"I promise not to see Riita anymore," I told her and she came back home. The following summer Jill and I were married. This was the beginning of a twenty-year journey into mainstream America. My life had turned 180 degrees. I did think of Riita from time to time, especially when the marriage got hard.

Twenty-five years later, Riita came back into my life, and for a moment, it seemed like something was going to happen between us. This time there were no barriers, except the voices in Riita's head. [6] Well those voices never did tell her to come to me and she faded back out of my life again, but the gift for me, and I'm grateful for it, was that I no longer had that haunting feeling about her, always wondering what might have been if I'd made other choices.

Chapter 22

The Whole Catastrophe

After Jill and I married, we decided to do a little exploring. We wanted to settle down and eventually raise a family, but neither of us felt that Columbus, Ohio was the place to do it. It was amazing how much we managed to pack in our little V.W. Rabbit. We had a camp-kitchen, a dog and a cat as well as my newly purchased guitar and all our clothes. We even had a place for a small bed. It's hard to believe, but we did. At last, we said goodbye to our friends, hopped in the car and headed west, camping along the way.

We stopped in Boulder, Colorado and even walked in Bluebell meadow where memories lingered in me as if from another lifetime. We continued through the Rocky Mountains, spent some time in Colorado National Monument reading *Zen and the Art of Motorcycle Maintenance* to each other on the canyon rim, and then drove across Utah.

We swam in the Great Salt Lake and even stayed in that same desolate campground I had stayed in with my friend Party several years back. I guess I was showing Jill my past in some unconscious way. We traveled across Nevada along route fifty, self proclaimed the loneliest road in America, and at last ended up in California.

My friend Bill from Bowling Green and his girl friend Mary had moved to San Diego, so we stopped there and had a nice reunion, played lots of music, and even took some Peyote in the desert where we encountered the benevolent spirit of Mescalito among the southern California cacti. From there we headed north to San Francisco.

My brother was away on a trip to Alaska and so we stayed in his small, one-bedroom house, the same house whose door I had knocked on just two years before after the bike ride from Oregon. This was the end of the road for Jill and me. After all we couldn't drive any further west and didn't want to go further north. Somehow, it seemed important to be back in the bay area again. We tried to find social work jobs in this vibrant city by the bay, but in 1976, that proved to be impossible. People with Ph.D.'s were lined up for low-paying social work jobs and we with only Bachelor's degrees couldn't find anything.

I had thought to start graduate school in a new discipline called Transpersonal Psychology at a school in San Francisco called the California Institute of Integral Studies. That family imperative for the advanced degree was strong. But I needed to get work first, since I had virtually no money, and somehow going into debt for school just wasn't an option. After two months of trying to find a job, our time and money were running out. My brother would be back soon and we would have to find somewhere to live, but we couldn't rent a place without a job, and it seemed we couldn't get a job without being a resident or having more degrees. We were caught in a catch-22 situation and things were getting desperate.

"Never mind what I want to do. What can I do?" I asked myself. I was having some real self-esteem issues, and doing some deep soul searching. I really needed to make something of myself, to be a success in the world, and I also felt the responsibility to provide my new wife. In other words, all the cultural conditioning that I had been fighting against for several years of hippie life was coming back to haunt me! But all the doors were closed. Something had to give.

I'll never forget the moment the new door opened. I was walking in the streets of downtown San Francisco with all the high-rises and business people scurrying about, and I was in the depths of despair. There I was just walking along aimlessly with my head hung low, eyes in the gutter.

"What am I going to do?" I lamented.

Then I noticed something lying there in the gutter under my dejected gaze.

"Hmmm. What's that?" I asked myself and bent down to pick up a small object. It was a matchbook. I took it in to my hands, turned it over, and read the words in front of me.

"How would you like an exciting career in computers? No experience necessary. Call 555-1212 today."

This was to be the beginning of a twenty-year computer career working in Corporate America. Over that time, I'd have three kids, a house, two cars, a dog and two cats, a riding lawn mower, and all the other things of a middleclass American. To quote Zorba the Greek from the movie of the same name, "Yes! I had a wife, kids, a house. I had the whole catastrophe."

After finding the matchbook, I made some inquiries and ended up taking an entry-level job with NCR Corporation. The only catch was I had to cut my hair, buy a business suit, and move to Chicago. So life took us to Chicago, and it was there that our first child was born. During this period of my life I maintained a split identity. Every morning I donned my three-piece suit and went off to be with conservative people to tend to business, and every night I'd come home, pull off the tie, and climb out of the suit and back into hippie clothes and my hippie persona.

Bill kept in touch with me for the first few years, mostly by letter, but one day he called me with some news.

"Did you hear what Fran did?" He asked a little bit into the conversation.

"No, what?" I replied, my curiosity piqued.

"She left Jerry and went off to India to be with some Guru!" I could tell from his voice he was shocked. I was envious. [7]

***

Though I couldn't go off to India, I still pursued my spiritual interests and even met some spiritual teachers during this time. Swami Rama was one of them.

The Swami was born to a northern Indian Brahmin family in a small village in the Himalayas. From an early age he was raised in the mountains by his master Bengali Baba and, under the guidance of his master, traveled from temple to temple and studied with a variety of Himalayan saints and sages. After returning to his master in 1952 and practicing further for many years in the Himalayan caves, Swami Rama was encouraged by his teacher to go to the West, where he spent a considerable portion of his life teaching, specifically in the United States and Europe.

Swami Rama was a formal scientific research subject in mind-body experiments in the early 1970's. He demonstrated his ability to stop blood from flowing, causing his heart to either stop or beat at three hundred beats per minute. The Swami managed to change the temperature of different parts of the palm of his hand by eleven degrees Fahrenheit, and he also demonstrated psycho kinesis, the ability to move matter with his mind. He didn't perform these demonstrations merely to impress people about himself, but rather, he wanted to show the immense potential of the human being in mastering otherwise unconscious abilities.

At the time I met him, Swami Rama was the head of the Himalayan Institute in Chicago, a graduate studies program in Yoga Psychology. When I heard about the institute, I was very excited. It was right there in Chicago where I was living, so I went to an informational meeting. About ten of us were gathered on the floor in the large living room of a spacious house in Evanston, Illinois that was the home of the institute. After several minutes, Swami Rama entered the room. He appeared like a Roman Emperor, tall and stately in a long off-white robe with a luxurious sash placed over one shoulder. He spoke calmly and succinctly and told us of the importance for all seekers and aspirants to choose a definite path and practice it.

"Without practice nothing can be attained," he said and then told us that we were blessed to be on the path, and that one day we would reach our goal and attain freedom from all pains and miseries.

As he spoke and afterwards in his casual presence, the Swami seemed somehow unapproachable, even aloof to me. Frankly, I was afraid of the man. I realize now that he was an exaggerated version of my own father who carried himself with a certain sense of importance. The people close to the Swami, however, were very personable and communicative and soon I was initiated into Swami

Rama's yoga practice, given a seed mantra to aid in meditation and began studying Yoga Psychology at the Institute in the evenings.

I enrolled in several classes including one whole semester course on the science of breathing. Occasionally Swami Rama would speak. His main message was about how the mind was in direct control of the senses, breath, and body and that our spiritual practices, all our techniques and disciplines were just a means to train the mind. Then he told us that the foremost part of the training is to make the mind aware that reality lies beyond itself, thus pointing to the immortality of the soul.

With new resolve I maintained a morning meditation practice and studied at the institute some evenings, but after a few months the heads of the institute announced that they were moving the whole school to some property in Pennsylvania. Unfortunately, I was just getting started in my computer career and Jill had just given birth to our first child, Aaron. I just couldn't justify leaving my job and uprooting the family to go with them, and so I let go of my studies and that source of spiritual connection. In one of the final talks I heard from the Swami, he told us that the simple method to enlightenment was to first know ourselves and that we didn't need much external information; we already had true knowledge within. Then he encouraged us to study and learn from the greatest of all books, the manuscript of ourselves.

"Above all else, remember this one thing," he said at last. "It is easy to meet that *infinity* within you— to attain that awareness, you just have to be silent and listen."

After the Swami left, I continued with my meditation practice in the early morning hours using the mantra that I was given. During business hours, I worked hard at NCR installing and programming electronic cash registers and as a reward I was given the opportunity to learn computer programming. Meanwhile Jill and the baby bonded and thrived.

***

After I had two years of work experience and had completed my computer training, Jill and I decided to move to Colorado. We had enjoyed it there on our trip west and, of course, I had been in Boulder for Naropa a few years back. Baby Aaron was another big reason for the move. We didn't think inner city Chicago was the place to raise a child and thought Colorado would be much more conducive, so we drove out there to see if I could find work.

When things are meant to be, they happen effortlessly, and that was the case with the move to Denver. I found a computer-programming job there in two days. First we rented a small house and then we bought a condo. After only one year we sold the condo for a nice profit and bought a bigger house. Then, after our second child Zachary was born, we sold that house and moved to our dream house in the mountains. We had five acres of land surrounded by National Forest that was an old gold mine up around nine thousand feet. [8]

It was in Colorado that I met Swami Satchidananda. Remember? He was the Swami that opened Woodstock. He was a beautiful man with long white hair and a long white beard. He was a pundit who was also a master of puns, and loved to laugh. (This last sentence is an example of what he loved to do with words). When I met him I was giddy like a schoolgirl. Yes, it was strange. I felt toward him the way I feel when I fall in love with a woman, totally head-over-heals in love, radiant and full of bliss. But there was nothing sexual or possessive about it. I just wanted to be in the presence of this beautiful being, and when I was, I was overwhelmed by a warmth in my heart. Unlike Swami Rama, this man was approachable, and he exuded love and joy wherever he went.

When I had a one-on-one moment with this lovely being, I became completely speechless, and then I knew what Ram Dass was trying to describe when he talked about his Guru. I prostrated myself before Swami Satchidananda and he gave me his blessing, a spiritual name and a mantra for meditation. Unfortunately, I had already received a mantra from Swami Rama and for years these two mantras would vie for my attention in meditation. The lesson: If you want a guru, stick to one, or at least stick to one mantra, but what to do? I didn't plan any of it.

Ah... with Swami Satchidananda it was a pure heart connection, and I just melted in his presence. His message was one of love and devotion to the yogic path, and I became a good yogi. He was to move to Virginia and open a retreat center that is still very active today, but it was my karma to stay in Colorado and turn my attention to my work and my family.

As I put my energy into work, I began climbing the corporate ladder. I changed jobs several times, and now I was a weekend mountain man and a weekday corporate manager with a window office on the nineteenth floor of a brand new office building in the heart of downtown Denver.

Although in the world, I still tried to keep a thread to the spiritual dimension through a daily yoga and meditation practice, but gradually life and the demands of keeping a house and a family drew me further and further away from spiritual matters. I worked hard to provide for my growing family. I chopped wood (we had three wood stoves to heat our mountain home) and carried the proverbial water the Zen masters love to talk about. I survived corporate buyouts and mergers and the oil crisis of the 1980's. But sometimes I was frustrated and felt like I was living a false life.

We moved to Louisiana as part of one ruthless corporate buyout, and after feeling undervalued there and missing my beloved mountains, I brought the family back to the Colorado foothills and found work with a computer software company. Throughout it all, I would occasionally read spiritual books, and I continued my yoga and meditation practice, but I was alone in this pursuit and most of my free time was spent helping to raise the children. The great thing about Colorado was that there was plenty of wilderness to nourish the soul. The mountains were my Buddhas and the elk and deer were my spiritual friends. When things got particularly turbulent at home as a household with three young children can get, I could simply step outside, go for a walk and sit on a mountaintop. This was my main spiritual practice at this time. But, unbeknownst to me, life would not continue this way forever. Earlier in my life, seeds had been planted deep in my soul, and they would eventually take root and sprout.

Chapter 23

Walking the Dog, Part 2

It's now that fateful Thursday evening in late August of 1993. I've just grabbed my dog Maggie's leash and stepped out the front door of our Colorado mountain home and into... another world... a world where everything is shimmering... a world where the trees, the grass, the rocks, and even the mountains in the distance are all alive and super-charged with energy.... a place where everything feels like one thing... one energy... of which I, too, am a part.

"What's going on? Am I tripping? Am I having a flashback?"

It's late at night, and I sit here in front of my computer writing my autobiography.

"If I can just get this story down on paper, maybe I can make sense of it all."

After several hours of writing, my body is tired, even if my mind isn't, and so I crawl off to bed, lying there with visions of my life flashing before me. I finally drift off to sleep and my dreams are intense, but just out of reach.

I wake up to my daughter Dawn's alarm.

"Oh yea, today's a school day," I recall dragging myself out of bed. The day is fairly routine, except that my parents are expected to arrive in the afternoon. They are coming to visit all the way from Florida, so I do what everyone does when his or her mother comes to visit. I clean the house. I start with the bathrooms, my least favorite part of cleaning, just to get them over with. I clean the toilets, the showers, the sinks, and the bathroom floors. Then

I dust and sweep the rest of the house. There's something very centering and grounding about this work and as I focus on it, my mind relaxes. I do a little work on my computer and then mop the kitchen floor. The vacuuming is the last thing. After finishing, I have some lunch and go back to work in the home office. I am just finishing a key section of a training document I'm preparing when the doorbell rings. My parents have arrived followed shortly there after by Jill returning home from the mental health clinic where she works. There is visiting, talking, starting the charcoal on the grill, cooking, eating, drinking a little wine, having some dessert, talking some more, and then sitting down to watch my daughter Dawn dance to some renaissance music. Throughout the evening, my dad is struggling for his words. He has been diagnosed with Alzheimer's disease and is pretty deeply into it by this time. He hardly makes sense at all when he speaks.

In the midst of all the activity, I begin to feel a new rush of energy and a heightened awareness again. It feels like I'm seeing the very fabric of the space around me.

"It's happening again," I whisper to Jill, and I notice a little concern on her face.

Yes, I'm "flying" again, and it is the smoothest, clearest, and most inspired experience I've had yet. Using this energy, I play the guitar for my parents, and I play like I have never played before. I don't know if they notice, but I sure do. At last everyone retires to his bed and I am back at my computer keyboard writing feverishly as high as Mount Everest, while everyone else sleeps. As I write, some words from one of my songs come to mind.

"Feeling mighty weary eyed, gotta get some sleep, but that's just when the creative force is trying to earn her keep...." [9]

And so the day ends with my mind turning to my autobiography and tales of the past. As I ruminate over the events of my life, I make a mental note to ask my mother to tell me something of my childhood, and at long last drift off to sleep.

The next morning I realize I have slept pretty well, have had some dreams and feel rested, but I wake up *high*. It feels like a door has been opened in my mind and left that way. I start the day by driving my oldest son Aaron to his friend Sierra's house. He and I talk the whole way, which is unusual. We usually don't have that much to say to each other, but this morning we discuss his favorite topic, computers, and the time goes very quickly. After leaving Aaron at his friend's, I feel really good that we have connected so well.

When I return home, the others are up and I propose that we all take a short hike in a place called the Three Sisters just a couple of miles from our house. Everyone agrees, we go, and it is an incredible hike. It is so great to be out in nature with this heightened perception of the world around me. The wildflowers are glorious. The golden Asters are sprinkled with purple Larkspur and an occasional white Lilly along the trail that wanders through the trees up to our destination, the rocky lookout point at the top of one of the Sisters. As we walk, I am overwhelmed by the vibrancy of all that I see. My dad has a lot of trouble navigating over the rocks, but finally makes it up to the top with some help, and I can tell he wants to sit. So once we reach the lookout, we set ourselves down on a large boulder and gaze out at the world below us. From our vantage point we can see the neighboring meadows and forests of the Colorado foothills in which we live and the mountains beyond. There is a palpable stillness in the air, and I find myself breathing in unison with every tree and rock as one interconnected organism. I am in bliss.

On the way back down, Dawn and I play a little game of who can get back to the car first. She is the rabbit, I the turtle, and my slow steady pace almost outdistances her as I inch past her near the finish, but she alertly notices and finishes first as I become distracted by some more wildflowers.

We return home and after a late lunch and a small argument with Jill over the timing of it, Dad and I sit down on the couch and have a long talk. Actually, he talks, and I strain every known brain muscle, if there is such a thing, to listen to him and try to understand what he is saying. He is desperate to communicate and has so many points to make, but they are all just beyond my grasp. It doesn't help that he is losing his voice. At times he is reduced to a whisper, his voice just a tiny thread of a sound, but he is not deterred and continues to talk, mostly in vague abstractions, much of it about the work he was so passionate about for many years of his life, his research on the threshold of perception. Then without warning he changes the subject and begins telling me how consciousness is like the skin of an onion. At least I think that's what he is trying to say.

What he actually says is, "You know, it's like an onion."

"What's like an onion, Dad?"

"You know, it's like an onion," he repeats with the palms of his hands raised toward the sky. I infer the rest. Alzheimer's is supposed to be a neurotransmitter problem, and I can see that he is struggling to get the signal through the layers. Then I have a thought. We just need to turn up the gain.

"Wow! Psychedelics! That's what my dad needs. Give him a hit of L.S.D. That'll open those channels," I think to myself.

Then I have another crazy thought. "Maybe this is why I had my L.S.D. trips in the first place, why I experimented with psychedelics, so that I could help my dad through his Alzheimer's."

It's funny how everything I think and experience takes on heightened significance when my consciousness is expanded. It's as if everything is part of some grand conspiracy for good. I can really see how that same tendency turns sour for Schizophrenics when, somehow, trust is lost and benevolence turns into paranoia. After I settle down from the effects of this brainstorm, I begin to doubt the wisdom of giving my dad something like L.S.D., even if I could find some. In his state, he could find tripping very frightening.

Letting go of the idea, I return to just sitting, my dad and I transfixed for hours, and after awhile I begin to have the feeling that my dad is giving a sort of spiritual transmission, that he is the Guru and I am the disciple, and that our conversation is the most important one of my life. I have the overwhelming impression that if I can just concentrate, if I can just listen a little more intently and for just a little bit longer, I will get something vitally important from him. I'll hear the ultimate truth. Then, just as I feel that I am on the verge of getting this important something, I am suddenly thrown into doubt, and everything he is saying becomes nonsense.

"Wait a minute Dad, what are you saying? Who put you in the simulator that looked like your car? Are you talking about driving through Texas? That's no simulator, Dad. That was a five-day car trip from Florida. That was no simulator, that was Texas! And you couldn't stop it because Mom was driving!"

Just then the whole conversation becomes incredibly weird and I begin wondering what is really happening... questioning reality itself.

Some time later, as the conversation gets crazier and crazier, my mom comes in the room and breaks it up. I can see that all the crazy talk upsets her. She has had such faith in the brilliance of her husband. Jill is also upset that we have taken up so much time and have excluded everyone else. I tell her I am sorry, but that I just want to understand and to be there for my dad to help him unsnarl those tangled threads in his brain.

Later as I reflect on the process I've been through with my dad and my struggle to understand him, I realize that this is nothing new. He has always been difficult to understand, especially when he discusses his science. You see, he is a certified genius and always talks in high-level abstractions. His words now are still quite obtuse, but there is an added quality to it, or at least in my state of mind I am detecting another dimension to the conversation. I have the feeling that my dad is imparting something to me on a totally different level of reality while we talk. As I speak about it to Jill, I start to cry and then to laugh. I am crying and laughing at the same time.

"My God! Where did all these feelings come from?" I exclaim.

I don't even realize I am feeling anything and suddenly it is all poring out of me. I am in ecstasy. I've never been so happy nor so sad, and both feelings are coming at the same time.

Then Jill says something in a language I can hear. "Perhaps what has happened is your heart Chakra is opening."

Yes, that's it. My heart chakra is being blown wide open, and what a trip it is, what an incredible high! Then I wonder how long it'll stay this way, but then decide that it's okay if it closes again. I've had a deep, authentic sharing with my Dad, the deepest sharing I've ever had with him, and it's such a blessing. I've had the invaluable gift of being present and really communicating with my father... before it's too late.

At dinner, when I ask my mother about my childhood, she shares a few memories.

"You just didn't want to come out," she tells me. "I dropped three weeks earlier and had a false labor, but of course you finally did make your appearance."

As my mother says these things, I think to myself, "I couldn't come out a Leo. Two Leos in one family would not have worked."

Then it occurs to me that Laird was born premature.

"Hmmm. I wonder. Was he supposed to be the Virgo, and me the Leo?"

That's a funny thought... mind blowing really.

My mother goes on to reminisce about building the playroom in our Ann Arbor house, and how that allowed Laird and I to finally have separate rooms. Ah yes, before that we shared a room with bunk beds. I was given the lower bunk because they were afraid I'd fall out. I didn't. Instead, I was deathly afraid of being crushed by the big, scary, saggy lump that was my brother in the bunk above. We reminisce about my fears of the Boogie Man, a favorite quilt made by my grandmother, and all our playroom toys.

"I constantly fought with you two to pick up all those toys," my mother interjects. "You always made such a mess!"

Yes, we take a real trip down memory lane, but at last everyone else goes to sleep, and I am left alone sitting at my computer, writing again. Hours later, I finally crawl into bed.

I find myself awake the next morning at 3:00 A.M. or so. Sleeping the previous night has been next to impossible and now I lie in bed having some of the most interesting and bizarre thoughts... about dying and having a rebirth and about reengineering my life.

"Let's start by redefining my job," I say to myself. "My God, my work is on the computer and I've got a laptop! I can work anywhere, anytime. I don't have to be so stuck in my rut sitting in this little room all the time."

"Step outside and smell the flowers," a friend who worked with me at one of my corporate jobs always told me. He had had an out-of-body experience and nearly died from a reaction to Penicillin, and since that time had a deep appreciation for the simple things of life.

Jill is awake now. She rolls over as I am about to get out of bed.

"Where are you going?" She asks, half awake.

"I'm getting up. I'm wide awake," I tell her.

"What time is it?" she mutters.

I don't answer, but if I had I would have said, "It's the dawning of a new age!"

And then all of a sudden my whole body begins to shake. I'm trembling all over... and Jill holds me.

"I'm so scared," I blurt out.

"What are you afraid of?" she asks.

"Dying," I say without even thinking about it. "What if I reengineer everything? Where will I be?"

"You'll still be there", she says soothingly.

"When I look in the mirror, will I recognize myself?"

Chapter 24

Journeys on the Edge of Madness

I am lying in bed a couple of hours before dawn, shaking and feeling very vulnerable. Jill tells me that everything will be okay and I hear that, like I heard those words from God spoken out of the mouth of a sleeping man back in the flying saucer commune so many years ago. Then Jill asks, "What can you do for yourself that would be soothing?"

"Hmm. Let's see. I could play music, but not now. I'd wake up everyone. I could go for a walk. That's it. I'll go for a walk."

"In the middle of the night?" Jill questions.

"Yea, you're right. That's crazy. I know. I'll do some yoga."

"Okay," She says. That idea passes her 'crazy-o-meter'.

"Why didn't I think of that in the first place?" I wonder. "Oh well, it doesn't matter."

I go into the family room and find a spot on the floor, and then as I begin my yoga routine I have the feeling that all those years of yoga practice were just preparation for this moment. I start with the sun salutation and I immediately feel immense gratitude for the gifts of the sun.

"So this is why the Kundalini yoga folks (3HO) get up so early," I think to myself as I deepen into the early morning stillness.

As I begin my practice, my mind wanders and I recall a conversation I had the day before with my Mom. I had told her I was writing a book, and that I had started it two days ago. "It's an autobiography." I had said.

"Yes, that's where most writers begin," she had replied.

"Well, it's always good to write about something you know," was my retort.

As I recall the conversation, I realize what a real joke this is, the idea that I'm writing about something I know. I really don't know myself at all. Then a stream of memories begins to fill my brain. I recall when I was little and I tried to use the manual lawn mower and how the handle was so high I could hardly reach it. Then I remember the time I got stuck under some stairs on the playground and I felt so helpless. Stories, stories and more stories... just fragments of mind... just little nerve bundles... like Freud said, "just a bunch of synaptic loops" all firing in random succession.

Then, for a moment, I step back and see all these thoughts passing by and realize that this is all reality is, just a bunch of firing synapses. Then I try to imagine what it would be like to lose my mind or to get amnesia and suddenly have no idea where I am or who I am, not to mention how to get home. Could I handle it if it happened to me? It seems to me that the secret to handling amnesia is just to be right here, where I am, and go from this. After all, lost or not, I am here and I am now, and there's a certain reality to this that I will always know for sure, even if I don't know where *here* is in some larger construct of the mind.

All of a sudden I realize that my mind has drifted off in the middle of doing yoga, and with new determination I go through the next set of postures, this time focusing my mind by chanting the names of God.

"Rama, Rama, Rama... hare Krishna, hare Rama...."

At last the yoga, some breathing, and the mental chanting begin to do the trick. Twenty years of practice has paid off after all. I am finally finding my center, and the mind is quieting... at least for a moment or two.

"I've got to do this every day," I say to myself, and then realize I am sliding into an old pattern of mind, trying to hold on to my experience beyond this moment in an attempt to make it last. It's such a strong habit. When the experience is good I want to hold on to it.

After I finish my yoga routine, I sit back down at my computer in hopes of capturing a few more of the "brilliant" ideas that are spilling forth from my overactive brain. As I sit in front of my computer screen, I suddenly get a vision of the future.

"Hmmm. The computer is going to provide the platform for the transformation of a generation."

Then, I awaken my computer and begin typing.

"Oh lord, thank you for blessing me with screensavers, and may I have the strength to jiggle that mouse. Yes, Microsoft Windows, you are a window into my soul. Many hear, but few call... no, let me correct that. Few are called, but now we have e-mail. Oh dear God, did you get my message?' Please God, check your e-mail. Is this the right address? Do I have a dedicated line? What's your baud rate? Damn. What's the protocol. If I could only find my protocol converter...."

"... Oh blessed morning has come and here I am beside myself. I'm sitting on the floor in Lotus position beside my old self there in the chair, reengineering my life, reengineering the work place. I'm beside myself with joy. I need a dummy for the chair. How about a stuffed animal Clown. Dawn, may I borrow your clown, for the rest of my slow plodding turtle life?"

I turn off the computer and go take a shower to try to relax, but the mind won't quit, and so, still dripping wet, I write the following on a piece of paper, which I turn into a letter for Jill:

"In the shower I figured it all out. I know what's been happening to me! It's my midlife crisis! Wow. Forty-four down and forty-four to go. As I stepped out of the shower, my heart skipped a beat. I struggled for air, and then I prayed to be allowed to use the second half of my life to teach the world to sing. Now my heart beats to a different drummer. I suppose some could call me crazy. It's all in how you frame it."

In a moment of internal quiet, I am able to reflect back on what I've been going through... and I wonder... "Am I Crazy?"

The answer that comes is, "Yes, I guess so... but *God filled* crazy I'd like to think."

Later that morning, my parents load their suitcases in the car and head off to Estes Park for some quiet time alone. After seeing them off, I return to my computer. That day and for several days after, writing becomes an obsession for me. The words are pouring out of me in often disjointed phrases as I try to keep pace with the ideas that are flowing through my brain.

Later in the day I decide that sitting in a chair at my desk is no longer appropriate, so I climb up on my desk and sit cross-legged on top of it. My kids really start to think I am nuts, and Jill keeps them away from me as much as she can. I try to work on the training materials I am supposed to be preparing for my job, but work is very difficult to stay focused on because everything is so beautiful and every thought triggers whole chains of secondary thoughts that lead me away from what I am trying to pay attention to. Despite my difficulty staying focused, I notice that I am feeling very illuminated and full of presence. Framing it in Eastern yogic terms, I decide I am having a spiritual awakening. My heart chakra is opening and I feel incredible love pouring out, and everything that I see, hear, think and feel is so beautiful that I often find myself just crying.

I do become fearful at times, when it feels like there is just too much energy in me and that my heart will burst from all the love it's holding. Music calms me during these times and so does riding my bicycle, which I ride for hours through the Colorado mountainside just to work off some of the energy. I also do a lot of yoga. The yoga seems to help ground me, and as I practice, it occurs to me that this is why the yogis created this practice, to help in the awakening.

"Yoga strengthens the nerves so they can handle the increased energy of an awakening," I recall Ram Dass saying, as I'm doing my routine one morning.

***

Jill is now talking to me about something she calls "Bi-polar Disorder," which used to be called "Manic Depression," and suggests that I get a formal diagnosis so I can start taking Lithium.

"I'm not crazy," I protest. "I'm having an awakening!" I certainly don't want to suppress this experience.

I'm playing and writing a lot of songs during this time and I end up writing a song to express my feelings about Jill's preliminary diagnosis: "They say I'm obsessive, manic depressive. Oh so sublime. But I say the veil has lifted and the sand has shifted, how could I have been so blind. Awake from a dream is what it seems, after all these years, I am here." [10]

As Jill continues to talk to me about bipolar disorder, I begin to get paranoid that she will have me *put away* for what she perceives is my own good. I can see her side of it. She's afraid for the safety of the children and that our marriage and our nice middle class life might be in jeopardy. As it turns out, she's right about our nice middle class life. It is in jeopardy.

"They say the next episode will be stronger," cautions Jill, and I think about my friend Rob who was diagnosed as Bi-polar and has been put on Lithium.

In Rob's case, during his *episode* he was filled with crazy purpose and went barging into the office of the CEO of the large corporation for which he worked. He told the man in charge all the things that were wrong with his company. This did not go over well with the CEO and he had Rob's wife called. She came and got Rob and took him to the psychiatric hospital. He was on lithium before the day was out.

"I'm not Rob," I tell Jill.

"And even if I am having a manic episode," I tell myself, "I'm not going to be crazy enough to do something like Rob did, or run around naked in public, which another friend of mine once did that landed her in the psychiatric ward."

Then Jill tells me about a bi-polar patient of hers who is obsessed with sex. I guess we know which Chakra he opened.

Although I know how to play it cool, it's true that I have always been fascinated with craziness. Maybe it's because of my father. Losing his mind was his greatest fear, and in his case his greatest fear came to pass. It's amazing to me that as I am having my *crazy* spell, my father is spinning deeper and deeper into the darker corners of his own mind.

Because of my father, and also Jill's fears about bi-polar disorder, the next day I begin to do some research into the matter. I first begin reading a little about the disease, Bi-Polar Disorder, which used to be called Manic-Depression. In my reading, I come across an article about something called "Unipolar Mania" and I think that sounds more like me than bi-polar, because I don't get depressed. But then I read on and find that there really is no such thing as "Unipolar Mania". In other words, what goes up must go down. However, the article goes on to say that some people who are not particularly emotional only manifest the down swing of the disease in subtle ways: by being more tired, sleeping more, being 'mellow'. I decide that if I am Bi-polar, this is probably my situation.

The biggest concern with the Bi-polar thing is the down swing. The manic side is great, although too much energy can drive some people over the deep end. But I feel like I can handle it. I have a lot of tools. I've been doing yoga and meditation for twenty years. But what about the lows?

Then I remember something Swami Satchidananda said. He said that what we're all searching for is peace and harmony and that only these things last. For every high, there is a low. I know that to be true, and it's my belief that balance comes from integrating the two poles at a higher level of consciousness. I feel like I am staying centered with the high end at this point, but wonder what will happen going forward.

After further reading I am convinced that Bi-polars, Depressives, Attention Deficit sufferers, people suffering from Anxiety and even Schizophrenics all have related diseases. Brain chemistry and the handling of energy at the synapses seem to be common threads. Scientists are beginning to understand what is happening in the brain bio-chemically. Research is showing that dopamine, the brain's chemical messenger, is involved in all these illnesses, and there is evidence that excessive amounts of dopamine four are accumulating around the neuro-receptors in all the patients studied, which would dramatically intensify signals in the brain.

This could be enough to create hallucinations, delusions and paranoia, all the things that incidentally are often a part of an L.S.D. experience and a spiritual awakening. And now research is showing that the key to my father's disease, Alzheimer's, is also in the neuro-transmitters. Ah, this whole game is beginning to get very interesting.

Of course, there's another way to talk about all this stuff. If we use spiritual terms, the story goes something like this: God cannot be revealed to a simple mortal without blinding him. For this reason, the human nervous system is coated with a protective substance so that God's messengers, the neuro-transmitters only give a person what he can handle. But this veil over the nerves may be lifted to let in more light. What causes the veil to be lifted is just God's grace, but one can be prepared for this heightened level of awareness. It also helps to have the proper road maps, the proper framework, and the proper set and setting. These are the things Ram Dass, and Timothy Leary kept telling us in their experiments with L.S.D. Many of the ancient yogic scriptures are helpful. They tell us to tune our bodies and our minds to prepare for what they call "the awakening".

It's clear to me that there is a slim distinction between hallucination and spiritual vision, between mystic experience and psychosis. What makes the difference may be just a matter of how a person relates to his experiences. Anxiety is actually excitement when properly channeled, a manic episode is creative inspiration when directed properly, and perhaps even Alzheimer's is letting go of rational thought to awaken to spiritual revelation, if a person can just allow it to happen.

***

I have another so called manic episode the following evening. It starts out as heightened energy while I am reading Dr. Seuss' *Horton Hatches the Egg* to my daughter Dawn. I'm really getting into the character of the loyal and steadfast elephant and those around who ridicule him.

Jill leans over as I am reading and whispers to me, "You're a little manic."

Now, I ask you, who wouldn't be a little manic reading Dr. Seuss? But that's just my perspective.

***

I find another piece to the neurological puzzle a few nights later. I am reading a book about finding love in your marriage and suddenly I am in the midst of a discussion of neurotransmitters, specifically Epinephrine. It seems that people in love have more of it. They're all having manic episodes! When I was a teenager, it was said that I was in love with love. I was falling in love all the time. Jill says that when she first knew me, I was falling in love every six months (not necessarily with other women, but with causes, Gurus, etc.). I'm reminded of how I felt with Swami Satchidananda.

So... what is mania? What is crazy? And what is normal? Am I having a manic episode or a spiritual awakening? Zen mystic Osho was known to have said that insanity may be the only sane response to an insane world. I suppose it doesn't matter what we call the experience we're having. However we label it and the state of consciousness that accompanies it, the words "this too will pass" are appropriate, at least in my experience. No states seem to last and no experience seems to be the ultimate experience. In fact some teachers of consciousness are now suggesting that awakening is not an experience at all, but simply a recognition of the truth of things.

But still, it seems to be the nature of consciousness to experience the world, and the nature of the mind to see these experiences as real and to "learn" from them. Perhaps this is part of the natural unfolding of the human being... like the flowering of a Washington Lily or the skyward thrusting of the mighty Sequoia tree... and maybe it's all just happening by itself while the minds of men give it labels, make up meanings and attribute significance to it all.

Chapter 25

Life Breaks Apart

A month passes, and I am back to my normal self... or am I? The truth is that something has opened up in me that will never close, and as a result I can't go back to the way things were. The pedals of the flower that is my life have begun to show themselves in the new spring. Or to use another analogy, I'm like the mythical character Rip Van Winkle who awakens after twenty years of slumber and doesn't want to go back to sleep. I have had some extraordinary insights and feel an energy inside me that I haven't felt in a long time, and I desperately want to bring what has awakened into my life, but as a result, my marriage is in trouble and I am losing focus at my corporate job. I just can't go on with life as usual.

That next year is to be the hardest one of my life. I am traveling a lot for my job, my marriage is crumbling, and my family is showing the effects of it all. Jill and I seek out marriage counseling to try to save the marriage, but the more we get into it, the more I realize I don't want to make it work anymore. Something essential has been broken during the "manic" time, and I realize that relations between Jill and me will never be right again. In the process of the counseling, I see that Jill and I don't even want the same things out of life. I want to be carefree and creative and live the hippie life, while Jill seems to want to immerse us more and more deeply into the materiality of the American dream. Despite my seeing these things, I am extremely resistant to actually leaving the marriage. My parents were my models for relationship, and they stayed together for nearly fifty years as they persevered through their conflicts. From them I took on the belief that marriage is a lifetime commitment.

There are also the children to be concerned about. I know what often happens to children of divorce, and I don't want my kids to suffer. But of course, they are suffering with every argument Jill and I have. Finally Zack, our middle child, begins acting out. He appears to be the escape valve in the family dynamic. He begins leaving the house without telling us where he is going and often stays out all night. He is also cutting himself with razor blades, doing drugs, drinking and even sniffing gasoline. He is definitely out of control and on a downward spiral, and so after much debate, Jill finally convinces me that he needs treatment. One early morning, we force him into the car, drive him to the airport, and escort him to a residential treatment program in California. The place we take him is supposed to have the best program in the country, and it is very strict. Jill says it's what he needs. I feel that we have violated his freedom and betrayed his trust. I'm sure some of my feelings stem from my own fear that Jill might do the same thing to me during one of my "episodes," for my own good of course.

After Zack has been locked up for a month on a behavior modification program, Jill and I and the other two kids drive out to California to get him, and after a few family therapy sessions in which we work on the family dynamic and hone our communication skills, especially about feelings, Zack is released back into our care. On the long drive back to Colorado, we begin to re-integrate Zack into the family. The treatment has helped him. For one thing, he has learned how to better express his feelings rather than holding them in and getting depressed and rebellious. There is hope. But over time, Zack slowly gets worse again. That's when I realize that staying in my marriage for the kids is not working. Looking from Zack's perspective, I see him looking at my life and me as his role model and saying to himself, "If this is what life promises, then I don't want it."

***

In the middle of all this, we go off to a long-planned family reunion in the Tetons of Wyoming. My mother has arranged it. I think she sees it as a last chance for all of us, my brother and his wife, Jill and I and our kids, and she and my dad to all be together. Dad is going downhill fast and he won't be around much longer.

After a two-day drive, we arrive at Togotee Lodge in the Grand Tetons. We unpack, play some ping-pong and shoot some pool in the lodge recreation room, and we all try out the Jacuzzi. My parents arrive around five-thirty the next afternoon after a difficult journey. I immediately notice that my dad has gotten very thin and he seems to be quite fragile. Has Dad gotten worse? Yes, he probably has, but it is also true that my heightened awareness had provided the extra energy and acute attention required for us to communicate for such a long time the previous year. I'm wondering if there will be any heightened awareness this time. There is no sign of it so far. My brother Laird and his wife Melinda arrive from Tahoe, where they now live, sometime that night after we have gone to bed.

The next day we go for a long walk in the Tetons and some of us go swimming in one of the lakes. The water is cool but not cold and it feels exhilarating on the body. It's difficult at times to walk with Dad. As he walks he begins leaning off to the left as if the whole world were on a different axis, but the more we pull him in one direction, the more he counterbalances in the other until he becomes completely rigid. It is especially hard to get him to sit down or once sitting, to get him up to standing again.

Dad is still talking quite a bit, but no one can figure out what he's saying most of the time. I've pretty much given up trying to understand him during this visit, but instead try to relate to him on another level, beyond words, through open attention and more touching. This is a new experience for me. All of my conscious life, I have related to both of my parents verbally. We were a family of intellectuals.

Later in the afternoon Laird makes an announcement. "Melinda and I are going to drive to Jackson! Who wants to go with us?"

I am pretty mad at Laird for planning to just take off like that, while I feel obligated to stay behind and help my mom take care of my dad. Then I realize that I have always been jealous of Laird's life, his adventures and his freedom.

I'm meditating a lot during this time and it's helping me gain perspective. I am not reaching any deep transcendental states, but I am learning the art of letting go one thought at a time.

"Just let it go... and that one too... yes and also that one. Now gently bring the awareness back to the breath," I hear a voice inside me say, and it's all helping me identify less with what is arising.

As a result, I am coming to some understanding, particularly about the things I have to let go of: feelings of victimhood, the notion that life is not fair, and most of all about my tendency to compare my life to Laird's. The next morning after my meditation, I have a better perspective on this tendency, and I see that I have actually been given a lot in my life, and that my resentment of Laird is simply a sign that I haven't fully taken responsibility for the choices that I've made. From that more centered place, I can see that those choices are what have made my life what it is. No one else is responsible for what comes into my life. It's my dharma, say the Buddhists. It is my karma, say the Hindus. It is my free choice, say the humanists.

There is a very intense moment with Mom and Dad the next night. We can't get Dad to the toilet and he makes quite a mess. Finally we get it all cleaned up and get Dad on the bed for a nap. That's when my mom brakes down and begins to cry. I hold her and cry with her and then suddenly my mother wipes her tears and apologizes to me for wrecking my fun.

"Mom, what's more meaningful than this? Have we ever been so close?" I ask. "Don't you see that this is where the treasure is? What life is all about? It's not just about having fun!"

The next morning, I take a hike with Laird, just the two of us, and as we hike I express my desire to be closer to him. I've only seen him a handful of times since he left for college so many years ago. Then I tell him that I was mad at him for just taking off the day before.

"You could have gone, too. There were two adults there for Dad." He says a bit defensively.

"It's funny. I didn't even see that as an option," I say and then remember what I discovered in meditation the day before... that I stayed behind because I wanted to be with Mom and Dad, and in the broader context of my life, I chose to have children and to be in a role of responsibility, I chose to work in Corporate America to provide for my family, and I am still making a choice to be with my children and to be with Jill. My life is what it is because of my free choice. Then I recall something Ram Dass said back in Boulder those many years ago. "I have free will - that's my karma talking." He went on to explain that at one level of consciousness we each have the freedom to choose our directions in life, but at another level of consciousness, we're just playing out our karma, doing what we have to do, what we are inevitably called to do. Either way, fairness has nothing to do with it, and still I notice how strong the habit is to look over the proverbial fence at the grass on the other side and to regret my choices, and how much of my life I spent being jealous of Laird and his experiences, wanting to be on his side of that fence.

"Come with me on a backpack trip next summer," Laird says as we walk. "I'm celebrating my fiftieth birthday next year by hiking a hundred miles from Sierra Buttes to the middle fork of the Feather River. It's one of the most breath-taking sections of the Pacific Coast trail."

I hear him speak and at first say to myself, "Oh I can't do that," but then I realize that's the old me talking... and now the new me begins to see the possibility open up in front of me. "Yes. I can do that. Life isn't black and white. It isn't a case of either responsibility or freedom."

"I'd really like to do that!" I say to him. "It sounds great. Let's see if we can work it out," and as I say this I wonder if I can really make it happen.

***

Back home after the interlude in Wyoming, I can see myself falling back into the same old rut of a life. I need to do something to fan the flame of the awakening that is dimly flickering inside me. But what? Then I see an advertisement in our local paper for a free session with a massage therapist in town. She advertises her sessions as Spiritual Massage, to help spiritual energy move.

"That sounds like just what I need," I say to myself, but I am a little apprehensive. I've never had a massage. But my need for change finally overcomes my reticence, and I make an appointment. Before she starts the session, the therapist, also named Jill by the way, tells me that she likes to think of her massage work as "beyond Rolfing". I've heard about Rolfing, a practice of deep massage invented by Dr. Ida Rolf back in the 1950's, and how it could help a person make changes in his life by breaking up the patterns of holding in the musculature. I have even heard of cases where a person's physical appearance and personality shifted from this work, but I also heard that it could be very painful. I am scared as I undress and slip under the sheets on her massage table, but I'm also hopeful that maybe she can help in my awakening process. Perhaps she can help me make the real changes I desperately desire. She walks in the room and puts her hands on me, I take a deep breath and try to relax.

I begin the session with an open mind, and I come out of the session with an open body! The massage is an amazing, powerful, painful, wonderful, blissful, full body experience. I laugh. I cry. I tremble. I feel the energy coursing through me, and I feel some blockages. My hands, my back and my legs all tingle. What does she do? Well, she pushes on my ribs and she works on the upper part of my neck. As she works there, I feel a strong sensation of being suffocated and I have a small panic reaction. Then she eases up and I relax. Next, she begins massaging my internal organs: my intestines, spleen and liver. Then she tells me she is massaging the muscles along the inside of my spine. That's really painful! She goes so deep I feel like she is digging right through me and I have the weird sensation that I am insubstantial, that I'm nothing. When the session is over and I have gotten dressed again, she comes and talks to me.

"I got a funny taste in my mouth, while I was working on you," she says. "Candida," she adds. "I think you have a yeast condition. You should go see my Iridologist friend, she'll be able to tell for sure, and she can treat you. Tell her I sent you."

She gives me her friend's card and I go to see the Iridologist the following week. She is a slightly overweight woman in her forties with an intense gaze, and the first thing she says to me upon looking in my eyes is, "If you were older, I'd say you had a Vasectomy."

"I am older and I did have a Vasectomy," I tell her. Then she tells me that I have some left knee problems, and that a large lesion in the right eye indicates some lung problems. The knee I am aware of. The lungs I am not, but a couple of years later, I do have a bout of pleurisy. Then she confirms the therapist's hunch that I have a Candida condition in my stomach and she prescribes a whole series of herbal remedies including a Chinese herbal cleanse. I come home with an armful of pills in assorted bottles.

The next morning I climb up on my desk sitting cross-legged in front of my computer for the first time in months.

"I may not be manic anymore, but that doesn't mean I have to be conventional," I declare to myself as I sit listening to Paul Horn's flute in the Taj Mahal burping Chinese herbal medicine and waiting for a big bowel movement.

I have several more sessions with Jill the massage therapist over the next months and I continue with the Chinese herbs. Relations continue to be strained with my wife as she feels me pulling away, and I sense that something will have to give. The first step I take is to have my own space, separate from Jill, which I create in the basement near the laundry area. My thought is that if I have my own space, I'll be more free to explore my creativity, and it will also provide a place for me to sleep when I want to be alone. The idea of me sleeping in my own place is quite threatening to Jill, but it's less drastic than me moving out. So, for the sake of the children and our finances, we decide it's worth trying.

The first night I sleep alone, I wake up in the middle of the night feeling vulnerable, lonely and scared. My bones ache, my left hand hurts and I notice a funny spot on my leg. Then I realize that I am just afraid of being alone. I have become so habituated to having someone in bed beside me, and I want the security of someone who cares. I want a mother. I want Jill.

"Who will take care of me when I'm sick?" A voice in me cries.

"This is exactly what I must fight," another part declares. "Jill is not my mother and I can't go running for cover (Mother's skirts) every time I get a little scared. I need to be brave and stand strong."

I focus on my breathing and just watch the inner dialog.

"That's right, that's just a thought. Let that one pass, and that one too. They are just the gate keepers on the road to freedom."

The mind quiets, the body relaxes, and I eventually go back to sleep.

Chapter 26

A Failed Attempt

Now that I have my own space and I am on my own schedule, I begin meditating for longer periods of time. In meditation, my thoughts are still strong, one thought often catapulting tangentially from another, but I keep coming back to the mantra, the one I was given by Swami Satchidananda so many years ago. I also begin a reflection practice I learned from a yoga class I'm attending. The statement I choose to reflect on is: "I am whole and complete as I am." As I continue to reflect on these words I notice that the "I am" I'm reflecting on is something beyond the thoughts I am having. Then I realize that it is the very nature of thought to separate, distinguish and create a time sequence for experience, which in turn leads to the feeling of not being whole and complete. It's suddenly clear. As long as I am identified with my thoughts, they by their very nature are keeping me away from wholeness. Then I see that the place where "I am whole and complete" is beyond all that. But of course, I am thinking this as well, and then I remember what Ram Dass used to say about the Jnana yoga path... the path of the intellect.

"That's the interesting trick," he had said. "These are tools that are able to take us outside the rational mind by way of the rational mind."

"I am whole and complete," my mind says again, but then it adds, "I may be whole and complete but I have needs that aren't being met. I need to have this and I need to have that, blah, blah,

blah...... Om Nama, Om Nama, Om Nama. Breathing in, breathing out. Breathing in, breathing out. Om Shanti, Shanti, Shanti. Om, peace, peace, peace."

As I become more centered in myself and less dependent on Jill, I notice that Jill seems to be more resentful, and eventually our relationship is reduced to just passing each other in the hallway. Over time, the whole thing takes on a hellish quality, and there is a tension permeating the household that begins wearing on everyone.

"Things just can't go on like this," I say to myself.

Although I feel a lot of fear and am filled with doubts, my overwhelming sense is that I have to move out. It's clear to me that I have started something in motion that just has to complete itself. I grab the daily paper and look through the want ads. In no time, I find a room for rent at a reasonable price not far from home. I call and before I can second-guess the decision, it's all arranged. I am to move in on January first!

The timing of this is awkward, but then there's never a good time to leave a twenty year marriage. Jill is furious. Just to add another level of complexity to the whole process, a day or two before my move date, my car dies, so I have to buy a new car. So, on New Year's Eve, I load a few essentials, a CD player and CD's, my guitar, a drum, some yoga stuff, a couple pairs of pants, a couple shirts, a sleeping bag, a piece of foam, and my laptop computer into Jill's car, and Aaron drives me down to the car dealer to pick up my new car. Jill makes it clear when I leave that I am not to come back home, so when I get my new car, I load my things into it, say goodbye to Aaron and, not knowing what else to do, drive to a nearby shopping mall to hang out and see if I can figure out what to do until I can move in to my place the following day. My yoga teacher is having a party at her house in the evening, so I decide I will go there, even though I am not in a party mood. Then, thinking about the night ahead, I wonder if she'll be open to letting me stay the night? I'm feeling a bit insecure about it. After all, I don't know her that well. In fact I've never been to her house, just been to her class at the town recreation center several times.

As I sit in the shopping mall thinking over what to do, I pause and look at what has become of my life. It occurs to me that I've been so caught up in my family, the house and my job, that I have no friends anymore. As I consider to whom I might turn at this time in my life, I realize that I've completely lost touch with my old friends from graduate school, and that I haven't really made the effort to make new friends. Sure, there are some people that Jill and I get together with from time to time, but I have the strong feeling that they are really Jill's friends and won't be supportive of what I'm doing. I'm left feeling very alone. Then I reflect on my last few moments in the house. Jill is yelling and Dawn is crying and it breaks my heart.

"What have I done?" I ask myself. "How did things get like this?"

I do go to the yoga teacher's party, and as it turns out, I am the only one who shows up, which is really strange, but it's a blessing. I am pretty rattled by what's happening in my life and need someone to talk to, and so I end up spending the evening with someone I hardly know and sleeping on her coach that night. The next day, I move into the new place. I have the downstairs of a house in a pretty remote mountain setting. My housemate Linda, as it turns out, is a T.V. watcher and compulsive video-taper. Every day, while she is at work, she programs the V.C.R. to record all the daytime soap operas. She even tapes cartoons! Then she sits on her coach every night for hours on end watching what she has taped. When she isn't watching T.V., Linda is very talkative and very friendly, in fact, too friendly for my taste. After a day or two, I am beginning to have serious questions about what I have gotten myself into. It seems like Linda has had ulterior motives in renting the space to me and I'm starting to feel much trepidation.

A day or two later, Jill calls and is very nice to me. She asks how I am, and when I tell her my concerns about my new housemate, she asks if she can come over to see me. I agree to the visit, she comes over, and the meeting goes well... too well, really. We end up sleeping together and the next thing I know I am moving back home, wondering what all the fuss was about. I have to admit that it feels good to be back in familiar territory, and I can tell the kids are glad to see me back. But, in returning, I have made a promise to myself that, although I am back home, I will be more insistent in taking care of my own needs from now on.

As I settle back into being home, I come across a book about traveling and meeting holy men in India, and this leads me to think about my old friend, Fran. The last correspondence I'd received from her was a postcard she had sent me from India where she had gone to follow a Guru named Osho. That was at least fifteen years ago.

"What's happened to Fran," I wonder, and as I think about her a vacant feeling comes in to my heart, like there's a piece missing out of the middle of me, and I can't help feeling that Fran has that piece. I can't say I really understand the feeling, but it gnaws at me never the less. Then I have the thought that maybe there is unfinished past-life business with her. That's when I remember my old friend Bill who was also Fran's friend.

"Bill might know where Fran is," I think, but then I realize I haven't heard from him in years either.

"Let's see, the last time I saw Bill, he was living in San Diego," I recall and dial long distance information. This is back in the days before Facebook and even before e-mail was widespread. I try to get his phone number, but the operator says there is no such person in San Diego. Some weeks later, as circumstance would have it, I have a business trip to San Diego. It's the first time I've had business there, so it feels like divine providence. On my first night in the hotel room, I open up the telephone book for the greater San Diego area, and there is his name, address and phone number staring out at me in black on white. It turns out he actually lives in Chula Vista, a suburb of San Diego. I guess that's why the operator couldn't find him. I call Bill from my hotel room as soon as I have some free time and he comes over. We have a wonderful visit. It's as if we have never been apart. Toward the end of our time together, I ask if he's heard from Fran.

"Oh yes," he says and he gives me her address.

When I get back home from the trip, I write Fran a long letter. After a few weeks the letter is returned with "Address Unknown" stamped across the front. I am crushed. I call Bill.

"Oh yea. We got another letter from her," says Bill. "She's moved. Here's her new address." He recites it to me carefully.

I write Fran again and when the weeks go by and I still have heard nothing, I resign myself to the possibility that I will never hear from her again.

Then, one night I have an amazing dream. I am sitting in a classroom and someone is lecturing. As he is talking, I look over to the right and see that there is a TV in the room and it's on. Some people are having lunch on the TV and one of the guys having lunch is reading the newspaper. The paper is open to the comic section. The TV camera zooms in on the comics being held in the man's hands, and on the last frame, we see a speaking bubble. The camera zooms in further until the words in the bubble can be seen clearly. They say, "Hey, Bryan!"

It's such an adrenalin rush for me to see my name in bold print like that, and I have the distinct impression that it's a message from someone.

A few weeks later, I have to go to Boston to my corporate headquarters for some important training. Due to the PC network revolution, my company, a mainframe database software company, is in trouble. A new management team has just taken over and everyone is scrambling to get on board with the new team and the new technology. We all know the alternative is to go out of business. Since I am going to be on the East Coast anyway, I decide to combine the trip with a long desired weeklong yoga retreat at the Kripalu center in the Berkshires. It's part of my new resolution to take care of my own needs. I plan on taking a bus there after my business meeting and then flying home the following weekend.

Just before I leave on the trip, I begin to feel some lower back pain and go to a chiropractor that my yoga teacher has recommended.

"This guy is amazing," she says. "He's got a gift, a kind of third sight, and he's a real healer."

I go to see him. I go with an open mind. I sit on his table, and he tells me to relax. Suddenly, before I know what's happening, he grabs my torso and twists my spine violently. My body tries to protect itself, but his movements are just too quick.

"Relax," he says and then suddenly gives my torso another violent jerk. Something pops in my back.

"Good," he says, but despite his reassurance, my body is trembling with fear.

"I move fast so that I can override those protective mechanisms of the body," he tells me.

I am not convinced that I want those protective mechanisms to be overridden, but after one more quick movement, he is done. When I get up from the table, I am feeling a lot of energy all through my spine. Still, it has to be one of the scariest experiences I have ever had.

Two days later I am on an airplane heading for the East coast and the following day, sitting in meetings all day, I begin to experience a lot of lower back pain and sciatica. Everyone there seems to be feeling the uncertainty of the changes ahead for the company, which makes the meetings very stressful, and as the week progresses, as if to mirror this stress, the pain in my back and left leg intensify to the point where it becomes increasingly more difficult to sit in a chair. I wonder how I will ever manage at the yoga retreat, but stubbornly hold onto the idea of going. It's that Taurus moon of mine, I suppose, staunchly adhering to plans made.

"It'll work out somehow!" I tell myself.

Finally the week comes to a close, and by the time I reach Kripalu I can barely walk. Some sessions of hot yoga and time in their sauna begin to ease the pain a little and I manage to get through the week and back home to Colorado.

At home, I continue to experience back pain. I have had back episodes before and bed rest seems to be the best remedy, so I call in sick and stay in bed. One morning, after a couple of days rest, my back seems better, and so I get out of bed to do something with my computer. Just as I am getting up, something snaps in my back, and I crumple to the floor like a rag doll. The pain is incredible, like being electrocuted. I have the distinct sensation that something essential in me has come apart, and that the whole support structure of my body has been compromised. I lie there on the floor for a while afraid to move, and then finally find the strength and courage to drag my body every so slowly onto the bed. I can't move my legs at all, and so I just lie there on my stomach not moving for a couple of hours.

"Thank God it's Wednesday, the day Jill always comes home for lunch." I realize, and as I lie there waiting for help, I relive the event over and over in my mind. I feel such intense fear... body fear.

At long last, I hear Jill open the front door, and I call out to her. She finds me lying on the bed hyperventilating from the pain and fear. I am still unable to move while the sensations in my body go from throbbing pain to numbness and back to throbbing pain. I particularly notice a tingling and pulsating sensation in my hands and feet along with the sharp stabs of pain in my lower back and legs. The pain is so intense that I wonder if I will be able to bare it. Then my mind jumps ahead to the future, and I wonder if I will ever walk again? As my mind races, my body begins to go into shock, and I am overcome with the feeling of helplessness! Jill, always good in a crisis, calls the local Chiropractor, a very gentle and noninvasive practitioner, not a so-called "healer" like the last person I had. She tells the Chiropractor my situation and the woman offers to come over after her office hours.

That evening the Chiropractor does come, she looks me over, asks some questions, gives me some acupuncture treatments and suggests that we apply alternating cold and hot compresses on the injured area. After she takes the needles out of my back, we start with ice and as the ice begins to numb the area of my lower back, I am finally able to calm myself.

For the next several weeks, I do nothing but lie in my bed, look out the window and think about my life. My kids are very sweet to me during this time, changing my bedpan and bringing me my meals as I relax into my unfamiliar role of being served. With Jill, it's a different story. She is carrying resentment and I can feel it every time she enters the room. Still I have to depend on her, I have no choice, and she is helpful and attentive, despite her obvious feelings. As the time goes by, I develop an intimate knowledge of pain as I observe it in my body. What I notice is that if I just allow the pain to come without trying to resist it, it doesn't last too long. Pain, it seems, comes in waves.

Time has a way of standing still and yet slipping away. Each day lying in my bed is an eternity and yet each eternity is just a day, and the days pass. As I lie there day after day, one question keeps coming into my mind over and over.

"Can I really change my life in any fundamental way?"

Then it occurs to me that a better question is, "What is good about being flat on my back?" This question is more of an honoring of where I am right now, and the answers to this question come easily. First, I am being treated kindly by my children. Second, I have plenty of time to read, listen to music, look out the window at the tree that has become a companion to me, and let my mind wonder wherever it wants to. Third, I don't have to go downstairs and work on that computer of mine. Fourth and most importantly, I am learning about *being*, because all my *doing* is pretty much out-the-window for the time being... literally, since all I can do is look out the window. And so, for so many reasons, I am grateful for this time to do nothing. I have been acting and reacting long enough. In sickness is the potential for a tremendous let-go, and I am beginning to take advantage of the opportunity.

***

As the days go by, time's demarcations are beginning to blur. Is it Tuesday or Thursday? What week is it? What month? It is so easy to lose track of those meaningless abstractions. I am currently reading a powerful book called the *Inner World of Mental Illness*. It's a first hand account of insanity, and the woman is writing from her bed while those around her are screaming in their straight jackets. And so here I am in my bed, in my own version of a straight jacket, just barely able to roll over and use a bedpan. I have been forced to step, or rather crawl, off the wheel of life and I lie on my back suspended in an eternal moment of nonexistence.

***

I have been watching Joseph Campbell on videotape for a few days and the theme for this day is *Out of Death Comes life*.

"It's a common theme, especially of the plant cultures," he says. "Death is the fertilizer for new life."

I wonder what I am fertilizing? What will rise up from this deathbed? I have had enough of dying. I'm ready for the resurrection, and yet shear will won't do it. Loving, nurturing, patience seems to be all that is called for at this moment, and so I wait and wonder if there will be a transcendental moment near by? I can see that everything I have ever done, all my experiences, thoughts, actions, loves and choices are bringing me to this one moment, and I see that every moment is a potential turning point.

And then, as time passes, I realize that if there is going to be any kind of resurrection, the body is going to need to be attended to. The chiropractor is making regular visits and applying her acupuncture needles whenever she comes, but my body is not responding. In fact, after so much time in bed I am beginning to lose the feeling in my left foot, and I also have a lot of tingling in my legs. Then the thought occurs to me that maybe I really am dying, not just metaphorically, and I start thinking about what that would mean. I think about my life, my family, and my goals. Then it occurs to me that if "getting to God", as Ram Dass used to say, is my main goal, dying might be the fast path. But as soon as I have that thought, I quickly realize that I am not ready to die. I still have things to do. I'm just getting my life together. There is my music, my writing, my yoga. Besides, my family still needs me.

Chapter 27

Taking Steps

About this time, two different people from different parts of my life recommend the same physical therapist. This catches my attention, and I decide to go see this person, but I need a doctor's prescription in order for physical therapy to be covered by insurance. This means I have to go see a doctor. Reluctantly, I make an appointment (I don't like to go to doctors), and at the appointed time, Jill, with much effort on her part and lots of pain on my part, loads me into the back of the car and drives me to the doctor's office (The doctor doesn't make house calls). He examines me, takes some x-rays, does some blood work and declares that I am in good health. Great. I am going to live. As for the ruptured disc, he suggests an MRI to start with, and then probably surgery. I definitely don't want to go down that road. I've heard too many stories about people who have had back surgery and were left with a lifetime of pain. I tell him about the physical therapist, and he reluctantly consents to me seeing her with the understanding that if I don't see immediate results I am to schedule the MRI. He writes the prescription and then Jill loads me back in the car, drives me home, and finally gets me back into bed. This has been a real ordeal, and I'll need to regain my strength before going out to see the physical therapist.

The next morning my mother calls. She tells me she has to go in to the hospital to have surgery for a lump, presumably cancerous, in one of her breasts and wants to know if I can come and be with my dad while she is in the hospital. At this point my dad needs constant care. My mother doesn't know what has happened to me.

"I'm sorry mom, I wish I could come, but I'm lying here flat on my back unable to walk."

When I hang up the phone, I feel so bad for my mom. I know how scared she must be about the possibility of cancer, and I notice how she can't even let herself experience that, my dad's needs having priority. I feel sad that I am unable to help her. She so rarely asks for anything, and now when she finally does, I have to let her down. It all seems like one of life's cruel turns of events.

A day later the snow is falling gently outside my window, and an Om Nama Shivaya chant is playing on the tape player. The boys are out of the house pursuing their interests, Jill is at a workshop for her job and Dawn is in school. Ponda, the cat, stretches his big fury body and begins to clean himself after a satisfying nap. Maggie, the dog, is sleeping under the small hand-me-down desk in the corner of the room, and I lie in my bed holding boredom at arms length with the tangle of my own thoughts.

As I lie here, still ruminating about my Mom, my helplessness, and humanity's seemingly futile collective destiny, the tree outside my window catches my attention. There it stands, through sunshine, clouds, wind, darkness, dawn, and now, as I watch, through falling snow, and amidst it all, barely moving, it seems at peace and fulfilled. As I gaze out at this tranquil champion of just being, I notice by contrast how much more I expect of myself, and perhaps because of it I find no such fulfillment. I tell myself there is really nothing for me to do and yet my mind pours over the possibilities and pressures of life's agendas that seem to be only momentarily held at bay, like the Dead Sea by that heroic parting the *Bible* talks about, all just waiting for the right moment to come crashing down around me. There's expectation in the air as if there were a clock ticking away the last few seconds before the dawn of a new day, and somewhere inside me, I feel the pull of the universe wanting me to wake up and come to life, but my body still says "No!" Here I am still lying on my back in this bed, and my left leg seems to be getting worse again. There is more numbing and more pain. My hope is that it is the last fling of pain before the final healing, but a part of me doubts that.

"The doubting part is the part I need to work on," I tell myself.

I have read the new age precepts about how we create our own reality, and I know I just need to have faith in the natural healing process, so I try making an affirmation.

"I am grounded in my own power. I am secure. I deserve to enjoy life. I can ask for and accept what I want with joy and pleasure. I can have health and wholeness and I can have it now."

But making an affirmation and truly believing it are two different things. Affirmations don't work unless you really believe them, and if you really believe them, there's no need to make them. It's a Catch-22.

But despite what the mind does, despite faith or lack of it, nature seems to have it's own way, and after a couple of days I am strong enough to be driven to the physical therapist. As the therapist gets me on her table she explains that she has just returned from "back school" in California. Then she moves me into a certain position on my side with one leg straight and one bent and starts putting slow, even pressure on my spine. I begin to experience relief immediately!

"I can't cure you without your active participation," she says, and she shows me a series of back exercises that I can do myself to strengthen the muscles needed to keep my back in place. I go home and begin to move, and after several more visits to the therapist I finally feel like I am on the road to recovery. I start by getting myself to the bathroom by crawling on my hands and knees, and then the day finally comes when I feel ready to stand again. I'll never forget this moment. It's like how I imagine I felt taking my first step as a toddler. I pull myself up onto my feet and, looking down, I feel like I am a mile above the floor. Then I take my first step. I am so wobbly and weak. That first day, I take three steps and collapse in bed. The next day, I shuffle to the bathroom and back. It's a major accomplishment. After a week and another visit to the therapist, I feel like I am ready to walk outside. I shuffle over to the front door, pull it open and look out at the glorious world, and I am reminded of the time, not so long ago, when I went out to walk the dog and everything in my field of view was shimmering. This day the world is just a normal gloriousness, but miraculous just the same. I peer out from the front porch steps, and set my sights on my goal, the mailbox at the end of the driveway. The first day, I take a few steps in that direction, the next day a few more, and then, two days later, I make it all the way to that box and bring in the mail myself.

Just about this time, Bill calls me from San Diego. He has no idea what I am going through. I guess I'm not very communicative. He calls with a proposal. He and Mary and a couple others are planning a trip to Arizona in April and want me to come along. Their destination is a place called Havasupai. It's an Indian reservation along the Colorado River just down stream from the Grand Canyon.

"We're going to hike down into the canyon and camp in one of the reservation camp grounds next to Havasu falls and then explore from there," Bill explains.

"How long a hike is it?" I asked timidly, "and do we pack in?"

"It's eight miles down to the Indian village of Supai and then another two miles to the campground, but you won't have to carry anything but a daypack. We'll hire horses to carry our gear."

I tell him I'll have to think about it, and after getting off the phone, crazy as it seems, I have an overpowering urge to say "yes" to him. The trip is six weeks away and I know it will take a lot of work on my part to be ready. I am very weak, but in my heart I feel that somehow this trip might be exactly what I need, a real incentive to get me up and well again.

Later that day I walk out to the end of the driveway again, and there in the mailbox is a letter from Fran. I feel like a kid on Christmas morning as I tear open the envelope. I can hardly believe I have finally gotten a letter from her after fifteen years. Her name is Prem now, she explains as I begin reading. It's a name her guru gave her. As I read her tale, I can see that her life since I've last seen her has been quite a journey. For all these years she was either in India with her guru or back in the States trying to scrape up enough money with odd jobs to go back. Reading her letter and feeling her presence again leaves me with a burning desire to see her, and it occurs to me that perhaps I am hearing from her now because she has a part to play in my awakening, that it's all somehow part of the divine script.

"I have sent you many messages over the years in the ether," she says.

I guess I was too busy with my life, or just not sensitive enough to hear her. Then I think about that dream I had not too long ago, when the cartoon bubble spoke to me. "Was that her?" I guess she finally had to break down and communicate the old fashioned way, in pen and ink, and call on help from the U.S. Postal Service.

The next day, I realize that my mother must be out of the hospital, and so I call her to find out how her surgery went.

"The lump was benign," she says and we both sigh with relief.

As my healing continues, I begin reading the, *The Artist's Way: A Spiritual Path to Higher Creativity* by Julia Cameron, and start a practice she has suggested called "morning pages". Morning pages are three pages of stream-of-consciousness writing with no pauses. No time is taken to stop and think, there's just a spontaneous flow... a brain drain, a clearing out of the mind garbage.

"Here goes my first attempt at mind dump where I just keep writing without stopping for three pages. Well, let's see, I'm feeling better I guess, why crawl when I can walk. I guess that feels good, although my foot's still a bit numb, I'm kind of cold sitting here on the couch and the pen is a little awkward. My hand hurts already, and I feel strange sensations in my hip. But gotta keep going. Wonder if I'll ever be back to normal. I wish I could go to the Havasu Canyon with Bill, but I think that's pushing it, plus the time away from work, and it's not fair to Jill. Obligation, blah, blah, blah and that reminds me of my obligation to keep supporting the family with this job, my work responsibilities and all that. I wonder how Ali's doing. He's a guy from work who just got fired. I don't know how to get a hold of him. As I think about him, I appreciate what I have. The job's not so bad. At least I've got a job... but it ties me down. Or does it? Why should it? I can go anywhere, live anywhere and still do this job. Remember, they closed our office and sent us home. Another voice argues, I want to be free... just go... suspended in time... hope I can go backpacking with Bill and Mary. That should be a great suspension of time. Can I do it? Can I keep up? Gotta get in shape. I wonder if I should lift weights. I'm such a stickman. I've gotta work out to bulk up a little. But not too much though. I don't want to be too big. Also don't want to hurt my back again... and so it goes. Everything has a 'yes' followed by 'but'. But, why did I come back to Jill? I certainly couldn't have made it through the back thing without her. The security, the safety, the nurturance. I must remember that anything I see in her is really in me! She's crabby and self-centered. I guess I must be crabby and self-centered. Certainly self-centered but at least I leave other people alone. But maybe I leave other people too much alone. What is aloneness anyway? Am I just afraid to relate to other people? Do I leave people too much alone? Because of that tendency I was never much of a parent. Yes, the role of parent is certainly not my natural role. I'm more of a teacher/guru type. I'd like to go back to school and become a professor. Yes, that's it. That's my place. Bag this computer garbage. But how do I get there? Is there another way to get there that would be less painful financially? What could I do? How long do I have to wait? Maybe I could .... well no probably not ... um... write a book... become famous... get an honorary degree. No. I need a real degree. How about a correspondence course. Yes, that could work. Or let's see... become a yoga teacher and then a yoga therapist. Probably can't do a lot of physical stuff with this back though. I'd like to form a commune. My yoga teacher could live with us and let's see, who else? Fran. Boy, I'd like to see her.....

Oh, oh, I violated the covenant. I stopped writing and started thinking. Maybe the mind dump is finally coming to an end. What else is there to say? Just lots of this and that... ideas about what to do with my life. When does that stop? When do I actually just *be* and the heck with the rest of it. Heck with what I'm doing, what I'm accomplishing. It's not important. Just *be* in the moment. That's it. That's all there is. No more. Nothing else. And so that's the end of the mind dump for today. Thank God. Amen."

I have a dream about Fran or I guess I should call her 'Prem' now. I meet her at this place where there are a bunch of other people and activities going on. Maybe it's Kripalu or some place like that. She has dark red lipstick on. We kiss. She tells me that I need to explore black magic so that I will no longer be afraid of anything. I am skeptical about that, but excited to see her. I go back to my dorm and get on an elevator to go to my room and think about when I can get back to see her again.

After the dream, my heart aches, and I yearn to go visit Prem now that my subconscious has opened to the idea. I am feeling so sad and alone, even though I know that on another level I am connected to the whole universe. Despite these feelings I faithfully do my back exercises every day, and each day I head outside to walk. At first I walk to our mailbox, then I make it to our neighbor's mailbox and then finally I get all the way to the end of the block and back.

Every day I am getting stronger and stronger and when April finally comes along, I do hike down Havasu Canyon. I walk the full ten miles, and I bathe in waterfalls and swim in the crystal clear waters of the natural pools that are formed by them. I sleep on the ground and share campfires with my friends. I hike and explore, laugh, play music and eat gourmet cuisine, each day feeling stronger than I did the day before. Then when it's time to go, I hike all the way back out of that canyon. As I take step after step along the arduous trail ever onward and upward, I begin to feel like a Phoenix rising out of his own ashes, and when I arrive at the top, I am reborn.

But for the rebirth to be complete, there are a few more things that have to occur. As life would have it, shortly after I return from Havasu canyon, I have a business trip to Albany, New York to give some computer training. This is my chance to go visit Prem. At this time, she is living in upstate New York in a little town called Ithaca, the home of Cornell University where she is teaching meditation.

Ithaca is about a three-hour drive from Albany, so after I finish teaching for the week, I extend the lease on my rental car and drive out to see her. I am filled with excitement and anticipation to see

Prem again after all these years. I wonder how it'll be to see her again and how we will get along. I have some definite fantasies. I first met Prem at the impressionable age of twenty-two and have been smitten ever since. At the time I met her, of course, she was married, but now she is single.

"I wonder, is she available? But twenty-three years have passed since those days. I am now forty-five and she is forty-seven. How would that change things?"

These are the thoughts that go through my head as I drive through the countryside of upstate New York. At last, I pull up in front of her house. It's Friday night and she has told me that she will be showing an Osho video and having a group meditation at her house that evening. I'm early. Her door is open and I walk in. There she is, sitting in a hammock chair suspended from the ceiling looking out the window. I knock gently as I enter and she turns and smiles, and in that moment all the years between us evaporate like dew in morning sunlight.

"Hey. There you are!" She says and gets out of her swing to give me a hug. "I cooked a couple of frozen vegetable pies. Have you eaten? They're really good. They're Amy's all-natural.... Say, how are you?"

And just like that I am swept up into her world as if I'd been in it all my life. An hour later people start arriving for the meditation. There are some younger people and some older, and they are all people who instantly feel like friends. We start by watching a video of Indian Mystic Osho. I am mesmerized by this man all dressed in white with long beard, intense gaze and radical perspective on life.

"This is a video from the Pune I days," Prem comments and then we dive deeply into his words and gaps of silence in between.

In the video he is answering a questioner who says he doesn't have any real questions. Osho's response is that there are no real questions in existence, and that all questions are false, unreal, nonessential, because life is not a problem to be solved, but a mystery to be lived. He says that only the fools go on questioning and go on thinking that some answers will help them. The truth is that no answer is going to help because every answer will only create more questions. At last he tells us that a moment will come when there are no questions left, and that this is the moment when one attains to wisdom.

After the video is over, my mind tries to grasp my own questions, but just can't seem to hold on to any. Then everyone begins clearing away the cushions to prepare for a special sort of meditation.

"These meditations are *active* meditations designed specifically by Osho for the western man," Prem explains. "The one we're doing tonight is called *Kundalini Meditation*," she goes on to say. "There are four parts. We start with some shaking, then we dance. Then we sit and listen to Tibetan bells, and finally lie down to bathe in the stillness. Let the music guide you through the first three phases," she tells us, she demonstrates the shaking, and then puts on the CD. We all stand in the main room of her small apartment and begin this full body release. Then as the music guides us, we move into joyous dancing, then sit and listen to the bells, and finally lie down to bask in the silence. By the end of the mediation, we are all feeling open and relaxed, and we sit on cushions on her hardwood floor and talk while Prem brings out a little food to nibble on. Actually, I don't talk much. I'm just taking everything in, watching Prem interact with these wonderful people, and remembering how she has always been the life of any party.

At last, when all the snacks have been consumed and the talking dies down, people, one-by-one or in some cases two-by-two, begin to leave, and then it's just Prem and I.

"Tell me about your journey and about this man Osho," I suggest.

Over the course of the next two days, she distills fifteen years of a journey in devotion to this beautiful being from India, and pours it all in to me. I am the empty vessel, and she pours long and steady. I am profoundly affected.

On Saturday evening we take a break from all the talking and attend a performance of a local satirical comedy group in the old downtown theater. I don't remember much about the performance except that it is irreverent and funny, but what really stands out is a certain moment, sitting there in the back of the theater next to

Prem, when we have a brush with eternity. Just there, just then, time rolls forward and we live the entire remainder of our lives, grow old and die together. And somehow, just like that, the whole dream of a lifetime is complete. I know it sounds strange, and I'm having trouble describing it, but it's as if the clock moves forward from that moment into the entirety of the potential we have together, and the whole thing gets played out.

Eventually, the next moment comes and we are back in the theater applauding the performance and then walking back to her house. In this reality, I am just taking a few days out of my life to visit an old friend.

"Did you ever get the feeling you lived the wrong life?" Prem asks looking me in the eyes, as we stand in front of her house in the dim moonlight.

The next day, after I leave her to take the long drive back to Albany, something breaks open in me. It's like a dam breaking. All at once, I begin crying tears from the depths of my being. I cry and cry and cry. The tears pour out of me for three straight hours. I cry so hard I can barely see to drive. I need windshield wipers for my eyeballs. The strangest thing is that I have no idea why I am crying. I have no story to go with it. I just have the overwhelming feeling that I have come home!

When I return to Colorado, there is no question what has to happen next. The final step in my rebirth process has to be taken, and it proves to be the hardest one of all. I have to leave my marriage of twenty years. And this time, like Lot running from Babylon, I can't look back. The break finally occurs at the end of June, and I move into a little cabin I have rented on the outskirts of the mountain town of Evergreen. Packing my things and loading them into the rental truck has been gut wrenching. I pick a time when Jill is out of the house, but the kids are there and noticeably upset, especially Dawn. At last, I unpack my last box in the new place, and my new life officially begins. As I sit in my little cabin letting the feeling of being on my own sink in, I think about the phone call Jill got a few days prior. It was from Cindy, the wife of my old friend Ben from college.

"Ben left me, and at first he spent some time hanging out in strip joints. Then he moved in with one of the strippers in a seedy part of town," she blurted out obviously very upset about the whole thing. "And now he's gone off to Florida to be a crewman on a boat headed for South America."

"Wow. Must be something in the air," I think to myself and then feel some comfort in knowing that my break has been tame compared to his. I have only moved five miles away. And yet I have moved away. As that fact begins to sink in, and I feel the inevitability of a new chapter of my life about to unfold, I reflect on this whole period of my life, and am struck with the impression that everything I have experienced: having the "awakening", rupturing a disc in my back, seeing Prem again, and ultimately leaving my marriage, has all been part of one process, and that the initial awakening had been a call from my soul to come out of my slumber and begin living the life my soul had intended. From this perspective, I can see that when I failed to break free in my first attempt, existence took more drastic measures, and eventually I got the hint that I was not going to be able to go back to living the life I was living. I was being forced to face my life head on and make some drastic changes. [11]

The mind moves from one moment to another on a horizontal plane. It is like a railroad train: full of past and future. Consciousness on the other hand, is vertical and extends infinitely in that plain. Action is in time; being is beyond time. As I drop into being, I see that there is no way to turn back. In fact, there is no such thing as "back".

As I continue to expand into being, my life becomes one amazing adventure followed by another.

"Did you ever get the feeling you lived the wrong life?" I hear Prem asking me.

"No, not any more!" I can now say.

Now I would be much more inclined to say that this life has truly been a soul's journey, orchestrated to perfection to facilitate the process of unfolding, but I'll let the tale unfurl, as it will.

Chapter 28

New Love

"Did you know there's an Osho center in Boulder? You could go up there and join in some of the meditations they offer," Prem says in a letter to me that I receive a few days after leaving Jill and moving in to my new place. "I think *Dynamic* might be really good for you right now."

I find the center listed in the phone book and call.

"Yes, we have *Dynamic Meditation* every Saturday morning," an enthusiastic woman responds. "Come on up."

The next Saturday, I make the forty-five minute drive to Boulder, come into the center and am directed to a small meditation space with fresh flowers in a vase and a large picture of Osho on the wall, his compassionate brown eyes looking down over us. There are just a couple of people in the room. Then a guy comes in with long, wild hair, a beard, and a bit of a crazy expression.

"I'm Samarpan," he says, looking around the room, and then asks "Is this the first time for anyone?"

"Yes." I say. "First time."

"Ok. Well there are five stages to this meditation," he says with his intense eyes looking at me. "The first stage is cathartic breathing, a bit like the yogic 'breath of fire', only with no pattern. It's designed to break up the patterns of thinking and energize the body for the rest of the meditation."

He demonstrates. The breathing is rapid and deep, but totally erratic.

"The second phase is the let go phase," he continues with a bit of a smirk on his face. "Explode! Let go of everything that needs to be thrown out. Go totally mad, scream, shout, cry, jump, shake, dance, sing, laugh, throw yourself around. Hold nothing back and while doing that, keep your whole body moving."

When he demonstrates this, he looks like a madman in an insane asylum.

"The key is to be total," he emphasizes after he comes back to stillness.

He goes on to describe and demonstrate the next phase, jumping up into the air and shouting "Hoo, hoo, hoo."

"It's a Sufi mantra," he says. "Just let the music guide you, and then when you hear Osho yell 'Stop', you just freeze where you are. Try not to move a muscle. If you do that, you will soon feel a tremendous energy rushing through you. The final stage is a celebration. Just let the music take you. Everybody Ready?"

I really don't think I will ever be ready for a process like that... but here I am standing in the room and when the music starts, I begin breathing with every ounce of my strength. When the music changes, everyone in the room begins shouting, roaring, pounding, wailing, and I let myself be swept up in the shear madness of it all. The music changes again and I jump and shout "Hoo, hoo, hoo" until I am utterly exhausted from it. Then comes Osho's voice saying "Stop" and I freeze with my arms still in the air. I hear the pounding of my heart and feel the sweat running down the side of my face, and then the energy begins to rush through my whole body.

"This is great," I say to myself. "I feel so alive!" But then, after what seems like an eternity, my arms begin to ache.

"When will it end?" I hear myself cry somewhere inside. "I can't take it much longer." But I stay there holding the position, and after what seems like forever, the sweetest music comes into my ears and I begin to dance.

When the meditation is over we have a little time together to share our experience.

"How was that for you?" Samarpan asks me.

"Well... I really thought I was going crazy there in the catharsis," I say. "I was starting to loose a grip on reality!"

"Great!" he says. "Keep going!"

***

One morning a week or so after moving in to my little cabin, I take a walk along Evergreen Lake. The lake is just a few minutes walk from where I now live. There is a nice trail, which I have walked before, that runs along the water's edge to the dam at the east end of the lake and then down into the town of Evergreen. But today, instead of taking the trail, I just go sit by the side of the lake and look out on the blue-green waters. There is a slight breeze, and small waves are breaking along the shore in front of me. I look for the cormorant I saw the last time I was at the lake and finally spot him out in the water a few yards down from where I am sitting. There seems to be just one of these diving water birds in the lake, and I wonder if he is lonely. Well, I guess that's a bit of a projection. Still, seeing him there alone causes me to begin reviewing my life as I so often do when I am alone in nature, especially these days.

"Where is my life going?" I ask myself.

Just then, I see a duck flying at top speed from one side of the lake to the other. He is on a beeline course, neck outstretched and wings beating rapidly.

"Now's there's somebody who knows where he's going!" I exclaim to myself with a bit of envy.

And then, as if on cue, he suddenly slows down, turns around in mid-air and starts bee lining back the way he has come. Ha, the joke's on me. He has no clue where he is going. Still, I admire his lack of hesitation and his dogged determination. Then I think about Prem, my visit to New York, and all the feelings that were stirred up inside me during our time together. Taking inspiration from that duck, I decide to head full-speed ahead as if I know where I am going. This means writing her a letter and sharing my feelings for her.

When I get back to the cabin, I am scared, but as I start writing my feelings begin spilling out onto the page. When I seal the envelope and put it out for the mailman, I start having second thoughts about what I have written and hope my mania won't scare her off. The feelings I am having remind me of how I felt with Sandy, the girl I met at Naropa all those years ago. With Sandy, I was so swept away that I asked her to marry me right there on the spot. With Prem, it's a little different. I have known and secretly loved her for many years.

A week or so later, I receive a letter back from Prem... a fabulously wonderful letter. As I read the letter, suddenly one of her sentences jumps out at me and flashes through my mind as if it were written in neon lights.

"I might want to have a go at a lover relationship with you!"

There it is... in black and white. She is saying YES! It's all beyond my wildest hopes and dreams! The universe is giving me my heart's deepest longing! I can hardly believe it. I reread the words. Yes. It really does say what I think it says. I'm not hallucinating. What joy! [12]

I immediately write her back:

Dear Prem,

I just got and read your letter. My God, I feel like I might pass out. There's this surreal haze coating my perception. The world out of my eyes looks like an impressionistic painting where someone took her finger and kind of smeared the edges. All this because you say you are open to a lover relationship with me. Needless to say, I'm overjoyed!

I've read your letter several times now, and there is one particular passage that really strikes a chord in me.

You say, "there is some continual battle in me between a *side* which feels that *in love* is the closest to enlightenment as one gets, and the other side that thinks this is true, however feels it is a continual distraction to get lost *in the other* when the longing inside is for one's own soul."

Wow! This has certainly been true for me, but I'll state it much stronger than "continual distraction". For me it's more like living someone else's life! Losing much of my own!

Being cut off from my connection to God! It's more than a distraction!

But, does it have to be this way? I don't think so. I have a vision of a love so beautiful, like the love that the flowers have for the tiger swallowtails I sat and watched dance for several minutes on the top of one of the Three Sister's Peaks on Sunday. It's a love that does not limit, does not hold back, but is more like a springboard launching me, aiding me in my most exquisite dive into the pool of spirit.

Jill used to ask me (or tell me really) about priorities. She said that my first priority should be to Jill's and my relationship, and my second priority should be to my family. I felt quite a bit of guilt about this over the years, when my own priorities were not "right" as she saw it, and I would question my ability to love.

Standing outside looking in at this now, I can see the incredible folly of it all! If I had any more love inside me right now, I would surely burst and all that would remain of me would be a mass of blood and guts and body parts all over the floor. I can love, do love, am love!

My first priority is my work on myself. My only priority is my work on myself. The only thing I can do is work on me, and that work is to open up so that I can love the rest of the world.

So, back to the vision: It's a vision of two people, supporting each other to continue their individual growth toward the one, being separate creative beings as free as the birds and the butterflies to savor every flower in this marvelous world, staying open and loving to all the world has to offer, being absorbed in our creative sides without obligation or limitation, and being in each other's company because it is helping and inspiring each of us to grow, or not being in each other's company when it doesn't. Now, I'm getting pretty idealistic, I suppose, but what I see is the possibility for us to be egoless in our love with no holding on except to get a boost up to the next level of our unfolding.

It will take total honesty, I think we've made a good start there, and then being open and clear when our lower selves come knocking. Can it be done? Is it possible? Or is it best left an unmanifest dream? Will we succumb to the horrors of toothpaste tubes and dirty dishes left in the sink? Or can we laugh and dance at the cosmic wonder of it all?

You know, it doesn't really matter what we think about all this. We can analyze it, make a list of pros and cons; we can even think that we have decided one way or another, but there is an intelligence greater than we know at work here.

I like thinking of you in the land of waterfalls enjoying your *Self* and me in my mountains enjoying my *Self.* I'm reminded of a beautiful John Belushi movie called *Continental Divide.* Did you ever see it? It's probably for rent.

Yes... the space we each have for ourselves is very good, very clarifying and illuminating, and yet ... there's this hole in my heart. It's as if someone sneaked into my bedroom in the middle of the night and stole a chunk of it and has taken it far away. If I close my eyes and I'm really quiet, I can see and feel this thin thread, a silver strand coming out of my very center and extending a thousand miles over prairies and cities and rivers and farms and woods. Across busy streets and vacant fields. At the other end of this delicate strand is that chunk of my heart lodged inside yours.

I worship the one in you that's also in me. Namaste.

In love *with* you,
Bryan.

Letters continue going back and forth between us. It is a real writer's courtship. We are both in our element. There is only a small break in the flow when I go off to California to hike the Pacific Coast trail with my brother. It's a trip of ten days and a hundred miles across the high Sierras: backpacking, swimming in lakes, and seeing scenery that made John Muir speechless. My mother thinks I am crazy to go after my disc injury six months ago, but nothing is going to stop me. Not even the stories from Laird's friends at his birthday party just before we leave.

"He'll leave you in the dust," one of his hiking companions says to me, "Just like he did me. He's a hiking machine!"

I am intimidated, but learn something early on in our hiking, as we climb five thousand feet in elevation along a shadeless trail. Laird can't take the heat! And so, those first few days are a killer for both of us: for him the relentless sun and for me a resurgence of excruciating lower back pain. Just in case I can't cut it, we have arranged for Laird's wife, Melinda, to meet us on the second evening at a point where we cross a highway, and we can stop for one last meal before we are subject to more than a week of backpacker's fare. After sharing the meal, I turn down the offer to go home with Melinda. I am determined to make the full hundred miles. The next day my effort is rewarded. The back pain subsides and I soon get into the hiker's groove. I will never forget the spectacular views, the stunning stillness, the stimulating swims in icy lakes and the wonderful bonding time I have with Laird. It couldn't have come at a better time for me, the beginning of my new life.

Chapter 29

Hard Lessons

When I return to Colorado, I am greeted by another letter from Prem.

"I've got some time between teaching terms at Cornell," she says. "I'd like to come to Colorado to see you!"

Wow! The letters are one thing. But her coming is an entirely different matter. We have said so many wonderful things in our letters. How will it be in the real flesh and blood? I'm scared. I'm feeling shy and vulnerable, and I'm also feeling an incredible excitement. I try to busy myself, but the days and weeks before she comes crawl by as my feelings build to a crescendo. At some point I fear my heart will explode, and I'll be dead before she ever comes.

"Don't be surprised if I don't make it!" she says on the phone to me just before leaving. "I always think it's a miracle if I get where I'm trying to go!"

I stand at the gate watching the people come off the plane... and then... there she is, my beloved Prem. She has on her favorite tan colored cotton sweater and her curly, blonde, somewhat out of control hair is blowing in her face as she emerges from the jet way. Then she sees me, and her big, beautiful, perfect-teeth smile lightens up my heart. It's a dream come true! Am I smitten? Undoubtedly. Am I hopelessly, hopelessly smitten? Absolutely, and I don't care who knows it.

What blossoms from that beautiful moment is an endless long weekend filled with hikes into the mountains and long talks, a visit to a nearby hot springs and time just being together in the Colorado mountain air. We make love for the first time, and we are suspended in timelessness, merging with the infinite. We fall deeply into a valley of bliss beyond description. As we lie in tight embrace, I have the feeling that there is no other time but this, and all is fulfilled. After an especially passionate moment, I pull back to look at her face to remind myself that I'm not dreaming the whole thing, and I am struck by the realization that existence has handed me my deepest heart's desire. I am utterly complete and filled with gratitude as life teeters on this precipice for a long moment before moving on.

But move on it does, and in the next couple of days, two significant things happen. The first thing is that I receive a letter from Jill's lawyer. It's a plea for divorce. Jill has not wasted any time filing once she knows that reconciliation is no longer possible. The second thing is that one evening as Prem and I are preparing dinner, I receive a phone call. It's my mom telling me that my dad has died the previous night.

"While we were making love?" I wonder to myself.

A few hours before he died, he came out of his mental haze and spoke coherently to my mother for the first time in months.

"He was saying goodbye," my mother says behind muffled tears, "and then he just slipped away in my arms and now he's gone!"

Now, I have to tell you something about me and death. Death has never felt real to me. I had a couple of good friends in High School. One moved away and one committed suicide by jumping off a building. The two events seemed the same to me, and I wondered if I were cold-hearted. My father's death was like that for me, too... somehow unreal. But for my mother it was her whole world.

"I think what shocks me the most," she says to me in disbelief, "is that life went on as if nothing had happened."

Then she explains that Dad is going to be cremated, and that she will save the ashes until Laird and I can get to Florida to have our own private ceremony. I hang up the phone and tell Prem what has happened, and she holds me for a while.

"It's good that he died," I say at last. "It was getting harder and harder for my mother to care for him, and she couldn't bare the thought of putting him in a nursing home."

***

As I sit and write about these events now, I am amazed at how life seems to be orchestrated. I see how peaks are always accompanied by valleys and get the feeling that this is how life works, how it all seems to stay in balance. Some people say that each of our lives is perfectly orchestrated to help us wake up to a higher reality, a reality where there are no peaks and no valleys. I don't know for sure if there is a higher intelligence running this show we call life, but I do know that if I look at my life as if there is, then I'm much more accepting of the ebbs and flows, and I'm left with the impression that everything that happens to me is just "grist for the mill" of this awakening. But of course these are just ideas in hindsight, and the only thing that can be said for sure is that life is a very big mystery.

***

As my visit with Prem draws to a close, we begin to talk about our future.

"You could move out here to Colorado," I say tentatively.

"I've got my job and my friends in New York," Prem tells me. "Maybe you can come to Ithaca... move in with me on a trial basis... see how it goes."

I take a few moments to think about this offer. Yes... I could go to New York. I would probably be able to keep my job with the software company. After all, I'd be a whole lot closer to the corporate offices in Boston. But what about my children? I'd be a long way from them in Ithaca. But, here's the thing... and I suppose this is something only a man would do. I could leave my children and not look back. The truth is that when I left home I wasn't just separating from Jill, I was divorcing the whole family. Another truth is that I never really liked being a parent. I was more of a friend to my kids than a father. Jill, on the other hand, was a supermom. The children were her life, and I knew she would want full custody of them. So my usefulness was questionable at this point. Aaron was heading for college, Zack didn't want much to do with me, and Dawn took Jill's side in every argument. So it's only natural that I would choose to follow love. Besides, that's the way I was raised, to fend for myself and to value my own heart's calling over family obligations. I was not alone in this. Throughout history, men left their families to follow a "higher" calling. Even Gautama the Buddha did it. And for me, going to be with Prem felt like that... a higher calling, a soul's calling... so of course I would go.

"I'll look into it," I tell her. "I'll see if my company would have a problem with me moving to Ithaca."

"What are you going to do about that divorce paper? Get a lawyer?" she asks.

"No. I don't want a big fight. I'll just agree to whatever her lawyer says and be done with it," I say.

The next day I drive Prem to the airport and we say our goodbyes.

"Come when you can," she says, and after one last wave and a big smile she turns and walks onto the airplane heading back to New York.

I have some loose ends to take care of before actually making the move to Ithaca. First I have to make sure it's okay with my company for me to move. I have a pretty good case for it, since most of my training clients are on the east coast. I'd save the company money on airfare and I would be a lot closer to corporate headquarters. My boss talks it over with her boss and the move is approved. Next, I have to deal with the matter of the divorce. I decide not to get a lawyer of my own, but to just let Jill's lawyer handle it. Frankly, I just want out and I am feeling enough guilt about walking out on Jill and the kids that I really don't care what Jill gets from the settlement.

"Let her have it all!" I say to myself as I sign the agreement. What I don't realize is that Jill will not only take most of my current assets, but that I will be paying her a fixed amount of child support and alimony regardless of the level of my income. It ends up taking

224

over ten years to pay her off! If I had it to do again, I would pay a little more attention to the fine print.

The last thing I need to do before my move is to go visit my mother and help her dispose of Dad's ashes. Unfortunately, my brother Laird and I can't make it to Florida at the same time, so my mother actually splits the ashes in two! When I arrive, we take "my half" down to the beach at sunset, say some words and scatter the ashes into the breaking waves. At that very moment, as we are saying our goodbyes, as if on cue or as a sign from the universe, a dolphin jumps out of the ocean between us and the setting sun, and my mother and I are both in awe. I later write a song commemorating this stirring moment of farewell. [13]

At last the time has come for the move to Ithaca. It's the start of the Christmas holidays, when everyone in my company takes a week of mandatory vacation. I pack my few possessions into the car and head east on Interstate Seventy, across Kansas, through St. Louis, through Columbus Ohio where I spent much of my childhood, up to the Ohio Turnpike and finally cross the border into upstate New York. When I arrive at Prem's doorstep, I recall the last time I was there and am amazed at the turn of events. She greets me affectionately, and then we have the job of fitting my things into her tiny apartment.

Around that time, I decide to embrace her Guru and become initiated into what Osho called Neo-Sannyas. It's a renunciation, not of life, but of the attachments to life, and it is a dedication to one's pathless path to freedom. I read over the terms of the initiation, and I think, "Of course. This is what my life is already. I am devoted to truth and freedom." I sign the application and check the box that says, "I want a new name," and then send it off to the ashram in Pune, India. Although Osho is no longer in his body, it is said that the names that are given are channeled from him. It doesn't matter to me. I am so in love, I just want *in*, to be part of this life that was Prem's for so many years.

As I settle into being in Ithaca and in Prem's life, I am beside myself with joy. All my heart's desires are fulfilled, but it looks like I haven't learned love's great lesson yet. I still think it requires certain outside conditions to blossom, in this case my being with Prem. While I am happy and devoted to her, my devotion is a bit like that of a lost puppy. I know no one in Ithaca but Prem. I have given up my life to be with her, and now she is my life. While I am drowning in bliss, she is just plain drowning. Love on the rebound, especially on the rebound from a twenty-year marriage, and love that in that moment I sincerely believe is the "love of my life" or even the "love of countless lifetimes" can sometimes be hard to take for the recipient. I have Prem so high on the pedestal that it is impossible to have a give-and-take relationship, and so it doesn't take long for her to start feeling smothered by my overwhelming attention.

"Get a life of your own!" She screams out one day and my "dream come true", "happy ever after", "love of my life" relationship begins to deteriorate. Just as this is happening my paperwork from the Osho Commune in India has arrived. I am being born into Sannyas and given a new name, Swami Jivan Jashan. Jivan means life and Jashan means celebration. Together they mean "Celebration of Life". The name is a reminder to celebrate everything that comes to me in life. To finalize the initiation we have a formal ceremony, and since Prem is the head of the local Osho center she performs the initiation. Frankly, I don't feel much like celebrating, because the next day, I am moving out of her apartment after only three months. Not knowing where else to go, I move into a room in downtown Ithaca that I have been renting as my business office. I am alone and in deep despair. All my dreams have crumbled and I am deeply, deeply alone. Several months go by without me even seeing Prem.

At this time, one of Prem's friends, Veet is doing Osho's *Dynamic Meditation* every morning in an old theater in downtown Ithaca, and I begin attending. At 6:00 A.M. every morning, a few of us gather and go through the five stages of this intense practice. Morning after morning, day after day, during the catharsis stage of the meditation I run through the huge theater screaming and ranting, pounding on the floor, letting my hurt, pain, frustration and rage be expressed. One morning, in the first few weeks of us going there, someone hears us scream and calls the cops. He or she probably thought someone was being murdered. But by the time the police arrive with their flashlights, guns and walky-talkies we are in the "stop" phase of the meditation. As I stand there with my arms in the air, I hear one of the officers calling into headquarters.

"It's just some hippies, burning incense and doing some kind of crazy meditation."

They never bother us again and I continue this practice every day for six months. I scream so much that I lose my voice for a whole month, and wonder if I'll ever be able sing or talk in a normal voice again. At some point toward the end of those six months, I manage to scream out all of the pain. That's when Veet gives me a bit of news.

"Have you heard? Prem's moving to San Diego."

"What?" I say, full of disbelief.

"Yeah. She says she needs a change, and you know her oldest daughter and her two little grandchildren live out there."

At first I am stunned. Then I'm angry. So much for screaming out all the pain!

"Well, I'm certainly not staying here if she's going. I'm only here because of her!" I blurt out.

"Where will you go?" Asks Veet as supportive as she can be.

"I don't know," I say and realize I really don't know where I would go. I just know I can't stay here.

Just about that time, I bump into Prem. It's strange to see her again after not seeing her for all this time, like seeing a piece of myself that I'd given up for lost.

"I'm glad I ran into you," she says matter-of-factly. "Have you heard that I'm leaving?"

It's at that very moment, seeing her there in the street, that I realize how much I love her. It's a love that is beyond romance and seems to transcend lifetimes. I had lost her and then I found her, and I didn't want to lose her again. That's when I have the realization that lovers come and go with Prem, but friendships last a lifetime.

"You know Prem, I won't want to stay here in Ithaca after you are gone. I could go with you, help you make this move."

"What would you do in San Diego? You can't stay with me. I'll be staying with my daughter, my grandkids and my ex-husband."

"Well, our friends Bill and Mary live in San Diego. Maybe I can stay with them until I get established."

"You know, we won't be together," she says with some sympathy in her voice.

"I know Prem, but we can be friends, and since we're both leaving Ithaca, we can help each other." As I say these words to her I mean them, but there is also a place in me that thinks that something romantic is still possible for us. After all, it's a long drive to San Diego.

"I'll think about it," she says. "I'll be in touch."

She does think about it, and a few days later I find a note under my door.

"I thought it over and decided to accept your offer. I really could use the help driving that rental truck across the country. But remember, we go our separate ways once we get there. Give me a call and we can work out the details."

I call her without hesitation and we do work out the details, and I am happier than I have been in quite a while. We are going to be together again if only for the ride to California. I call Bill and Mary. They are excited about having me come, and tell me they'll clear out space in the garage for me. There is only one more detail. I have to tell my boss.

"I'm sorry, but we can't approve of you moving to San Diego. We need you here on the East Coast," my immediate supervisor tells me after checking with management for me.

"But I was the one who decided to move to New York," I say in protest. And then after thinking about it for a few minutes I say, "Look! My personal life requires that I move to San Diego and so I'm going! You'll just have to fire me if you don't like it," and I hang up the phone. Three weeks later, Prem and I load a U-haul truck with our possessions... mostly hers... and we head west. I still have my job.

Prem wants to stay off the freeways and use the back roads.

"That way we can really see this beautiful country of ours," she reasons.

It's fine with me. The longer the trip lasts, the longer we can be together. As an activity to fill the long hours of travel in the less exciting parts of the trip, we begin reading Herman Melville's *Moby Dick* aloud to each other. As one drives, the other reads… and so as we lose ourselves in the heart of America, we are also cast out to sea in search of the great white whale.

Our journey takes on a timeless quality and we become the best of friends again, as we wander through Oklahoma, Texas and finally into New Mexico. We pull into a beautiful place called Bandelier National Monument as it's just getting dark, and then in the early dawn we hike down into the ancient cliff dwellings of the ancestral Pueblo people. Although we are alone, it feels as if we are in the company of elders. As the sun begins to pierce the eastern horizon, we climb down into one of their sacred Kivas, sit cross-legged, and begin chanting. Our voices reverberate in this thousand year old holy chamber where the Shamans met to be with God, and before we realize it we have become one being, transported through time, through space, beyond the sun, and back again. It only appears as though two people climb out and continue their journey.

After crossing Arizona, taking in the Grand Canyon and going by Havasupai, we come into Las Vegas where I relive a vivid childhood memory of visiting this crazy city with my parents and hitting the jackpot on the ice machine. I'll never forget the sound of all those blocks of ice tumbling out into the desert sun.

My good mood begins to sober as we enter California. As promised, we are to go our separate ways when we get there. I just want to keep traveling forever.

"We haven't finished *Moby Dick*," I protest as we pull in to Prem's ex-husband Jerry's driveway. They have made a room available for Prem, the floor of which is soon piled high with her boxes. She will be crowded in this tiny space, but her daughter and her twin grandsons who are about three, are delighted to have her there.

"Grum, Grum," the twins both shout when they see her and jump all over her as if she were a trampoline.

I leave Prem at the doorway and drive the truck up to Encinitas where Bill and Mary now live. They are happy to see me, but I am feeling the shock of being separated again from what I feel is the other part of me. I am pretty sure I'll see her again, but don't know when... and I resist calling her, remembering my promise.

"We will go our separate ways, once we get there," I hear her say, her words still echoing inside me.

Chapter 30

Harder Lessons and a Bonus Check

It's Prem who calls me about a week later. Bill gets the call.

"It's Prem," he says. "She wants to talk to you."

I answer the phone hesitantly, "Yes?"

"I can't stand it at Jerry's house. It's chaos with everybody living there, especially the twins. I love those two dearly, but I can't work under these conditions."

Prem is a writer and an artist and I know from living with her that she needs enormous amounts of space for her creativity.

"But I can't rent my own apartment," she continues. "I haven't got enough money and my credit is bad." Before leaving Ithaca, Prem had to declare bankruptcy when hers bills piled up beyond her control. Her adjunct faculty position at Cornell really wasn't making ends meet.

"Maybe we could share an apartment," she says and then quickly adds, "just as friends, you understand."

I can hardly believe what I'm hearing, and I am beside myself with joy! It seems our adventure together is to continue after all. I don't care what the conditions are: lover, friend, partner, roommate. I am just happy to have her in my life. And so we rent an apartment in an area of San Diego called Hillcrest. It is primarily a gay community, but it's affordable and it's within walking distance of many nice cafes and the famous Balboa park, where Prem soon becomes an artist in residence.

Life is good, and we are happy together... until the inevitable happens. Prem brings home a lover! That first night he stays over, the pain is so intense, I think I will die. I can hear them making love in the next room as I lie on my bed and sob. For a while he is a regular visitor, and I must deal with the deep ache in my heart when I come home and see his size 11 shoes out by the door, parked neatly next to Prem's. [14]

Yes... I know, we are supposed to be just friends now, and I'm okay with not having a physical relationship with Prem, but in my heart I still love her, long for her, desire her, and the thought of this woman with another man drives me crazy. But... I sit with it night after night. I dive deeply into those intense feelings and begin inquiring into the very nature of love.

"If I really love her, I'll want her to be happy," I reason, but it doesn't lessen the pain.

"I'm just glad to have her in my life," I remind myself and then cry myself to sleep.

"If I had someone of my own, I'd feel better," I think to myself and begin searching through the personal ads in the weekly paper.

This leads me to a blind date with a woman who is a Yogananda disciple. We meet at the Jack-in-the-box for our first date. It was in her neighborhood. I think there is something a bit odd about her when I meet her, and then she tells me her story. It turns out she has had a non-cancerous brain tumor, and when it was removed she couldn't speak for an entire year. Then when she finally spoke, she could only speak verbs, no nouns. You see. Verbs describe what's real, what's happening. They're tangible. Nouns on the other hand are all abstractions. They're conceptual.

When I meet this woman (I can't think of her name anymore), she's speaking nouns again, but she still has very little capacity for abstract thinking. That's when I discover that my own thinking is about ninety-nine percent conceptual. Whenever I start talking about something I see her expression kind of glaze over, and I know I've lost her again. Needless to say the relationship doesn't last, but it helps me through that painful time. [15]

Prem finally breaks up with the guy with the big shoes, and life returns to normal for a while, but then there is the next guy, and the next guy. Finally I can't take it any more. There is a big group of Osho Sannyasins in Marin County in Northern California that Prem and I had gone to visit when we were first living in San Diego, and I get the idea that I will move there. As circumstance would have it, I hear that there is a room available in an Osho communal house up there, so I take a trip to Marin to check out the house and meet the people living in it.

After a long ride on the freeway, the hardest part of which is the drive through Los Angeles in bumper-to-bumper traffic, I come up past Oakland and across the Richmond Bridge into Marin County. Continuing west through San Rafael, I enter the little town of Fairfax. I pass two coffee shops and the health food store and then climb along a narrow, steep, winding road up into the woods and at last arrive at the house. It is a big place nestled in the trees with a good-sized parking area. As I step out of the car, I am greeted by a tall balding man with an English accent.

"Hi. I'm Mitra. I own the house. You must be Jashan. Please come in."

Inside there is an older woman also with an English accent and a couple of younger people.

"This is Amrita. She and her partner live in the top room up by the communal office," explains Mitra. "You'll meet most everyone else at dinner. Would you like to see the vacant room?"

"Yes. Please," I say.

"The house is called the Chakra house," Mitra explains as we climb a small set of winding stairs in the front part of the house, "because there are seven levels." At the top of the stairs we come upon two doors.

"Your room, I'd say, would be the third eye," he adds. "It's here on the left."

Mitra opens the door to a tiny room at treetop level with windows facing three sides. A big part of the room is taken up by the stairwell, and there is only space for a narrow bed.

"It will be a bit cramped, but I like all the windows," I say as I look it over.

"It's three hundred and fifty dollars a month," Mitra tells me, "and of course you have access to the rest of the house, and we can set you up with a desk up in the shared office space. You work for a computer company, right?"

"That's right," I tell him.

"I'm in the computer software business myself," adds Mitra. "You've got to love home offices!"

I share a wonderful meal with several of the people from the house. There are the older couple who live up by the office, I'd say they are in their late fifties, there are a few people roughly my age, and four or five people in their twenties who, I am told, are "Sannyasin kids." They're called that because they grew up around Osho, and their parents were Sannyasins. One of these "kids" is studying to be a police officer, if you can imagine that!

After dinner and a delicious dessert that Amrita made, I tell Mitra that I'd like to take the room.

"As I explained on the phone," says Mitra, "we will meet as a group and discuss the possibility. If everyone agrees to have you, we'll let you know."

I sleep on the couch that night and in the morning we say our goodbyes, and I head back to San Diego full of positive feelings about the place and the people. It turns out the feelings are mutual and a few days later I am invited to come live with them.

Now comes the hard part... leaving Prem. When I get my invitation, I tell her of my intention. She is supportive and understanding for which I am grateful. As I feel the pain of the impending separation, I remind myself that I am moving to a loving and supportive environment and will still be surrounded by Osho's energy. This eases the pain a bit. Even so, my heart is aching as I load my things into a small trailer hitched to the back of my car, say my goodbyes to Prem and head back north on highway 101. After putting a hundred miles between myself and San Diego, I notice that the ache is lessening and a new feeling begins to overtake me, a feeling of excitement that builds as I get closer and closer to my new home and my new life. I'm not just going, I'm going somewhere, and I feel a certain relief at the realization that a new chapter of my life is opening. Yes, hard as it is, I have done the right thing, and I know it.

It's early evening when I pull into the driveway of the big house nestled in the Northern California woods that is to be my home. When I arrive I expect a warm welcome, but no one seems to be around. Feeling a bit let down, I begin unloading the trailer. Then, as I am carrying my futon up the narrow winding stairs to what is to be my room, I hear yelling.

"You bastard. Where were you last night?"

"I went out... to get away from you!"

The yelling continues as I struggle with my futon on the steep and narrow stairs. As I reach the top, the right bedroom door opens and a beautiful, young, and very naked woman runs out, slamming the door behind her.

"Oh. Hello. Who are you?" she asks sweetly while revealing herself to me unselfconsciously.

"J-Jashan," I say with a great deal of surprise and a bit of embarrassment.

She smiles and then turns back into the room from which she has come. I hear more yelling and then a guy comes out, slams the door, and runs down the stairs and out the front door. A minute later I can hear a car door slamming, an engine turning over and the squealing of tires.

"What have I gotten myself into?" I wonder and realize my new life is not going to be dull.

Later, as I start moving in the boxes for my home office, I run into Amrita.

"I see you met Hari Deva and his new girl friend." She says with raised eyebrows.

"Well I met the girlfriend, at least," I retort. "It was quite a welcome!"

After I get my things unloaded, Amrita shows me around a bit. First she takes me in to the kitchen.

"We share food and take turns with the shopping," she says. "There's a list posted above the stove. If you want anything just add it to the list. We eat dinner together and rotate the cooking and cleanup. There's a signup list for that right here next to the shopping list," she points. "We also have a message board where we post announcements of general interest. For example, you'll see that this Sunday we are hosting the Satsang. It's held at a different place every week."

After showing me the community office upstairs and the small Jacuzzi out side in the backyard, we return to the large living room.

"So... welcome and make yourself at home, Jashan," Amrita says as she turns and heads back upstairs to her room.

"Thanks for the orientation," I call after her.

I do make myself at home and gradually get to meet everyone in the house. There are a total of ten people living here, and there is also a guest room, which is often occupied by Sannyasins passing through town, sometimes on their way to India, or their way back.

Chakra house is nestled in the forest, and after a few days, I begin exploring. Much to my delight, I discover that the house backs up to the Mount Tamalpais watershed, a giant preserve that includes meadows and woods and even a couple of small lakes. This is all in the shadow of a very old volcano, Mount Tamalpais, whose presence dominates Marin County. I spend much of my time up in those woods walking, just being, and practicing my violin. Sometimes the deer come to investigate the alien sounds I make.

That next Sunday, Chakra house is host to the Satsang, a meeting in the spirit, and about sixty or seventy Osho Sannyasins gather in our large living room for the program. At the appointed time, one of the musicians in the community begins playing some very beautiful meditation music on his electric piano, and then we listen to a short Osho discourse. In the talk, Osho tells us that the mind is our sleep and that meditation is our awakening. He tells us that at the moment we awaken, sleep disappears along with all our dreams, projections, expectations and desires, and then at that moment there is an unfathomable silence.

As his words fade out we sit for about forty-five minutes, and as we all settle into being there on the floor of the Chakra house living room, the collective energy takes us all into that place that he has so beautifully described. At last Amrita sounds a bell, and the meditation is over. Snacks are put out, and during the social time that follows I meet people from all over the world who are now part of this vibrant community.

Over the next several weeks, I begin to get to know my housemates better and feel more and more at home. Hari Deva continues to have stormy relations with his young girl friend, but she eventually moves out and my part of the house becomes more peaceful. So life is good, and I am happy with the right balance of alone and together time, and soon I am integrating myself into this large Osho community across the Golden Gate Bridge from San Francisco.

One day, I am sitting in the kitchen. We have just finished a very nice spaghetti dinner. The young guy studying to be a policeman makes the best spaghetti sauce. Then, it suddenly occurs to me, that I am back to living the life I was living when I was twenty-three and living in Ann Arbor. Only now I am twice that age, forty-six. And in that moment I am reminded of what Prem had asked to me when we were first getting reacquainted.

"Have you ever thought maybe you lived the wrong life?"

Well maybe I was living the wrong life, but now I see that existence has given me a second chance, a "do over" as it were, and now I am living the life for which I have longed for all these many years. So, as I settle in to my new routine, I only occasionally think of Prem. Then, after about a month, I get a phone call. It's Prem.

"I'm not really making it here in San Diego," she announces. "I can't really afford the rent by myself, and I feel stuck here. I think I need a change. I want to be around Sannyasins again. So, I was thinking... do you know if there's a room available in Chakra house?"

I can't believe my ears! Prem back in my life again? I don't know what to think, but my heart is pounding a definite "Yes" and when I inquire, it turns out that Hari Deva has just left for India and the room next to mine is available! It seems my dance with Prem is to continue. She moves in right next door to me the following month. I must say it's great having her back in my day-to-day life again. Most memorable are the early morning breakfasts we share with lots of stimulating conversation and laughter. In fact, at some point, one of the other members of the house complains about our early morning frivolity.

Prem has no lovers during this time, but I do. The first is a Scottish woman who was part of the Osho community. [16] I eventually break it off. The problem is that I am comparing every woman with Prem, and no one can measure up. After all, Prem is intelligent, witty, artistic, very conscious, and extremely beautiful. She is a tough act to follow.

"You know, Jashan, you should go to the Osho Commune in Pune India," Prem tells me one day. "You'll be blown away,"

"I'd like to do that sometime," I respond. And it's true. I would like to go to India some day. In fact, I have dreamed of going there for over twenty years, but never made it.

"Even though Osho is no longer in his body," Prem tells me, "his energy is still strong there, especially in his Samadhi where his ashes are." A wistful smile appears on Prem's face as she talks about the place. "And the groups! They have every kind of therapy group there, to help you break free of your conditioning."

"Hmmm. That would be good," I interject, "and of course to do Dynamic Meditation in a large hall with hundreds of people. That must be an experience!"

"But don't go for any less than three months," she adds. "You'll need that long to really arrive there."

"But that's not possible!" I tell her. "I've still got my job with the software company."

"We'll let the universe decide," she says and begins talking about something else.

A few weeks later, I am back at corporate headquarters and my boss asks me to step into his office. With a bit of trepidation, I enter.

"As part of a company restructuring, we're giving each employee a bonus check as payment for his stock options," he says matter-of-factly. He hands me the check, and when I look down at it, all I can see is INDIA.

"The universe has provided," I think to myself, and without hesitation I ask for a three-month leave of absence. A few days later, it's granted. (Looking back, I marvel at the flexibility of the company I work for. I really put them through the ringer, as the saying goes.)

"I know someone who can get you a good price on a ticket," Prem confides. "All the Sannyasins use him."

I make a phone call and a few days later, I've got my ticket. I am going to India after all these years, and I am going by myself. That part scares me.

"You can prearrange for a driver to pick you up in Mumbai and drive you straight to Pune," Prem encourages, seeing my worry. "Once you're there, you won't be alone."

With an eighteen hour flight, a twelve and a half hour time change and a crazy layover in Singapore, where I end up taking a tour of some points of interest including the prison where American soldiers were held and tortured during the second world war, I am hopelessly jet-lagged and disoriented when we arrive in Mumbai.

It is my first time in the third world except for a very brief foray into Mexico, and I am blown away by what I experience when I step off that plane. What I first notice is the smell. There is a characteristic scent that is India, a combination of burning flesh from the open-air crematoriums, incense from the many temples and the smell of Jasmine. It is unforgettable. Then there are all the people, hundreds of them all pressed up against the screen at the airport arrival area, holding signs or just holding out their hands. It seems like everyone is calling out at once for my attention. But then, out of the chaos, I see one particular sign that has my name on it. Boy, am I happy to see that. I rush over, the man holding the sign gives me a little bow, grabs my bag and then pushes his way through the crowd to his vehicle. He tosses the suitcase in the back, I hop in the front seat (on the left, like England) and we are off... for the ride of my life.

Chapter 31

Red Robes and Stacks of Money

The road from Mumbai to Pune is narrow, windy and mountainous, and the traffic is a nightmare of cars, motorcycles, bicycles, cows, chickens, goats, and mostly trucks spewing enormous clouds of black smoke behind them. But none of these things deter my driver from zipping along at top speed, passing trucks and cars on blind curves, passing on the left, passing on the right, scattering chickens and goats as he goes. All I can do is watch the passing show, swallow my horror, and surrender to our fate as we drive on into the night. This night, our fate is to have us arrive safely in Pune. I don't know how the driver manages it. Maybe the words, "Praise be to Allah" written on his windshield has something to do with it. In any case, it is 3:00 A.M. when we arrive in Pune, and I suddenly realize I have no accommodations.

"Are you in need of a flat, while you are being here," my driver asks in a thick Indian accent with a slight tilt to his head. "If so, I have a cousin who is renting a room. It's not far from the Osho Ashram. You wish to see it?"

"Yes. That would be great, but it's the middle of the night!"

That's when he says the words I will hear over and over during my stay in India: "It is no problem, Baba." And it's accompanied by the traditional bobbing of the head from side to side.

He pulls up in front of a concrete building that looks a bit like many of the buildings in London must have looked after the German bombings of World War II, more rubble than cement. He knocks on the door, and after a long delay a woman appears cinching up her robe. They talk for a few minutes and then the driver turns to me.

"Come," he says motioning me forward. "She has a room for you."

We climb up some rickety steps and walk down a dark corridor with three doors. She opens the last door, and I look in to see a mattress on the floor, a small lamp along side it, and a makeshift shelf of boards and bricks. There is a window looking out on a trash dumpster and a small closet with a squat toilet and a bare pipe coming out of the wall next to it.

"You see it is equipped with private bathroom and shower," the taxi driver tells me. "You pay a hundred and fifty U.S. dollars a month, and it is yours for as long as you need."

I look it over and decide that it will work, and although I was told that I could find a cheaper room, it is the middle of the night... and well, it's here.

"You say it's close to the Osho Ashram?"

"Oh yes. A very short walk. No problem."

I take the room and after the driver leaves and the woman goes back to bed, I enter my newly acquired room, collapse onto the bed, and sleep soundly for a few hours. Then at some point I become conscious again, and even before I open my eyes I can sense that it's daylight, but I have forgotten where I am. I guess I think I am back in my room in California. Then I hear the whoop of an exotic bird, a parrot I suppose.

"That doesn't sound like home!" I think to myself, and then the whole surreal trip comes back to me.

We don't have kitchen privileges in the house. As it turns out, the woman I have rented from and her family of five are living in the kitchen. It's the one room they can't rent out! But this is not a problem. I will be eating my meals in the ashram.

I eventually pull myself out of bed, take a drip shower, throw on some clothes, and still dazed and jet-lagged I wander out the door and down the road. The first thing I encounter is the trash dumpster. There is a large cow there digging through the heap for something delectable. As I watch, a pack of dogs come and chase away the cow. Someone forgot to tell them that cows are sacred.

241

As the dogs begin their own foraging I think to myself, "Ah. The dogs rule!" But it turns out not to be so.

Next come a small heard of donkeys. They chase off the dogs in no time at all and take over the place. Now I know that it's donkeys that rule. As the donkeys settle in for some good eating I walk on and come to the river, a wide body of lazy brown water slowly moving southwest toward the sea. Around the area there is some smoke and a peculiar smell in the air, and I soon locate the source of it. There, next to the river is a concrete platform covered with smoldering ash, and yes... human bones. This is one of the crematoriums or "Burning Ghats" as they are called in India. There are still a couple of people sitting beside the platform chanting quietly, a Shiva chant.

"Om Namah Shivaya, om namah Shivaya," they mutter over and over as they both rock back and forth with their hands together in prayer.

As I watch, a couple of children in tattered clothes come up to me with hands outstretched, apparently looking for a handout. I have nothing to give, and so they eventually move on.

I walk back to the road and continue in the direction the taxi cab driver pointed the night before for the Osho Ashram. Before long I come to a sort of shantytown: row upon row of shacks made of boards and tin. A woman is out in front of one of them with a broom sweeping the dirt. I stand and watch as she works meticulously at brushing the loose soil away from the front of her hut. Then I notice a T.V. sitting out on a big rock in the middle of this village with several men gathered around it. I can't tell what they are watching, but it certainly has their attention. I look up above the shacks and see a large billboard with the picture of a man in a business suit in front of a computer. The words read, "Have an exciting career in computer technology."

"Hmmm. That reminds me of something I saw many years ago in a gutter," I muse.

But seeing it here, in such sharp contrast to the primitive huts underneath it, I am struck by how crazy the world has become.

Then I walk up the next street and pass a Baskin Robbins ice cream store right there next to the shanty village!

"This is a crazy world!" I say out loud and must seem crazy myself to anyone hearing me.

Finally I arrive at a place called "the German Bakery," and I remember being told about this place. It's supposed to be a big hangout for Osho Sannyasins. Just then, as if on cue, I see someone I know! It's a woman from our Osho community in California just climbing onto the back of a motorcycle.

"Tatini, hi. I just arrived and it's my first time here," I blurt out waving her down. "Which way to the Osho Commune?"

"Oh hi Jashan. Welcome to Pune," She says. "Just walk up the main road, take a left and then take the first right. You can't miss it, but watch out crossing the road! Gotta go. See you around." Her words trail off as she disappears in a small cloud of smoke.

When I get to the main road, I see what Tatini means. There are four lanes of steady and chaotic traffic: cars, trucks, motorized rickshaws, cows, donkeys, and lots of people all crowding the roadway, and along the side are peddlers of fruit, clothing, jewelry, even a guy repairing shoes. Intermixed with the venders are beggars, some rolling around on small wheeled carts with crippled legs, some apparently blind, another with no arms. A couple of boys see me coming and start following me.

"You want to buy prayer beads?" One boy says holding up five or six strands. "I give a very good price."

"No thank you I say," but they detect the smallest amount of interest on my face and keep after me for almost a block before finally accepting my "no".

At last I come to two large wooden doors that suddenly open as two Western women come out.

"Is this the Osho Commune?" I ask and they both nod. I slip through the doors and step inside... into an incredible stillness... and I know immediately why I have traveled so far.

The next thing I notice is a beautiful fountain with several people dressed in maroon robes sitting on benches talking quietly.

Then I see a sign directing me to the welcome center. I step in and up to the counter.

"I've just arrived," I say to a woman with curly brown hair and a big smile.

"Welcome!" She says and begins to tell me about the ashram.

"As you probably know, we've got a program of daily meditations and a Satsang with an Osho video in the evenings. You'll need to wear red robes during the day here and a white robe for the evening program. You can buy the robes in our boutique. Daily admission to the Ashram is around two dollars, and you can also buy meal vouchers for our dining room. If you're interested, we also have therapy groups of all kinds. You can go to the Osho Therapy Center to check out the schedule for those."

"Wow!" Is all I can say.

"But, to keep everyone here safe," she continues, "the first thing you must do is get an AIDs test. You can do that right now, but it takes two days before we know the results."

I duck into a little booth and surrender a sample of urine.

"Come back in two days," the young woman says as I hand her the sample, "and if you test negative, you can come in, and then we can get you the robes and vouchers and assign you a locker."

The next two days are a blur. I am so jet-lagged from the long journey that I mostly just sleep. As I approach the gates of the commune on the third day, I think about how I would feel if I don't pass the AIDs test, coming all this way just to be turned away at the gate. But that is not to happen to me in this lifetime. After being confirmed AIDs negative, I walk into the grounds of this peaceful, meditative place and am reminded of how I felt back when I was eight years old and first arrived at Disney Land. Of course Disney Land was a lot noisier.

"What should I do first?" I wonder feeling a little bit lost.

Then I remember that there are some things I have to do. First I have to buy some robes. Everyone wears them when inside the gates. I find the boutique and buy two red robes for day use and two white ones for the evening celebrations. Next, I have to locate my locker and the changing area. When I find the locker, I am a bit surprised. The locker areas are co-ed! So are the showers. That takes a little getting used to, but I happily adapt and begin to appreciate the implicit intimacy. Once in my red robe, I now look like everybody else, and there is something very soothing about that. The robe is also very comfortable. I guess I always did like dresses!

"Osho liked them because it lets the energy flow freely," the woman had said at the boutique where I bought the robes, and I can feel what she means as I make my way around the ashram.

I check the meditation schedule and see that there is a meditation called *Nadabrahma* scheduled to start in a few minutes in Buddha hall. I follow the signs, slip off my shoes and slide onto the cool, smooth, white marble floor of this enormous open-air auditorium. The floor is like glass and faintly reflects the giant photograph of Osho hanging over an empty chair that sits on a platform surrounded by flowers in the front of the hall. I look around this great space and notice that the roof is suspended above the marble floor with no inside pillars. I remember Prem telling me that more than a thousand people could be seated in Buddha Hall. Right now there are probably two dozen all in red sitting on the floor on cushions. The meditation is scheduled to start in just a couple of minutes, and I have been warned that they start on time.

"Most of the meditation leaders are German," the woman at the welcome center told me, "so they *vill* be on time!" Then she laughed at her own attempt at a German accent.

Nadabrahma Meditation starts out with humming. Then there is a very slow circular movement with the hands, first outward with palms facing up offering energy out to the universe and then inward with palms facing down gathering the energy back in. The last phase is the let-go phase, simply sitting or lying down absolutely still. I love this meditation, and even with only a few people in the hall I feel a very beautiful, peaceful presence as I let go into the process.

"Now, I really have arrived in this place," I say to myself as I walk out of the hall, find my shoes, and head for the group therapy center. The Osho therapies are world-renowned and I have it in mind to drink as deeply as I can of them while I am in Pune.

"The place to start is a group called *Fresh Beginnings*," says a man who is working at the reservation desk. I told him that I have just arrived. "It's a twenty-one day process. The first half is *Primal Therapy*, the second half is *Tantra*," he tells me.

I read the words in the write-up for the group: "*Fresh Beginnings* is a powerful therapeutic process that allows you to express, understand and heal old wounds and life-negative programs originating from childhood and the teenage years."

It goes on to describe the first part of the process, the *Primal Therapy*, and the way it's designed to peel off the deep layers of childhood conditioning, and the second part, the *Tantra*, that focuses on the adolescent years, addressing the social, religious and cultural conditioning around relating and sexuality.

I have heard about *Primal Therapy* and know it will be hard work, digging into my childhood wounding. Of course I've also heard of *Tantra* and am definitely interested in experiencing that so I sign up. Paying for the group is the next challenge. The groups are inexpensive by western standards, but they are paid in Rupees, which requires large stacks of currency. At the time, there are no ATM's in use in India and the commune doesn't take credit cards, so I take a motorized rickshaw to a place on the other side of town called the Bank of Naruda. I'm directed to a special building where someone processes my credit card and then back to the bank to stand in a long line for the money. I'll never forget walking out of the bank with armfuls of cash in great stacks. It's absolutely crazy, and I haven't even thought of taking a bag so here I am standing outside the bank with enormous amounts of money like I've just pulled off a bank heist. I've never seen a rickshaw stop so fast. When he drops me off at the ashram gates the driver jokes, "they won't let you take that stuff in there. You'll have to give it all to me."

Chapter 32

From Padded Walls to Despondency

On the first day of the group *Fresh Beginnings*, and on every day after that, we start with a 6:00 A.M. *Dynamic Meditation* in Buddha Hall. There are hundreds of people gathered in the hall, but as the leader explains, for the sake of the neighbors it is agreed that we will only have one loud version of the meditation each week. On the other days the catharsis is done silently, and it seems today is not the designated day for clamor so I am given the opportunity to begin perfecting the art of the silent scream. Here we are, hundred's of us screaming and pounding and running around like raving lunatics, but all is strangely quiet like in a Charlie Chaplin movie. Despite this, the process is very powerful in moving energy and preparing us for what lies ahead, *Primal Therapy*!

After *Dynamic*, the group is led down some steps into a dark basement room with no windows. The walls and pillars of the room are covered with six-inch thick padding. There are about fifteen of us in this proverbial padded cell, and as the group begins we are given some pillows and instructed to lie on our backs for a process called *Rebirthing*, a form of breath work that is designed to enable us to re-experience the trauma of birth. As we breath in and out in a strong, steady rhythm for what seems like hours, I am overwhelmed with rushes of intense feeling: a mixture of fear and deep primal urges that remind me of my L.S.D. trip years ago with Kimberly when I re-experienced the womb.

In the next ten days we are immersed in the *Primal Therapy* process, a trauma-based psychotherapy that was created by Arthur Janov, who believed that neurosis was caused by the repressed pain of childhood trauma. He thought that this primal pain could be brought to conscious awareness and resolved through re-experiencing the disturbance and then fully expressing the resulting pain during the therapy. In the group context, the process is very similar to the cathartic phase of *Dynamic Meditation*, except it goes on much longer, for many hours each day, and there are therapists there to help guide us into the places where we are resisting. *Primal* proves to be a physically and mentally exhausting process... screaming and pounding the walls all day to the point of exhaustion... and at times the whole experience becomes quite scary, especially when some of the bigger men in the room come to the point of being completely out of control as they express their rage. It's in those times that I am glad the therapists are there to help keep us physically safe.

Each morning in what seems like an endless time in purgatory, we line up at the door to face the inner demons, and just before going into that hell-hole I can smell the fear oozing out of every pore of our bodies. The days go by, and in the process I release a lot of pent up anger and rage that I have held inside about my father. He had a domineering personality. It's easy to get in touch with my resentment of authority that developed as a result, and it's very freeing to finally let go of it. When we turn our attention to Mother, though, I am surprised to see how much of what I think of as *me* is actually my mother internalized. So... when we are asked to *kill* the mother inside, it is very hard for me to do. But with the therapists' constant encouragement, my own persistence, and lots of "fake it 'til you make it," I gradually begin to break free of that strong but subtle conditioning.

The goal of the work is to throw off all the conditioning so that we can be alive, fresh, and spontaneous in this very moment. Once Osho was asked by a reporter, "It is said that you are brainwashing the people who come to you. Can you comment?" His response was something like this. "It is true that I am in the business of washing the brain. Tell those people that it is not only a brainwash, it is a mindwash – it goes far deeper, to the very roots." You see Osho wants to empty our minds completely of their "so called knowledge" and make us no-minds. That's what he calls meditation.

At long last, after our thorough mind cleaning through what seems like an eternity of pounding the walls and screaming 'til all our voices are gone, we ascend from this hell into the light. We have been through a lot: have progressed from birth through childhood and shed a lot of guilt and anger. Now all the screaming is finished, and we have graduated to the *Tantra* portion of the group. And so, on the eleventh day, we are led up the stairs out of the padded cell and into a beautifully decorated "love palace," full of soft pillows, luxurious couches and lots of windows letting in the light. It's in this room that, over the course of the next ten days, we explore our sexuality. We start slowly with a rather innocent, adolescent touching exercise done in couples, then move on to puppy piles and many other exercises in intimacy, and then one at a time each person sheds all his protection and stands naked in front of the group.

In the course of those ten days, I get to face my shame at being seen, release repressed feelings around my body and the sexual urge, and play out several of my sexual fantasies. The experience is amazingly freeing. I didn't realize how much I had repressed around sexuality and the opposite gender, and releasing it allows me to be much more present with the opposite sex without so much game playing. When, at last, the group ends, the therapists suggest that we take it easy for a little while to help process the feelings that have arisen over the course of the group.

Every evening in the ashram, there is an event called *The White Robe Brotherhood*. It's a time when all the people in the ashram dress in white robes and come together to celebrate. Each evening, there is live music by a large band of musicians, people who have come from all over the world to join in sound, and the music is truly eclectic. When Osho was still in his body he would sit in his chair while the music was happening and then speak to the thousand or so people gathered before him. Now that he is no longer in physical form, an Osho video is presented on a large screen instead, but still Osho's presence is felt by all in attendance. This is especially true for me on the evening after my group is over. As the group name suggests, it has truly been a fresh beginning. I feel so alive and so present.

But only after a couple of days I want to dive deeper, and so I find myself back in the group therapy hall looking for the next thing. That next thing turns out to be a three-day inquiry group called *Who is In?* This was originally called the *Enlightenment Intensive* and was devised by an American spiritual teacher named Charles Berner, who became a disciple of Swami Kripalu and received the name Yogeshwar Muni. A former teacher of Scientology, Yogeshwar had been developing the use of interpersonal communication processes for personal growth during the 1960's. He observed that those who tended not to make much progress in their personal growth were those who did not actually know who they were - that is, they were "identified" with their false self-images, their egos or personalities, unaware of their true inner being.

Yogeshwar felt that traditional techniques for experiencing self-realization, meeting with a teacher once a day using the question, "Who am I?" as a Zen koan or using the question for self-inquiry as Ramana Maharshi did, took too long for the average Westerner seeking personal growth. But, when the inquiry was done with partners in a group context, then the process was accelerated.

The group sounds like the perfect thing for me. After having spent the last three weeks stripping away my childhood conditioning, I feel like I'm ready to look deeply at who I am.

I walk into a fairly large hall, and there are probably about a hundred and fifty people in the room. We quickly pair up, sit on cushions on the floor in front of our partners, and make eye contact. One person asks the question, "Who is In?" which in effect means, "Who are you?" The other person takes five minutes to answer while the person who asked the question just sits and listens, maintaining eye contact, without responding in any way. After the five minutes we switch roles, and then after forty minutes we find a new partner.

This process continues for ten hours a day for three full days. It's a residential program, which means that we all sleep there together on the floor. Then we are awakened in the middle of the night to continue the process. So now that I've described the method, let me share what happens to me during the three days. My process goes something like this. When it is my time to share, I start answering with the usual identity stories. I'm a man, a father, a son of Scientists, I'm American, I'm a computer specialist. I'm a songwriter, I'm a product of the sixties, I'm a Virgo with Libra rising. But as I say these things I can see that none of them are ultimately true, especially after saying these things over and over for so many hours to so many people.

After awhile, my responses become more basic: "I'm this body. I'm this mind." But as I speak even these seemingly obvious truisms, something in me is saying, "That's not really it." Over time, my answers get more cosmic, more esoteric. "I'm energy... I'm a pebble in the cosmic ocean... I am the universe breathing..." and then, after about two and a half days, my mind has exhausted itself and just plain gives up. After that, everything that's said becomes incredibly funny, as if it's all just one big cosmic joke, and I begin to feel an intense feeling of presence. Then as I sit in front of the last few people on the last day of the group, my mind is at last still, and I drop into a profound silence. At which point, I am overwhelmed with a blissful awareness of the unity of everything. I have gone beyond words and explanations into pure *suchness*.

And then the very last person comes in front of me and I ask the question, "Who is In?" Suddenly my partner begins venting: expressing incredible anger and hate toward all men for having betrayed her, wronged her, hurt her. How all that anger survived in her for all these days, I do not know, but I am in such an open, loving, merged, transcendent space that as her words pore out of her toward me, my whole being suddenly cracks open and I begin to weep. Tears are streaming down my face, and I feel incredible remorse for being a man that has hurt a woman so deeply. As she looks in my eyes, just as suddenly something cracks in her, all her anger dissolves, and she too begins to cry. And so we hold each

251

other sobbing and sobbing for the remainder of our forty minutes. Then the bell sounds, and the group is over. I never see that woman again, but I am forever grateful to her for bringing that pain to me to be healed.

***

As rich as this experience is, after a few days down time, I find myself wanting to take another group, but I've run out of money and have to go off to the bank to get more. I am told there is a new branch of the National Bank in Koragon Park, the suburb where I live. "They have a credit card reader," someone says, so I walk a kilometer or two to that bank and stand in a long line. At last it is my turn, and I hand the man my credit card.

"I need 15,000 Rupees, please."

The man behind the counter takes my card and swipes it through the bank's reader. No response. He swipes again. Nothing. Then he rubs the magnetic strip on his shirt and tries again. Still nothing.

"I'm sorry sir, but it is not reading," he says to me with some regret.

"Is their another bank I can try?" I plead.

"Our main bank downtown has a different kind of reader. You can go there. You might have better luck."

This would be no problem, except that there is a rickshaw strike in progress, so I'll have to take a taxi, and they are expensive. I check my pouch. I have only a hundred rupees left, about two dollars in U.S. currency. I flag down a taxi.

"How much to take me to the National Bank in Downtown Pune?" I ask.

"That will be ninety Rupees," the man says. I have enough to get there, and assuming the bank can read my card I'll have money to return. It's a gamble but what alternative do I have? I hop in. By now I am used to the craziness: cars, bicycles, cows, chickens, and pedestrians all sharing the road. I am still amazed that there aren't more accidents, though. He drops me off in front of the bank, I enter and then stand in a very long line. At last it is my turn, and I tell the man at the counter what I want.

"I'm sorry. You are in the wrong line. You must stand in that line over there."

He points to another long line, and I resignedly move to the back of the second line. "This is a test of my ability to meditate," I tell myself and try to relax. As I wait I become distracted by all the people coming and going. At last it's my turn.

"I am very sorry, but we no longer process credit cards at this bank," the man says.

"What!" I scream. I can't believe it.

"But your branch in Koragan Park said you do!" I cry out in utter frustration.

"We used to, but do not any longer," the man says calmly.

"Well... where can I go to get money from this credit card?" I ask in desperation.

"Just wait a few minutes and someone will come and help you," the man promises.

I wait about ten minutes and finally a woman comes out from behind the counter and gestures for me to follow her, which I do, and we walk down some back stairs and out a side door onto the street.

"Do you see that man standing over there?" She asks while making a vague gesture.

I see a hundred men standing around in the streets, but I try to look where she is pointing.

"A bus will arrive at that corner. Get on the bus and tell the driver you want to go to the Bank of Naruda."

Ah yes, the Bank of Naruda. I have been there by rickshaw, and I know it is on the other side of town somewhere, but I wasn't really paying attention to where we were going at the time. I walk to where she points and wait. A bus does come. I hope I have enough money. I get on the bus and ask the fare. It is only four rupees.

"The Bank of Naruda, please."

He says something back to me in Hindi, which I assume is confirmation. The bus goes along for quite a while and then we come to some kind of terminal. Everyone is getting off. As I climb down the steps onto the pavement the bus driver raises four fingers. There is no sign of the bank and nothing here looks familiar. Am I supposed to get on another bus? The number four bus?

I ask several people there at the terminal about the bus, but no one speaks English. I wait as busses come and go. I notice that there are numbers posted on the windshields of the buses. I've seen number seven and number thirteen, but no number four. I wait at least forty-five minutes. Then I hear a couple of Indian men conversing in English. I approach and tell them where I am hoping to go.

"Oh yes," one of the men says. "We are waiting for that same bus, but the bus numbers are not on the windshield, they are in Hindi, up above."

We talk as we wait, and the guy gives me an apple. I am grateful. I haven't eaten in a while. Then he tells me that they are in Pune to attend a business conference to discuss the possibility of bringing ATM's to India...

"Huh, That's the universe's idea of a good joke", I think.

At last the bus comes.

"It's this one," the man says, "but it's actually a substitute bus with an entirely different number." No telling how I was supposed to know that.

We get on the bus and give the driver the two rupees he asks for. When we come to the street where the bank of Naruda is, one of my new friends calls out to me.

"Get off here and walk down about two blocks. There you'll find the bank."

I thank the two guys, begin walking and before long, the surroundings begin to look familiar. When I finally get to the bank, I know just where to go: across the street and up the steps to a little office where they process credit cards. I bound up the stairs feeling quite relieved, open the door, and spot three large wooden desks with three bureaucrats sitting behind them, each with neatly arranged stacks of pencils and piles of paper. There is no line! I sit down in a chair in front of the first desk and begin explaining what I need.

"I am sorry," the man behind the desk says. "We are closed for the day. Come back Monday."

"But you are here," I protest. "The door was open. Please. I need to get some money."

"I am very sorry, but the bank is no longer open. We can't get any money."

I am crushed, and in big trouble. I only have four rupees left and I have no idea where I am or how I will get home. I walk back down the steps, back out to the street and sit down on the curb, head in my hands, and resign myself to my fate. Just then I notice a beggar sitting just like I am on another part of the curb with his head in his hands, and I think to myself, "the only difference between him and me is this piece of plastic here in my pouch that is the promise of money. In fact, there isn't even any money at home to back up this piece of plastic. I am living on credit."

This is an existential moment. I look at my predicament and realize I can see no way out. Then life gets bigger than itself as I sit and ponder my situation and all the events that led me to this very moment, here on this curb at what seems to be life's dead-end. I think about the groups I have taken here in India and the journeys I've been on. I have killed my parents and played out my sexual fantasies in *Fresh Beginnings*, and then exhausted my identifications in *Who is In?*

"So who am I in this moment?" I ask myself and realize I have no answers.

Then I ask myself, "Is this it? Is this how this journey of a lifetime ends, here on this curb somewhere in the hill country of India?"

Chapter 33

One Step Leads to Another

Time stops… or is it my mind that stops. There is a long moment of utter stillness. Nothing moves. No one breathes. The air is motionless. Nothing happens… and then… somehow… inexplicably…

…it all begins again.

This is when something inside me comes to a realization that I don't need to know ahead of time how to get out of my situation. In fact, it doesn't even matter what I do. I just have to do something, and then be present to respond to whatever existence unveils next.

I look up from where I am sitting on this curb in a medium sized hill town in Western India and see a road there before me. I get up, pick a direction and start walking. I wander along for a little while with no destination in mind and then come to a small, but obviously very ancient temple. I duck my head and step through a stone archway. Inside, there are lighted candles and flowers adorning a small shrine. I recognize the deity as Shiva, the ultimate warrior and destroyer of illusion. I kneel down for a moment.

"The Shiva in me, give me strength and discernment," I say quietly.

I get back up, turn and exit the temple just as some young Indian girls are entering. They smile at me and in the only English they appear to know they say, "Hello, American." This gives me comfort and I am left with the feeling that it's a benevolent universe after all. I return to the road and walk on. Before too long, I come to a river.

"I live near a river," I think to myself. "Is this the same river?"

I decide to follow the flowing water. I am pretty sure I need to go north and I am also fairly certain that the rivers flow south here, so I figure I need to head up-river. I now have a direction. Before long I notice some bus stops and several concrete shelters full of bus drivers. At least they all have on the same uniform I saw on my bus driver earlier in the day.

I'll ask someone if there is a bus to Koregan Park, I reason. I step into the first shelter and call out.

"Anyone speak English here?" People look up at me, but no one responds. I walk on to the next shelter full of bus drivers. What they are all doing here, I don't know. Maybe it's their break room.

"Anyone speak English?" I call out again.

This time, someone comes forward.

"Uhhh, yes. A little."

"I'm trying to go to Koregan Park. Is there a bus?"

"What?" He's not getting it.

I try again. "Koregan Park. Bus?"

He seems to understand me this time. He walks out to the road and points to what looks like a bus stop.

"Take bus... there... Koregan Park."

I go where he says, and before long a bus comes along. I hop on and hold out all the money I have. The driver takes two rupees leaving me with just two rupies left. It's a good thing buses are cheap in India.

"Koregan Park?" I ask.

He nods and motions me to find a seat. Will I know when to get out? My eyes are glued to the passing scenery, but nothing looks familiar. I feel so alone and scared. We leave the river and go through a very congested area and at last we come in sight of another river and pass a bridge. Apparently there is more than one river in this city. Suddenly the entire bus erupts in conversation, and I wonder what's happening. Then several people yell up to the driver and a couple others are pointing at me. The bus stops, and I realize that I haven't been alone on this bus after all. Every person on the bus has been looking out for me, and this is where I am to get out.

I run up to the front to get off the bus, and notice that everyone is smiling and waving. Someone points across the bridge and I get the idea that I am supposed to cross it. As I get about a half way across the river, I begin to recognize the burning ghats on the other side. I am nearly home. I have almost no money, but I am home. I walk up the street and across the busy road to the ashram, and the first person I see as I enter is Mitra, the owner of the house where I live back in California and probably the wealthiest person I know. He loans me money right there on the spot.

The rickshaw strike continues, and so once again I have to venture out to try and find the Bank of Naruda when the money I have borrowed is mostly spent. This time, I figure I'd take the same bus I took to get home the last time, so I walk back over that bridge and hop on the first bus that comes along. After riding down the road for a while the bus suddenly makes a sharp right turn.

"I don't remember a big turn," I say to myself.

Before long we start going out into the countryside, and I realize I need to get off the bus. I am going to the wrong place. I try to get the driver to stop, but he won't so I end up jumping off the bus while it's still moving, I lose my balance and fall onto the ground as the bus zooms off. Suddenly, here I am again: lost, nearly broke, and alone on a vacant street. This time I don't even know which way to start walking so I just sit there in disbelief.

"I can't believe I did it again!" I gasp and hold my head in my hands.

Just then, a car pulls up; someone rolls down the window and says in plain English, "Do you need some help? Maybe a lift somewhere?"

Sometimes to get out of a jam one needs to take the first step. Sometimes one doesn't. This time no action is necessary. I just need to say yes.

"Because of the rickshaw strike, I decided to drive around looking for taxi business," says the driver of the car. "Where are you trying to go?"

I explain that I have no money and that I am trying to get to the bank.

"That's no problem. I will drive you to the bank," he says.

"But I have no money," I say.

"But you will, once you get to the bank!" he responds. "I will wait and then drive you back home. You can pay me a small fee once you are back home safe."

This is an offer I cannot refuse, and so I hop in the car and ride in style, I get my money, and soon I'm back home safe and sound. All I can say is that life is certainly a mystery. Sometimes it takes going out on a limb to see it.

With money in hand I return to the therapy center to sign up for another group. I have become a group junkie. The next group is one co-run by Deva Pat a famous breath therapist, and Shunyo a woman who was Osho's personal assistant for many years. In the mornings we do the breath work: three or four hours of intense deep breathing. It's such a simple thing, breathing, but it creates one of the most powerful transcendent states I have ever experienced. The body becomes so alive with every cell awake, and there is a feeling of overwhelming love that consumes me along with a perception of incredible beauty.

At some point in the third or fourth day of it after a full morning of deep breathing, I am so blissed out that I feel like I am making love to God. I am in such a rarified space. But breath therapy is hard work, and it takes enormous energy for me to keep going, to keep breathing deeply. It's the power of the music, the intention of the group and the encouragement of the leaders that keeps me going until the time comes when I am no longer the one breathing, as if some force beyond myself takes over, and I am suspended in timeless awareness. Then everything becomes effortless, and there is nothing but breathing. At last the music softens, and we are called to return to normal breathing. This is when the waves of bliss, tenderness, and transcendental love rush in, every cell bathing in it. This moment is like sexual orgasm tenfold.

So, what do we do with all these overwhelming feelings? Well, in the afternoons Shunyo takes over the group and guides us in heart opening exercises. I don't even remember what we do; I just know that by the time the group is over my heart is blown wide open. It's

not that I love everything, it's that I am everything and I am love...
just spilling out everywhere.

What could I possibly do after an experience like that? I choose
a painting group led by a gifted Japanese painter, reasoning that
through painting I can attempt to express the beauty I see in
everything. The group more than meets my expectations by helping
me open to my creative impulse, and for that I am forever grateful.

Finally, my time in India comes to a close. It's been three
wonderful, amazing months, but just as Prem said, I feel like I have
just arrived. But before leaving there is one more thing I must do.
I must arrange to visit Osho's Samadhi. At designated times small
groups of people are allowed in to just be in the place that used
to be Osho's bedroom and now contains his ashes. As I prepare to
enter at my scheduled time, I remember what Prem had said about
the place when I was planning my trip.

"Even though Osho is no longer in his body, his energy is still
strong there, especially in his Samadhi where his ashes are."

We are ushered into the place called *Chuang-Tzu* and my first
impression is that the room seems more like the atrium in a five-
star hotel than a bedroom. The room is round with solid marble
floors and pillars, lots of glass and a magnificent circular chandelier
on the high ceiling. About twenty of us are brought into the space
and directed to sit on meditation cushions before a raised marble
platform.

"That was his bed," I remember someone telling me, "and his
ashes are underneath it."

As I settle in to being in this room, I gradually become aware of
an incredible silence pervading the space, and then begin noticing
a pure, heartful energy. As I bathe in this energy, my own mind
soon becomes quiet. I am... just there... still... silent.... And then our
time is up. The hour has flown by in an instant, and we are ushered
back out into what now seems like the hectic atmosphere of the
commune.

***

Now the time has come for me to return to California. As I am saying goodbye to everyone and everything, I vow to return to this place as soon as I can, and as I am gathering my things from my room by the burning ghats, the woman who has been doing my laundry (she was part of the room deal) says to me, "Next time I cook for you." I take a train back to Mumbai. I can't face another taxi ride. From Mumbai I hop on a plane, and thirty hours later I am back home in California. I never return to India.

As I sit in my room in Chakra House again, I am overcome with the feeling that a rug had been pulled out from under me. [17] My heart has been so opened, and I have been so tenderly nurtured by the energy of the ashram. Now it's extremely difficult to be back in the world, especially to be back in America, a place of such industry and material abundance. My first trip to *Whole Foods* since my return is mind-blowing; there's so much food and so many choices.

Going back to work at my corporate job seems nearly impossible. The truth is that I have been changed, as if a genie has been let out of a bottle. That genie is my heart, a precious newborn in need of delicate handling. I really want to quit working for the computer company, but I just can't bring myself to do it. I am making such good money and hardly working. So, instead of quitting, I just stop pretending to be busy, and I stop doing things that I really don't think have any purpose. I only do those things that actually help someone.

A few months later, Prem and I move out of Chakra house into our own apartment, still as friends. Group life has gotten to be too much for Prem, all the subtle expectations, and I am also ready for a change. It's then that the inevitable happens. I'll never forget that day. It's April first and my phone rings while I'm lingering over breakfast talking with Prem. I hurry into my room to answer it. It's the manager of my department at the computer company, a person I have never actually met. You see, in Corporate America bosses seem to come and go every time a company decides to reorganize, which is often.

"I am calling to tell you that we are terminating your employment."

"What? Is this a joke? You know, April Fools' Day."

"This is no joke. We are letting you go. Now there will be a severance package, and since you've been with us over ten years, it will be a good one. You'll be getting the details of this delivered to you soon...."

His voice continues, but I no longer hear him, and when he's finished I hang up the phone and walk into Prem's room.

"What is it?" Prem asks looking up at me from a pile of papers she's going through on the floor. "Your face is white, like you've just seen a ghost."

"I've been fired!" I tell her.

At first I am shocked. Then gradually as the reality seeps in, I begin to feel an incredible relief.

"It's over." I mumble to myself, and then I say it louder, "It's over!"

This is the last remaining piece of the old life, and now it's finished. A few minutes later I try to log on to my computer system to tidy up my files and discover that my login account has been suspended. I guess they are afraid of sabotage.

The next day I receive a package sent by Federal Express from the company. As I read over the documents they have sent, I find out that my severance package gives me income for another eight months. I can continue to make my hefty alimony and child support payments and pay my share of the apartment for a while, but then what? I have no idea how I'll earn a living. I just know that whatever I do will have to be more in alignment with who I have become.

I drive down to San Francisco a week or two later. I park the car, which is always a major accomplishment, and begin walking along one of the busy streets. That's when it hits me. I suddenly realize I am replaying the scene with the matchbook from so many years before.

"How would you like an exciting career in Computers?" The matchbook says.

"No thanks." I say to myself, and allow the matchbook to fall back into the gutter. Just then there is a break in the fog, and the sun starts to peak out. The whole world is waiting!

Chapter 34

New Worlds Open Up

Prem and I continue to read Melville's *Moby Dick* to each other, but only on road trips. Several times over the years that we are together, we drive to San Diego to visit her grandkids and our friends, and we take turns reading while the other drives. Reading Melville out loud is a real treat. There's something absolutely amazing about his run-on sentences and his over-the-top descriptions. He has an incredible command of the English language, and when there's no word for what he is describing he thinks nothing of making up a new one. Reading *Moby Dick* is a lesson in flow, a lesson in let go. There's a sort of zone I have to get into to actually be able to read this stuff, but once I am in that place I find reading it so very rewarding. It's a bit like what happens after sliding down the big hill of a rollercoaster. The momentum carries me inevitably onward through all the unpredictable dips and curves to at last arrive somewhere... in the case of the book to arrive at some profound conclusion.

"Consider the subtleness of the sea," Melville writes, "how its most dreaded creatures glide under water, unapparent for the most part, and treacherously hidden beneath the loveliest tints of azure. Consider also the devilish brilliance and beauty of many of its most remorseless tribes, as the dainty embellished shape of many species of sharks. Consider, once more, the universal cannibalism of the sea; all whose creatures prey upon each other, carrying on eternal war since the world began."

"Consider all this," he goes on to write, "and then turn to the green, gentle, and most docile earth; consider them both, the sea and the land; and do you not find a strange analogy to something in yourself? For as this appalling ocean surrounds the verdant land, so in the soul of man there lies one insular Tahiti, full of peace and joy, but encompassed by all the horrors of the half-known life. God keep thee!" He concludes. "Push not off from that isle, thou canst never return!"

Prem and I are about three quarters of the way through *Moby Dick* when it becomes clear that something has to change in our lives. My severance is running out, and I need to find a new kind of work. Prem is feeling a need for change as well. We have been living together for almost five years, and neither of us can seem to find a lasting lover relationship, much as we both try. I know that it's time for us to part ways, but like with the corporate job I just can't bring myself to be the one to do it. Must be that Taurus Moon, fixed and stuck in the mud. Prem also has a Taurus moon, by the way, so I guess we both have a tendency to get stuck emotionally. Finally Prem takes action.

"I've decided to move back to Rochester, New York," she blurts out one morning.

"Why would you go back there?" I ask, truly mystified at the idea.

"I'm done with California, and Rochester is where I was born. My roots are on the East Coast and it's time for me to go back," she says, and a few days later she begins the long process of boxing up all her stuff.

Some of her things she sends by train, some by U.S Postal Service, and the rest by UPS. While she is busy with that, I do some deep soul searching myself and finally decide to go back to school. At first I think I'll go after that long coveted Ph.D. in Eastern Philosophy that I was going to pursue when I found that match book so many years before, but I just can't get myself to do it. It just doesn't seem practical. I'd go deeply in to debt with no real tangible avenue for employment. Around the San Francisco bay area, there are lots of people with Ph.D.'s in some esoteric field pounding the pavement, looking for jobs. The educational road is just too long, especially considering my financial obligations, so I decide on a shorter course, the pursuit of a credential in high school teaching. It only requires one more year of school, and there seems to be lots of job opportunity. Once I decide, everything falls into place. The college where my brother teaches has a teaching credential program, and I can stay with him and his wife while I attend. The school accepts me only two months before the start of the semester, and so it's set. Prem and I are going to go our separate ways: she to New York and me to Lake Tahoe and to Sierra Nevada College. She is meeting a friend in Albuquerque. From there they will drive together back to New York. I have some time before school starts and decide to drive with her to Albuquerque and then fly to Reno to start my new life.

"I want to take one last road trip with you," I tell her. "Maybe we can finish *Moby Dick*."

We do finish *Moby Dick* as we are arriving on the outskirts of Albuquerque. As she turns the final page, I know a chapter of my life is ending as well. I am scared, but I'm ready... at least as ready as I'll ever be. She drops me off at the Airport, we embrace and then we each turn and walk away into our new lives. I hear later that Prem only stays in New York for two weeks. Once she gets there she realizes she has made a big mistake, but the trip serves its purpose. We are at last separate from one another. Over the years we maintain a beautiful friendship, but are no longer enmeshed. A while later I fall in love... for the first time since Prem, and although it doesn't last, I now know that I can love again. My heart is at last free.

A year goes by, I get that teaching credential and begin teaching high school mathematics in inner city Sacramento. Why mathematics? Well if I wanted to teach High School Psychology I'd have to be a History teacher, and I never liked History. Besides it's been more than thirty years since I've studied that stuff, and the only date I remember is 1492. Math is something I've always been good at, and no memorization is necessary. Never the less, good at Math or not, teaching High School ends up being the hardest thing I will ever do for work, partly due to the fact that as a beginning teacher, I am given the most marginal students, and these kids do not want to learn mathematics. They are busy being rebellious teenagers, and to them I am the authority figure. But the truth is I haven't finished dealing with my own authority issues yet, so this seems like the universe's idea of a joke.

***

It's about this time that I start Internet dating. I start with Match.com and later move to Green Singles for what I hope will be a more conscious clientele.

"I am a forty-nine year old white male, college educated high school teacher. I am a liberal-minded hippie turned spiritual seeker and a musician. I love to sing and dance and be in nature. I'm looking for a spiritually oriented, non-materialistic, openhearted woman, who is interested in a long-term relationship. I am searching for an intimate partner in the journey to awakening."

I can't remember all the dates I go on, but the process is pretty much the same with all of them. First, we respond to each other's posting on the Internet. Sometimes I make the first inquiry. Sometimes she does. Then we begin corresponding through the dating website. If this goes well, we share our email addresses and continue corresponding. If there seem to be common interests and some hint of chemistry, we arrange a telephone conversation. The final step is to meet each other in a public place. I meet people in cafes, bookstores, in parks, and even once in a train station.

Meeting the person is always a shock, because she is never the way I imagine her to be. It's the mind, you know. It creates such fantasies... dreams up a whole image of the perfect mate... but it's all pure projection. The reality of a person is never the same as the projection... nowhere close. This is always a let down. And then there's this thing called chemistry. It's a real mystery to me. We have so much in common, seem to be perfect for each other, and then when we meet there's simply no spark. Sometimes I ignore this lack of sizzle and continue seeing the person, thinking that maybe I'll get used to her, and the spark will develop over time. Like rubbing two sticks together, if I do it long enough I'll eventually

266

get the spark. But it never works. One person I meet through the Internet becomes a very good friend though, and another woman whom I date a few times, I meet again years later in Costa Rica, and she becomes a close friend of both mine and my second wife's.

Here's my most crazy Internet dating story:

We correspond for a while before arranging a meeting. She says she is a free spirit and a gypsy. I say I'm a spiritual seeker. She says she's of an athletic build. I say I'm slim. The only trouble is she lives in Oregon, and I live in California, but she says she drives down to Sacramento from time to time. We decide to meet at the Sacramento train station on one of her trips down. We both think of Bogart... all very romantic. I'm there a little early. I keep my eyes peeled and wait. She says she'll have a flower in her hair.

"Is that her? No. There's no flower. Hmm, how about her? Nope, she's with that guy."

Finally after an hour, I go back home disappointed. When I arrive home I email her. "What happened to you?" I ask. "I was there, but didn't see you."

"I wondered what happened to you," she replies. "I was there!"

We talk about a second attempt.

"Let's meet half way," she suggests.

"Hmmm... Let's see. Half way would be Mt. Shasta," I tell her, looking at the map.

"Great! Let's meet there. We can spend the weekend together in one of the campgrounds. I've got a big tent!"

"Ok," I say a little hesitantly, wondering to myself what I will do if it doesn't work out. Then I think, "What the heck, it's just a weekend, not a lifetime commitment." We set the place and time.

She had sent me her picture... a bit fuzzy... a photo with her son. I should have known there was some trouble brewing when I couldn't tell which person in the photo was she, but love and projection are blind.

At last the designated day arrives and I head north along route 101 in my little Honda CRX. Once again, I arrive a few minutes early, a habit of mine, and wait nervously. I see a very large Chevy Suburban drive up.

"Is that her?" I wonder. I don't see anyone get out of the car. The next thing I notice is that someone is peeking out from behind a tree, looking at me. And at last a woman comes out of hiding and approaches.

"Oh my God!" I think to myself, but try not to show my reaction. The woman before me has got to weigh almost three hundred pounds!

"Hi," she says shyly.

"Hi," I say politely... and wonder about the next two days and two nights we are supposed to spend together.

"Okay, have an open mind," I say to myself. "She's a nice person. I can try to let go of my judgment of fat people," I tell myself. "Besides what else to do?"

We find our campsite, and I help her set up the tent. Then she begins to inflate an enormous air mattress!

"I like to camp in comfort," she says as she pulls the mattress into the tent. It completely fills the large tent. I didn't bring a tent.

After we share a meal and some pleasant conversation, she pulls out a little blue bottle of some sweet smelling liquid.

"Love potion," she says sprinkling some on me and looking at me seductively.

"Let's take this slow," I say.

It's getting late. I'm getting tired. So is she. We climb into the tent and onto the giant bed. She takes off her clothes and I figure it's only polite to do the same.

"Here goes nothing!" I mutter under my breath.

Before I realize what's happening, her gigantic size is creating a sort of vortex in the center of the air mattress, and I'm being sucked in. Soon I'm fighting for my life as I cling frantically to the edge of the bed and finally surrender to the inevitable. After some kissing and some "heavy" petting, and I mean that in the most literal sense, we finally dose off to sleep. The next morning I tell her the romantic aspect of the relationship is not working for me. Just before I ride off from my aborted weekend stay, we tell each other we'll keep in touch as friends, and then we never contact each other again. Upon returning home to my own house and my own bed, I decide to give up Internet dating once and for all.

"Just do what you love to do and the right person will show up," I tell myself and then begin looking around Sacramento for something in which to involve myself.

***

A little while later as I'm looking through the local weekly paper, I find an advertisement for an organization being run by a psychologist named John Ruskell. I look them up on the web and find their mission statement:

"A non-profit educational services organization, the Aspire Foundation has offered an innovative process supporting personal transformation since 1987. The heart of the Aspire program is a well tested and nurturing experiential process, which inspires participants to take total responsibility for the circumstances of their lives. Thus empowered and encouraged, growth accelerates, and individuals move inevitably toward a state of harmony and integration – a state of grace. In essence, the Aspire Foundation is a group of caring people who enjoy assisting others along the way to Self-realization."

I'm intrigued and decide to attend their next Wednesday night open meeting. I'm a little scared as I walk into a small room lined with chairs in a large circle. I am always a bit anxious when meeting new people in unfamiliar surroundings, afraid to do the wrong thing I guess, but this time I have little time to be uncomfortable. I am immediately greeted by a lovely Asian woman with a big smile who makes continuous eye contact with me as she welcomes me into the room and to a seat. People continue to filter in and soon all the chairs are full. Then someone goes into the back room for a few more chairs, and the circle is expanded so that it's flush against the walls of the room.

"There's something going on here!" I say to myself. "So many people!"

Just then, a tall man with a penetrating gaze enters the room, and all eyes turn to him as he takes a seat in the circle.

269

"This is John," I decide.

The man is wearing tan pants and a cardigan sweater, sporting a short beard, a long braid down his back, and a London fog cap on his head.

"Welcome," he says. "I'm so glad you all came tonight. Who has something to share?"

What follows is a whirlwind of sharing, mostly about feelings or challenges in life, all very personal, things that challenge self-worth and/or trigger responses learned in childhood.

"I see we have some new people in the room," John says after much of the sharing is complete. "Will you please introduce yourselves?"

We go around the circle and several people speak up. When it's my turn, I look around the circle at the large number of smiling people, present, available and interested, and I share my name and my desire to be with like spirited people. A couple more people share after me.

"Now turn and find a partner," John invites, and I turn to a smiling young woman next to me. "Now please take five minutes each to share how you are feeling right now. The one listening, simply maintain eye contact and be present for your partner. Decide who will go first. Ready? Begin."

I gaze into my partner's eyes as she begins to tell me about some sadness she has been feeling since she broke up with her boyfriend. I maintain a neutral loving presence. When it's my turn to share, I tell her that I'm still feeling some anxiety about being here in a group of strangers, but as I look in her warm brown eyes, I realize that I am no longer anxious. In fact, I feel really good.

After the meeting comes to a close there are lots of hugs, and the room is buzzing with conversation. Feeling a bit uncomfortable again I begin to head for the door, but the Asian woman who I now know is named Lydia sees me and approaches.

"Did you enjoy the meeting?" She asks.

"Yes," I say. "There's a lot of love here."

"I want you to know about a half-day group that's taking place this Saturday," she tells me. "It's called 'Hello Myself' and it's a great way to get an introduction to the kind of work we do here. I hope you can come."

She hands me a flyer and I look it over.

"Hello, Myself: Your true inner beauty is reflected with this revealing look at yourself and your reflections. Through participation in a series of experiential processes conducted in an atmosphere of conscious reflection and support, you will have the opportunity to meet yourself in a new, transformational way!"

I decide to attend.

When I arrive on Saturday, the layout of the room is the same as it had been Wednesday night. I take a seat and there is a brief introduction.

"One of the core beliefs of Aspire is that everything and everyone is a reflection of *myself*. So today we are going to be mirrors for each other so we can truly say hello to ourselves. Remember, everything you think, feel and say about another person says more about you than anyone else."

With that, we begin to explore our assumptions, attitudes and beliefs about ourselves through deep presence with a partner who maintains eye contact and loving acceptance while we speak. There's something about the eye gazing and having someone totally present while I speak that strips away the layers of protection and falsehood, leaving me with a clear view of what's really true. It happened in the enlightenment intensive in India, and now it's happening again, here in Sacramento. I am encountering my unconditioned self. [18]

After a half a day of this, I realize I want more!

In the last few minutes of the morning session, Lydia gets up and begins to speak.

"Before you leave today, I want to give you some information about our four-weekend intensive series. These weekends are designed to help you go deeply into all the aspects of your life that hold you back from being your true *self*, the one who is happy and free. What we have explored here this morning is just a fraction of what we will experience in a forty-eight hour retreat together."

I take the literature and when I get home I check it out.

"The NEW BEGINNINGS Workshop Series is a compassionate and comprehensive program of Self-realization. A beautifully orchestrated and intuitive developmental process, this four-part Series challenges you to know your Self as never before, to improve your relationship with yourself and others, to learn to respond, instead of react, to be who you really are, not who you learned to be, and to experience love as never before!"

I see that "Level 1", as they call it, is being offered in two weeks time. I read the description in the brochure.

"Level 1 surprises us by shining light upon the obvious and subtle ways we have learned to hold ourselves back. We discover that we learned to survive, even to succeed in conventional terms, yet remain unfulfilled, disappointed, even depressed because we have not learned to trust, to create or fully express the great gift of life. Let yourself experience, if only for an eternal moment, the underlying joy within you. Come to know your transcendent self and the love that holds us all as one."

Chapter 35

Another Look at Myself

A car arrives to pick me up around 3:00 P.M. on a Friday. Four of us are in the car, and we are all Aspire first-timers. As we make our way out of Sacramento and onto I-80, we are caught in a snarl of slow-moving traffic. Hundreds of bay area skiers are heading into the mountains for the weekend giving us plenty of time to get to know each other. The four of us are all a little nervous as we talk about what brought us to this work and our expectations for the weekend. The talking helps pass the time and relieves some of the tension, and at last we arrive at the address given to us in the directions.

We pull into the driveway of a large house perched on a mountainside near the little town of Truckee, and as we step up onto the porch of that house we are greeted by the ever-present Lydia, and she shows us where to place our things. It seems we'll be sleeping on the floor on foam pads about ten to a room. It'll be cozy living and I can imagine that morning bathroom time will be challenging, but the implied intimacy feels good to me. After spots on the floor are claimed with our mats and bags we gather in the large living room of this luxurious house. There are almost fifty people in the room, which has been stripped of furniture before our arrival.

"The team please sit over here, the participants over there," said a blonde woman pointing the way. "We'll get started soon."

"The team" is a term used to describe the group of assistants, equal in number to that of the participants, who have gathered to facilitate our weekend-long exploration. I take a seat on the floor along one of the walls of the large room. There is a nervous energy among those gathered on my side of the room as we wait with uncertainty for what is to follow. At last John, with the long braid down his back and his London fog cap appears out from behind a closed bedroom door.

"We will be looking at some deep conditioning this weekend, and I just ask you to stay present in the process," he explains. "We will be exploring mother issues in level 1," he goes on to say. "Sometimes it will be fun, sometimes it may be more challenging, but remember that we are all here to help you have a safe and rewarding journey." Then he points at the wall behind us and says, "Participants please stand along the wall behind you. Team, you line up over here by me."

I stand along the wall and look across the room at all the people standing on the other side, most of whom I have met at the Wednesday night meeting. Then we are given the instructions to choose partners, and we begin the process. Stopping only to eat and sleep, we spend the next forty-eight hours confronting ourselves and our projections with various partners. Working in dyads, one person shares while the other simply keeps eye contact and remains neutral. At times, we are brutally honest speaking our judgments about the person in front of us. At other times we are playing roles.

At one point I have the opportunity to tell my mother what I've always wanted to tell her:

"Mom, I love you and appreciate all that you have given me: confidence, curiosity, a sense of wonder. You are the perfect mother for me... and Mom, don't worry about me. I'm finding my way."

At another point, I have the chance to tell myself what I believe my mother would want to tell me:

"I just want you to be happy and fulfilled in your life, and most of all to find someone to love. That's the most important thing."

In the process, I get to really look clearly at my mother projections for what they are, just projections, and I am finally able to let go of my long held belief that I didn't get what I needed from my mother and from life in general.

After experiencing a wide variety of processes during this long weekend, I start to see how deeply my mother still permeates my whole psyche despite the work I did back in India during that Primal group. I guess there are many layers to the work, but by the end of the weekend it feels to me that I have shed some more of them. I have also come to grips with the ways I experience love, feel comforted, and avoid my feelings in my life and in my relationships, and have let go of some of the underlying worry that I inherited from my mother. Having discovered some things about myself, dug a little deeper into my conditioning, and let go of some of the fear, I now feel much more available to love.

I continue to attend the Wednesday night meetings, and two months later I enroll in Aspire's level 2 retreat. Here's what the brochure says about this group:

"At Level 2, we learn to appreciate and celebrate the masculine, and reclaim the creative potency of inspiration. We'll discover together a new way to understand the gift of Responsibility in our lives…. We learn to heal with father, thus healing with our inner masculine, and, at last, become our own authority. Awakening to your authentic self reveals the limitless truth of your creative potential and creative power! You'll be more effective and more fulfilled at work, in relationships and in leisure."

Despite this big promise or because of it, weekend two so I have heard is the most challenging process for most people. The weekend is dedicated to working through *father issues*: authority, responsibility, work, and accomplishment. It's the heavy stuff, which is represented by Saturn in Astrology.

I carpool again, this time with people I already know from the level 1 work, and we arrive at the same house in the Sierras as before. Only this time it's a Friday evening in February, and there's snow piled eight feet high along the driveway as we pull in and park. I have mixed feelings as we enter the living room, and I recall the work I did in here a few months back. There's excitement, but this time there's a heaviness I didn't feel before. It seems we all have some father wounding, but being a father myself I realize that it's not a question of blame, but rather inherent in the role itself. In any case there seems to be a general consensus that facing this conditioning won't be easy.

As we enter the dyads and the weekend progresses, I begin to see the ways in which I have rebelled against authority and avoided responsibility. Despite all I have done to free myself, I see how I still cower from a domineering father, and as a result I often avoid contact with men preferring instead the company of women. But by confronting the men in the group and engaging in role-playing conversations with my own father, I begin to see that the separation I often feel from men is the result of my own projections.

By the end of the weekend, I feel like I understand myself much better and feel much freer to be myself. As a result, I begin to reclaim my own energy, come into my power, and actually dare to take up space for myself. "It's okay to be me," I assert and then, as I claim my space, I begin to find the real strength and the true meaning of being responsible, being able to respond to what life brings. This helps me move from a tendency to be authoritarian and reactive towards acting more from true authority.

When I return home from the retreat on Sunday evening, I feel strong and sure and ready to take on the world with new resolve. That next week at school as I stand in front of those rebellious adolescents, I am able to play my role of authority more confidently, and to see the whole drama with a little more detachment and even with a bit of humor. I am at last learning to embrace my own authority.

"Are you going to go up on the mountain with us this year?" Lydia asks me after the Wednesday night post-retreat check-in at the center.

"I don't know. Tell me about it," I reply, my curiosity awakened.

"Well, we all go up to Mount Shasta and camp on the mountain," she tells me full of enthusiasm, "each person in isolation for seven days, utterly alone with him or her self."

"Wow!" I reply.

"But that's not all," she continues. "In preparation for the trip, we all participate in a six-week purification cleanse before climbing the mountain and then we just drink juice while we're there."

"Whoa! You guys don't go half way into an experience. That sounds really intense!" I add, feeling both excited and apprehensive.

"And of course as an added preparation for the journey," she tells me, "a week and a half before the Mount Shasta trip is a Level 3 weekend, right in the middle of the cleanse! This is where we look at issues of victimhood."

"That's good. After all that cleansing, I might feel like a victim," I joke.

As I think about the retreat the next day, I notice the creature comfort, earth sign part of me thinking, "you've got to be crazy". But another part of me... the Neptune in Libra on the ascendant or maybe the Uranus in Cancer on the mid-heaven... is excited by the intensity. It seems that ever since my "Walking the dog" experience and then taking Sannyas, there has been an overwhelming drive in me to do whatever it takes to peel away the layers of my psyche and find true freedom.

"Yes, I am ready to meet myself," I declare and the following week a group of us meet to learn about and prepare for the cleanse.

"Thanks for coming everybody," says Lydia as we all settle into our chairs in a tight circle. There's about twenty of us in the room. "I think you all know Rita," Lydia tells us. "She'll be coordinating the cleanse for all of us."

Ah yes. I have met Rita, a very cute and petite Italian American with shoulder-length black hair and a twinkle in her eyes. She was in both Level 1 and level 2 as one of the "team" and I was paired with her on a number of occasions. I have also been to her herb shop in town where I met her three small children and learned that she was divorced.

"I'm going to explain to you how the cleanse works, give you guidelines for eating during the cleanse, and give out the herbs and supplements that will aid in the process," she explains as she starts pulling out bottles of pills from a large bag in front of her. "We will be primarily taking this Psyllium husk and Bentonite powder to aid in the cleansing process." She points at the bottle. "There is enough in this bottle for the whole six weeks of the cleanse and the week-long fast on the mountain."

She grabs a stack of papers and hands them to the person sitting next to her.

"Can you pass these around to everyone?" She asks and waits until everyone has a copy.

"The sheet I just gave you contains a recommended dietary schedule for the cleanse. You will be gradually eliminating certain foods as the cleanse progresses, continuing to simplify your diet. By the final week, we want you to eat only one thing at each meal, unprocessed food of course. For those who are concerned about weight loss, that one thing might be avocados. They are high in fat content. Are there any questions?"

"What about enemas?" Someone interjects. "I hear we're supposed to give ourselves enemas."

"Yes, that's right. It's fairly easy really and is a big help in the cleanse. After a few times you will all be pros at it."

"Will the cleanse make us sick?" someone else asks.

"You might have some symptoms as part of the cleansing process, but I'm providing you with adequate supplements to maintain health, including acidophilus for the colon."

She pauses for a few moments.

"If there are no more questions, I'll start dispensing the bottles, everything you need. Instructions for the enema are on the back of the cleanse schedule that I already gave you."

When the meeting is over, I gather my allotted assortment of pills and powders, place them in my backpack, and head for the door. Sasha, a friend I met at level one who runs a massage school, approaches me as I am about to leave.

"If you want, we can be buddies in the cleanse," she suggests. "It'll be good for each of us to have some support."

"I really appreciate that," I say. "I could certainly use it."

Over the next several weeks I gradually reduce and simplify my food intake while using the enemas and Psyllium husk. After awhile

I do get used to giving myself an enema. It's not quite routine, but not so difficult. Sasha is a big support, as we compare notes about our food consumption on a regular basis. I gradually become thinner and thinner, but after feeling bad at first, I begin to feel better and better as the cleanse progresses. At last it's time for the Level 3 retreat, the last step before the journey to the mountain and the juice fast. By this time I am eating bananas for breakfast and avocados for dinner.

The theme of the retreat is victimhood. In their words:

"In Level 3 the un-illusioning is complete. We break through the sacred wound and sense the great truth, purpose and meaning at the core of our life experience. We see 'the game of life' and experience bliss, being and beauty as reality. In our readiness and willingness to surrender, we discover that peace and power are one and the same. In surrender we discover wholeness and holiness. Our lives are consecrated in service, fully accepting and expressing what we are."

As I dive into the process, there is a lightness to my being as a result of the cleanse, and I am able to see clearly how many of the limitations I have experienced in my life are self-imposed. At some point I begin to shift my habitual attitude that "life will always be a continual disappointment" to a clear sense that life is full of unlimited possibilities, and that what seems like a limitation is really only the effect of my own belief in what is and isn't possible.

In this retreat, we share many deep personal experiences, and holding nothing back we reach a very deep level of intimacy. In the process, I release a lot of guilt and shame, and this in turn allows my feeling of victimhood to dissolve. What remains is a strong sense that each of us on this journey is none other than myself disguised in another's clothing. As I walk out of the retreat space on the last day, I feel a strong sense of being... like a peaceful warrior... ready to face myself on Mt. Shasta.

Here's what the brochure says about Level 4:

"Level 4 is a 10-day retreat, a profound experience of letting go. This is a quiet, contemplative, meditative, Self-revealing space where illusions fall away, revealing an underlying and ever-present

279

mastery. We arrive at the end of a cycle of deep cleansing, and discover the beginning of a new life, a true life. Level 4 is giving yourself the gift of you."

On the first day of Level 4, forty-two of us hike in, each person finding a spot in isolation on this mighty mountain. There we remain for seven days only venturing out to pump water from a nearby spring, just drinking juices and water, reading spiritual books, and meditating. The last three days are group processing and celebration. While on the mountain, I keep a journal.

Chapter 36

On the Mountain, A Journey In

Day I, August 2001

Today will be the first day on the mountain. We all help to pack the trucks and make the final preparations, rearranging our packs one last time and ceremoniously weighing them. Mine weighs in at exactly 50 pounds, and since my body weight is a slight 120 pounds after the 5 week cleanse in preparation for this special journey, I am glad the scales do not register more. I bring only what I consider to be essential: my camping gear, some warm clothes, a few spiritual books, the water filter I had used with my brother in the Sierras which I considered to be superior to the filter Aspire provided each of us, and some frozen grape juice concentrate which will be my only sustenance.

We inch our way up the mere hint of a trail, twenty of us heading for a place called the "bowl" and another place called the "ridge". I am a bowl person and finally split off to the left with Roger leading the way. Before too terribly long we arrive and begin choosing our sights for the next seven days of silence. It's hard for me to stop walking. I really want to push on ever higher toward the mighty, looming snow patches of Mt. Shasta, but my sore back and hips convince me it's okay to surrender to *here*. At last, just as the sun ducks behind the mountain, the last tent stake is in place, the latrine is dug, and my camp is laid out. I can allow myself to drop into the silence of this magical place. What will happen in the next seven days I do not know, but I hope to capture the essence of it here on these pages. Will there be spiritual insights? Perhaps a great peace? Maybe I'll be facing my boredom like a good Buddhist. If nothing else, I am sure I'm in for some great sunsets and sunrises, amazing stars and a commune with nature in this place of just being.

Day II

I watch the clouds dance across the mountaintop as the winds roar to celebrate the rising sun. I awake to the sound of rain on my sleeping bag and hurriedly gather my things and scamper for the shelter of my tent. It's a small price to pay for the glorious spectacle of last night's shooting stars. It took awhile to find my sitting spot, but the morning has revealed it to be right by my tent. There is a perfect stump for resting the back and an unparalleled view of the mighty mountain. It's funny how I looked everywhere else on my little knoll before seeing this spot right here. Hmm. Is life an analogy for life?

Today's word from the Osho Neo-Tarot deck of spiritual stories is "Challenge". This is the story about the farmer who is unhappy with all the storms and droughts he has had to endure and bargains with God to let him control the weather for one year. The farmer made perfect weather day in and day out, but when it was time to harvest the wheat, which had grown very tall and full, he found it had no seed. It seems a little adversity is needed to grow nourishing wheat. I shall watch how this plays itself out today.

The wind is an orchestra playing my heartstrings as the clouds gather to dance. Is adversity knocking at my door? A large ant explores my crotch as I struggle a bit with this fountain pen. Is there really a voice beyond my mind? An "I" beyond this personality? Birds come to the trees around me. Maybe they know the answer to my questions. I'll listen and wait.

Hmm. I seem to be having some challenges around technology. My stove wouldn't work last night, and then my water filter required being taken apart and cleaned before it would cooperate. Is my seed growing?

***

Now I am being attacked by a very pesky grasshopper who seems to have a taste for cotton. No matter how often I chase him away, he returns. Two wills, two egos defending and attacking. Self-preservation, or at least the preservation of my cotton, is what it's all about. He seems to prefer the rope on my Tarot card bag. I guess I'll let him have it for the moment and return to reading Krishnamurti's *Reflections on the Self* and his thoughts on ego and identification. Krishnamurti says that the very act of seeking God makes it impossible to find. It seems that time is the culprit for it is only in time that seeking is possible. When there's no time there's no seeking, because there is no doing.

***

Grasshopper eventually gets his fill. The only cost to me in letting go of my battle with him was a little fraying of my pouch string.

The wind picks up again as the sun approaches the far ridge. It's always good to dance at such times. The flies seem to know this, but the birds, with a higher perspective, still remain silent. Is there anything for me to do, now? "Be still... and know... I am... God."

***

283

Here's something I've had time to observe in the twilight as I boil some water for tea: A watched pot does eventually boil as long as you don't watch it for too long at a time.

Day III

My arrogant self has been humbled just a bit. My water filter, my pride and joy, keeps clogging and failing. I finally gave in this morning and used the Aspire filter. It worked like a dream, no better than a dream. Dreams are often strange and unreliable.

The word for the day is "Greed". I shall watch how my mind does not trust and is greedy. A case in point was my water filter, which I was hording for myself thinking it better than the one Aspire gave everyone. It turned out to be a false coin and simply a means of creating separation.

***

I was chased out of my sacred spot by the powerful winds and have taken shelter behind a wonderful rock with a smooth surface to rest my back. From here, I look out on the meadow full of darting chickadees and the mountains in the distant Northeast. Now I hear the roar of the gusting winds but only feel a gentle breeze. It is said that John Muir could tell the kind of tree by the sound the wind made passing through it.

Is it true that this consciousness is but the consciousness of a cell in the body of God? It seems so separate and distinct. What sense does the idea of greed make with this perspective? Krishnamurti says that identification is the process by which we construct the separate self. This can be identification with objects: my car, my job, and my body. It can also be a more subtle identification with things like my knowledge and experience. It was my so-called knowledge and experience that led me to my arrogance and ultimate feelings of separation around that water filter. There would be no greed without that identification.

***

Now I feel that the wind is trying to find me. Who? This body that feels its chilling touch? This mind that judges the experience and fears its repercussions? Who?

A couple of days ago when we were packing the truck to journey to this place, I was given an impossible task, to fit so many chairs and coolers into one small Toyota pickup truck. Somehow, miraculously, I accomplished the task. I felt quite proud. Not more than thirty seconds later, the order came down to unpack the truck to get some juice out of the big cooler on the bottom. I was pissed off! Why? That was me they were dismantling back there. Yes. I had identified myself with the packing.

***

I feel like I'm losing control of the days. Today slipped by so fast. Can the sun really be by the mountain so soon? I've been doing some deep breathing this afternoon, and now everything has a special luminance in the diminishing light. Wispy clouds appear like angels drifting above the mountain hinting at the presence of celestial choirs. The wind has calmed itself for a moment, and there is a timeless quality of being that hangs in the air, but a trace of fear lays over it like film on a glass. I take another deep breath. Ah. There is no better moment than now to let go.

***

I often wonder where thoughts come from. It seems that they are all just floating around in the ether waiting to be plucked out or fished out with a hook and pole. Who am I without these thoughts? As I watch them more closely, I notice that there are different kinds of thinking. There are thoughts related to remembering, bringing back past experience for reflection. Then there are thoughts that spring from sensation, such as "my bladder is full, I think I'll go pee" or "I'm thirsty". The third kind are the creative thoughts that hatch from new ideas. Are these truly different? It seems that all types could arise in the process of solving a problem. I shall observe some more.

Day IV

The wind picked the card for the day and it was "Rebirth/ Moment to moment." This is the story of Buddha returning to his wife after being gone for seven years attaining enlightenment. She was so caught in her anger at him for leaving without telling her, that she didn't see who stood before her. When Buddha asked her to look with fresh eyes, she suddenly saw the enlightened one and dropped to her knees. I believe the card is asking me to drop all prior knowledge and be open to what might be discovered this new moment.

Today seems to be the day of the bees. First one kept landing on me as I sketched. Now one is humming loudly as he communes with my water bottle. The grasshopper isn't chewing string anymore. Yesterday he was hanging out in my pee spot. The last I saw him he was piggybacking a newfound mate and they were hopping off down the hill to the south.

***

The most incredible thing has just happened! I was just visited by a small fox. He was so sleek and curious, cautious, alert, but unafraid. He came up behind me from the left as I was sitting in my spot. He walked within a foot of me, then pranced around my tent, peeked at me again, hopped up on the log in front of the big rock, and then disappeared. What is the message of the fox? I shall have to check the medicine cards when I return to the "world".

***

And now I have another surprise. I pick up my pouch to get my Osho cards out and there is that grasshopper, hiding underneath and feasting away on that pouch string he loves like there was no tomorrow. Hmm. He may have a point there. Grasshopper. Are you gnawing at my heartstrings?

***

As the day progresses, I spend some more time thinking about thoughts, meta-thinking I guess you could call it. It seems that most of my thoughts stem from sensation coupled with past memories. But some do seem to arise with no provocation. Could thought really create experience as some have said? "First there was the word."

In *The Impersonal Life*, Joseph Benner says that first there is an idea and then the desire to express that idea. That desire then compels thinking, which in turn causes action, which finally produces results. It occurs to me that perhaps I only see the thoughts, not the idea which may be the true creator of experience. So, what is an Idea?

I have an idea: Let's go get some ice cream. Here's another idea: Let's get a big piece of property and live communally.

***

Roger just came by for a daily checkup with a message written on his tablet that said to let go of ideas and just be. Hmm. How did he know?

***

Krishnamurti says that to come to a conclusion is to build a wall around oneself, which prevents understanding, and that only awareness of what is, is liberating.

Chapter 37

Nature's Symphony

The Bow!

Ah... it's that one special time of the day when the sun shines through the trees to the west onto my sitting spot and altar. I have become so aware of the movement of the sun relative to this tiny spot of mine cradled in the arms of Mother Shasta.

Once again I honor the parting of the sun as it inches its way down behind the trees making its daily descent. It has been a good day, a precious day, with many riches being showered upon me. Bees in my face to keep me present, a silent fox to bring me to my senses and Grasshopper in my tent biting my hand to wake me up to myself, reborn moment to moment. I ponder the miracle of fire as I watch the sun disappear. Fire. It's a little piece of the sun that you can hold in your hand if it's dancing on a candle. Both have the same exquisite radiance.

***

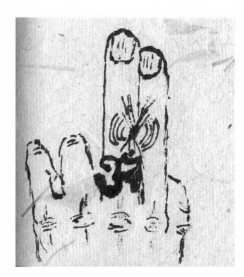

Try looking at the sun through the gap between two fingers. What an amazing energy mandala it creates.

***

There is a sort of *Twilight Symphony* that is unfolding in subtle and delicate sequence tonight. As the light begins to wane and the earth's aura begins to appear, a band of darkness seems to rise in the east. It is then that we have the first movement, the swallow overture with their darting and swooping. The second movement of this piece of music is the syncopated fluttering of a small moth across my window to the world. Next comes the third movement, the boldest yet. It comes as a surprisingly frantic burst of bats beating their wings past my ears and disappearing only to just as suddenly reappear zipping over my left shoulder, flapping frantically as if they had been pent up in the darkness for eons. Just as suddenly this movement comes to an end. The bats are gone, and ever-so-slowly with quiet steadfast resolve, the stars appear. First come the planets and then the patch quilt of light that reminds us that we are not alone after all.

Day V

A fly picked the card for the day. It's "acceptance", the beautiful story of the Zen master Hakuin who is accused of fathering an illegitimate child. He just says to the accusation, "Oh, is that so?" and takes the child into his keep. After much time, the mother of the child, filled with remorse, confesses her lie. They come to take the child and apologize to the monk. As he gives up the child, he simply says, "Oh, is that so?" He was accepting life as it comes.

I find my mind back on the topic of thoughts. Yes, the mind is certainly intrigued by them. Krishnamurti says that the thinker and his thoughts are one. The observer is the observed. If this is true, then without thoughts, do I exist? If I don't exist, then who is watching? Who is aware?

Never mind who is aware. That's just mind stuff again. There are stories for that, but they are irrelevant. A better question is "What is awareness?"

Perhaps awareness is observation without judgment, without comment, and without thought. With it, there would be an acceptance of what is, and it would occur in this very moment. This. Here. Now.

I've noticed that the easiest way for me to enter in to this awareness is by observing nature; watching the birds follow their pecking order as they hop from branch to branch, noticing the gentle dance of the pine branches in the wind, listening to the flies zoom past and the wind slowly make its way here from distant valleys to meet my face in a magnificent crescendo. I have no judgments about these things, no opinions. They just are.

The next step for me is to notice the thoughts and feelings as they come to me with the same openness as I had for nature. Then, when I've mastered that, the final step is to enter into relationship with others with the same lack of judgment. Clearly, with each subsequent step, it becomes more difficult to maintain this open acceptance.

***

I just observed a grasshopper laying its eggs in a hole in the rock where my water bottle lies. Is this the female I saw in tight embrace the other day? Ah... the paths of the mind down which a simple question takes one... and now I return to a taste of what is.

***

I feel so out-in-the-open today, so exposed. I had felt a certain security in my little place here, tucked away in this woody knoll.

But, today there is no place to hide. I am raw and exposed to the world in all its intense splendor. This is not a frightening experience, for the world feels like a loving place, a benevolent host. When I let go into it, I feel a certain quiet, merging expansion happening, and there is a flavor to it all, a tangible essence that is like sweet nectar. Even the flies and bees are part of it, and I am no longer shooing them away.

***

Wow! I have no idea how cracked open I have become until I encounter another human being. John has come to pay a visit and the love and gratitude pours out of me and all I could do is laugh and cry at the same time. Ah... I remember this happening before... that tell tale sign of being in the presence of the divine.

***

A little later, I go to a nearby spring for water and encounter another person seemingly just hanging out by the watering hole. With this encounter, I have a very different reaction. I feel annoyed, because we're supposed to remain in solitude. Doesn't she know what a pure state I am in?

And then in that very moment I see that I am not honoring the space she is in. Wow, from bliss to annoyance so quickly. This choiceless awareness I have been pursuing is so much harder when there are other people involved. Oh yes... I am reminded that the unconscious act of this woman is just a reflection of my own unconsciousness, and I see how I suspect my own motives in the world. I feel my own blundering ignorance, which I want to deny because I'm on a "deep spiritual" quest. Is what I'm doing here really all so pure and spiritual or am I just hanging out in the woods with my things, scratching marks on hand-made Indian paper? Who do I think I am?

When I return to the camp, I go back to my reading and find a passage where Krishnamurti talks about the power of insight, a phenomenon all together different than thought which springs from accumulated knowledge and desire. Insight, he says, is an immediate recognition of a higher truth of something. It has the power to completely dissolve prior limitations. I reflect on this idea and then notice that through my insight into the situation with the woman hanging out at the watering hole, I find myself suddenly descending from the mountain of my own making and now I feel much more accessible.

***

Amazing! Can it really be that time of day again? The sun is once again spotlighting the place where I sit. Afternoon is beginning to draw to a close, and another day will vanish from this earth like a pile of gold coins in a den of thieves. And now I can feel my time on the mountain coming to an end. The unread pages of the books I have brought are dwindling, and there is a certain quickening happening in the fabric of time. Tomorrow is the last full day on this glorious mountain, and I can't help wondering what I will carry out with me as I descend to what we call the worldly pursuits.

But, my mind gets ahead of itself. Presence is all that's required. There are many more pages in this journal, this journal with the frayed string to wrap it closed. Yes, I said, "frayed". Grasshopper has been up to his tricks again!

***

I am but a vessel for divine expression, a flute in the hands of the flute player. Smooth my edges. Hollow out my core and clear out my holes that you may play beautiful music. The Persian poet Rumi reminds me to stay true to my passion when he suggests that the beauty I love be what I do.

***

involved.

Lassen Peak
to the South

As sun sets, I sit on the hillside facing south and watch Lassen Peak disappear into the sublime light. Wow, look at the subtle elegance of those clouds immersed in a sea of pastel luminance. Every human being contains this beauty if I could but strip away the cobwebs of my own making, clean my own lens, polish my own silver... and yet, having said that, I wonder if all the polishing is really necessary? Maybe it's just a matter of focusing differently. Spots on a camera lens are not visible with a long depth of focus. But enough words now. Let me be with the passing of this day.

Day VI

The day begins with a glorious orange ball rising out of the mist. The shadow of the tree branch dancing in the sunlight chose today's card, "Failure". Is it about my failure to capture the subtle beauty of Mt. Lassen with my humble pen on parchment when I tried to draw its likeness yesterday? Or maybe my failure to be present each and every moment of this precious day?

"I talk to my inner lover, and I say, why such a rush? We sense that there is some sort of spirit that loves birds and animals and the ants – perhaps the same one who gave a radiance to you in your mother's womb. Is it logical you would be walking around entirely orphaned now? The truth is you turned away yourself and decided to go into the darkness alone. Now you are tangled up in others and have forgotten what you once knew. And that is why everything you do has some weird failure in it."

These words of mystic poet Kabir remind me how often I get caught in thinking I've got to be the doer, when in reality, being is all that is required.

✳✳✳

I want to follow the voice of my higher self, the God within, but how do I discern whose voice is speaking? That it's not the voice of fear, my conditioning or ego?

"Be still and listen to the wind," a voice inside says. "Do not identify, but rather remain simply present with what is. All is provided. All you need to do is accept it."

✳✳✳

Here I am in the wilderness with expansive views, nothing but trees and rocks and birds and the wind and the sky for as far as the eye can see, and I wonder, what is space? Do I have space? Is space unlimited or is it the size of the box I think inside of? The size of what I think is possible? In this sense, it seems that knowledge is the opposite of space, because to know something is to place it in a box, to categorize it and to limit its possibilities. Ultimate space is ultimate freedom, and it's accompanied by the feeling that I have expanded to fill the whole incredible world. When that happens anything can occur, and I am no longer preventing it with my concepts, judgments or fears. To see what is... unencumbered by the mind... is space... is freedom. Then everything is just happening and I am but hollow bamboo being played by the wind.

✳✳✳

This seems to be the day of flies. How many flies can I have on me at one time? There are three at the moment. Oh, they're all gone. Oh, now they're back. They tickle the hairs on my hand a bit, but they have become friends. Amazing creatures really. So quick, so agile.

I've saved a spot for a portrait of Grasshopper in my journal. I wonder if he will grace me with his presence again. Meanwhile, I've decided to give myself a full reading with the Osho deck as a preparation for leaving the mountain tomorrow. Hmm. Decided? Who decided? Was that higher mind? Oh well, lower mind is also God. It's all good if done consciously. Hmmm. Sounds like a good rationalization anyway. Oh my God, am I undoing a whole week's work in a single statement? Ah! What Failure! That is the word for the day after all.

So, apparently I was thinking there was something to accomplish up here on this mountaintop. Another experience to add to my reservoir of mental reminiscences? Another specimen for my collection of rare and exotic experiential artifacts?

Chapter 38

Down From the Mountain

I sit here with my back against this stump and look down at the Osho cards sitting right here in front of me. No grasshopper will be disturbed if I pick them up, and the planet can only be better for my earnest inquiry. God knows I've got the time. I begin shuffling. The reading requires picking five cards. The first card represents the issue the reading is about. The issue card I pick is "Laughter". This is my favorite story in the whole deck – about the three laughing monks who go from town to town. In each municipality, they go to the central square and just start laughing for no reason. It becomes infectious. "If you change your sadness to celebration, then you will also be capable of changing your death to resurrection. So learn the art while there is still time," says Osho.

Ah... laughter is celebration and my name means celebration... so the issue is my very being. Me.

The next card I draw tells me what I need to be more open to in my life. The card I draw is "Self-accept". I must be more open to self-acceptance. This card tells the story of the trees that are comparing themselves to the other trees. The willow feels bad that it isn't tall and straight. The rose bush wishes it had a big trunk. The truth is, existence called forth each unique flowering. Ah, good reminder. Don't compare.

The third card tells me what I should put out into the world. This card is "Trust". It is the story of the "naïve" monk who was told to walk on water and trusting his master, actually does it. The other monks had played a trick on him to watch him drown, but his trust was enough.

The fourth card is the outcome card. My outcome card is simply "acceptance." How perfect! We already know that story of the monk who just says, "Oh, is that so?" to every situation that comes his way. Acceptance means choiceless awareness. Acceptance allows me to step out of the way. Acceptance allows me to hear the divine voice. Acceptance is the key to freedom.

**

Hold everything! Grasshopper has returned for his portrait and so I pause to sketch him with my pen.

**

And now for the last card, the master's insight into the issue. Will it be as perfect as the other cards? Of course. How could it be otherwise? Hmmm. The card is "Intelligence." This is the great story of Rabiya who is searching outside her hut for her lost needle. When asked by passers by who wished to help where she had dropped it, she tells them that she actually lost it in the hut, but that the light for looking was better outside. When they tell her how silly she is, she tells them, "Then you, too, are silly because that's what you go on doing all your lives, looking for what's lost outside of the hut where you have lost it." Ah yes, the master is just reminding me not to go looking out in the world for what I have lost. Everything I seek is inside me. It is a beautiful reading for a beautiful six days on this blessed mountain.

So the issue is my very being of Celebration. Then, I need to be more open to accepting myself as I am, I must continue to walk in trust, and the outcome will be the acceptance of all things. I just need to remember to look inside for all that I need. This reading is so in line with what I was exploring about non-identification and

297

open acceptance. First I practice this non-judgmental observation with nature. Then I bring that to my own thoughts and feelings (self-acceptance) and finally take that into my relationships in the world (Acceptance of everything).

***

Grasshopper seems to like the laughter card.

***

Oh look, it's that time again when the sun has come to the opening in the trees to spotlight this place where I sit. Another day begins to draw to a close. Remarkable!

My pee spot has become a watering hole for grasshoppers, bees, ants, and now flies. I have, no doubt, altered the course of history and possibly prompted a whole new folklore.

***

 Now I draw Grasshopper up close and personal with my black fountain pen while he chews on my finger.

"Ouch!! Easy with those mandibles, fella!" He actually drew blood!

***

The sun is into the trees again and the mountain is looking dreamy. A nut cracker perches on the very last branch of the highest tree and takes it all in while this one, here below, sits complacently and just watches with nothing to do but ponder the vastness of it all.

Let me say more about the watering hole. There seems to be a pecking order here. The grasshoppers are at the spot during the day, but in the very hottest part of the day, they clear out with the arrival of the bees. It isn't until after the sun goes down behind the mountain that the big ants come to visit. They seem to be willing to share with the gnats. Flies visit off and on all day. They seem to be less particular about who else is here.

Day VII

This morning I awake to the howling of the wind – a message of movement. Yes, today I pack my things, sweep away the markings I have made on this place, and walk away into a new beginning. Though I can remove the impressions I have made on the Mountain, I cannot nor wish not to remove the impressions the Mountain has made on me. May these impressions stay forever. As I depart, may I carry with me the gratitude and clarity I have found here. May I stay surrendered to the divine within me and hear loudly the voice of my higher self, calling me to divine acceptance and service. May I stay free of identification and love myself completely, even when I don't stay free of identification. May I love everything and everyone without judgment just as I love dear, beloved Grasshopper!

Aftermath

I sit in a beautiful yard of a beautiful home in the countryside outside of the town of Weed. I listen to the sound of the lawn sprinklers as they hit against the leaves of a nearby tree in their regular cycle. I look out in the morning at the evening side of Mt. Shasta and can see myself sitting on the other side, high up in mother Shasta's cradle, looking up at the sunrise side of the same rock and ice. From here, the energy of the mountain is soft, warm and gentle.

Yesterday was a jolting day. Like a space traveler, I needed a bit of quarantine before I was ready to be exposed to the energies of civilization. I found that gathering with my fellow journeyers, speaking, riding in a car, and especially hanging out in a gas station waiting for a flat tire to be fixed, all extremely unsettling.

Judgments were rampant in my mind, but, miraculously, in the middle of the condemnation, there was something inside me that arose with benevolent humor and loved even the judging mind. Once this happened, my heart began to soften and I was filled with the feeling that each person I was judging was, after all, a divine expression who was just loving in his own way. Gradually I relaxed into the new moment and began to open up again.

I have grown to admire John, the leader of these adventures so much in this process. I see how he has orchestrated my experience to nurture the tender newborn inside of me as we are cradled for two more days in loving support before being cast out into the world again. I take a deep breath and relax into being in this ever-present moment, celebrating my humanness in this vast and mysterious world.

My Morning Prayer

I surrender to the divine within me. May I always hear the voice of my higher *Self* and feel the love that is ever-present, both within me and all around me.

***

Fox Medicine

The Medicine cards tell me that fox medicine is a sign that I am to become like the wind, which, although it cannot be seen, is able to weave into and through any location or situation. It would be wise, it goes on to say, for me to observe the acts of others rather than their words. This is a further invitation for me to bring that loving, open, watchful presence that I cultivated on the mountain with all the beautiful creatures of nature to my own thoughts and feelings and then to my relationships with other people. Through this practice, I will experience a deep self-acceptance and then finally a full acceptance of everything and everybody around me.

***

A few days have passed, and I find myself sitting at my favorite spot on Limantour Beach in Point Reyes National Seashore. Today the tide is high and the flies are plentiful, really putting to the test my ability to be centered and at one with ten to fifteen flies on me at a time. It is the clearest, most radiant day I have ever seen at Limantour. The ocean is a deep, crystal blue and I can easily see all the way to the hills of South San Francisco, the Farallon Islands and Point Reyes. What a perfect reflection of the clarity I am experiencing inside. Everything I have done since coming down from the mountain has been effortless, and blessings abound. Interactions with people have been amazing. Love and connection is everywhere. I now have a new teaching position at Casa Grande High School in Petaluma and have moved to a hip little town nearby called Sebastopol. With only one phone call, I was given a beautiful little apartment with great, loving neighbors. Sebastopol seems like a wonderful, heartful community. I feel so blessed to have dropped into it so easily. I owe it all to my new openness. When the heart is open, so are doors.

***

A week or two have passed and I find myself once again by the ocean, this time on Sonoma State Beach. It seems the ocean provides me with the best opportunity for meditation and reflection. There's something about that constant roar and the crashing froth that quiet my soul, at least for the moment. Tomorrow I start my teaching year with new resolve to create an atmosphere of respect for a higher collective purpose. I am a starship on a quest to enter unexplored territory. I feel a little shaky. Are there no fellow voyagers with whom to rally support? The answer is an emphatic yes. In Sebastopol, I find a community of singers, dancers and poets. I believe they can help sustain my spirit. And, of course, there is a community of loving beings in Sacramento who will always live inside my heart. For that I am forever grateful.

***

As I find my way around Sebastopol, one of the groups I find is a band of Sufis. This particular order of Sufism, a mystic sect of Islam, is from the lineage of Hazrat Inayat Khan and one of his disciples named Samuel Lewis, better known as Sufi Sam. It was Sufi Sam who began the *Dances of Universal Peace*, a practice of spiritual folk dancing: singing and dancing to songs from all spiritual traditions. He began these heart-opening dances back in the sixties in San Francisco. You may remember my first experience of these dances back in Ann Arbor when I first started on my "so called" spiritual journey. It's in one of these dance circles in Northern California that I meet Chantal. We are progressing partners in the dance, and I hear her voice first... and what a voice!

"Who is that?" I wonder and then she is before me and I gaze into her eyes. She radiates love and joy.

We continue bumping into each other at dance meetings for another year before we finally arrange to meet and sing together. As other relationships fall away for both of us, we end up together feeling the warm promise of being truly kindred spirits. Having finally learned love's lesson, that love is what I am, at last I am ready to meet it in another, my beloved Chantal.

After spending a year together living in a Yurt in the middle of a Sonoma county apple orchard, Chantal and I marry in the summer of 2005 at a neighborhood park in Sebastopol and invite all our friends. Prem gets a temporary minister's license and leads us through the process. We sing songs, participate in some Sufi dancing and much more. It's not just a grand party. It's a send-off. After a little Internet search, I have gotten a job teaching at an International School in the Democratic Republic of the Congo. The stories of this adventure, I'll save for the book, Calculus in Congo. Let me just say here that it is an amazing four years.

After returning from Africa and not wanting to return to "normalcy", Chantal and I pack up our few remaining things and move to Costa Rica where we currently live. She works as a massage therapist at Blue Spirit, a branch of the Omega Institute, and I am writing, recording music and doing lots of surfing. Together we lead Kirtana at yoga retreats and on the beach for an occasional full moon. At some point I add the Sanskrit word "Ananda" to my name. It means bliss. I have to admit that it's hard not to be blissful in this beautiful piece of paradise.

And so the story ends... for now. And yet the story continues... and life is lived every day. I sit on my mountainside deck as the last rays of the afternoon sun illuminate the forest that stretches out to the sea, typing these last words.

"Look, the sun is just setting, Ananda," says Chantal. "Don't miss it."

I look up to see the brilliant display of colors in the clouds over the ocean and then notice a mother Howler Monkey with a baby clutching her tight pulling herself up onto one of the branches of a tree just in front of us. On a higher branch sits her mate whom we call *Yellow Tail* for self-evident reasons. *Yellow Tail* raises his head up to the sky, opens his mouth, and lets out a characteristic roar at the parting sun... and I reflect over my own place in this vast, mysterious universe and what I have learned from all my experiences....

And I wonder. Is there a lesson to be learned? Does my life make some sort of sense? Is there some sort of divine purpose to it all?

Epilogue

The Inner Journey in Search of "Who Am I?"

Unlike the outer journey, which is bound in time and experiences, the inner journey is always in the here and now. So what's true right here, right now, and what can I say about the pathless path from here to here?

Well, as for what's true, I know that "I" am, and the universe is, or at least my experience of the universe is. I appear to be looking out these eyes, listening through these ears, sensing through this skin, thinking and feeling. And I notice that the world within and the world without are constantly changing. There's continuous activity, an ongoing interplay of sounds and sights, and this body that is my vantage point is in constant motion, at least until this amazing thing called sleep happens, some part of which contains whole other worlds of my making, while other parts don't seem to exist at all. But still, time passes. The earth turns and the skies eventually brighten, the roosters crow and here in Costa Rica where I live, the monkeys howl the coming of the new day.

When do I first realize that *I am*? I hear stories about being fearful as a small child, holding on to mother's skirts, deathly afraid of everything new, but especially people. I realize at some point that I am a young male, a white middleclass Homo Sapien, and I am a younger brother, a tag-along bothersome younger brother at that.

305

At some further point, I come to realize that I want to be loved. I think that I need to find that love outside of myself, specifically from girls. If a pretty girl loves me, then it means that I am all right. I'm loveable... after all.

And who am I anyway? I notice I am aware, sensitive, observant, smart, but also serious, scared, and a bit of a nerd. But I'm not cool... at least I'm not popular... and I want to be.

So I become cool... a track star.... and I start buying cool clothes... orange bell-bottoms and a red and white poke-a-dot shirt. I'm the first kid on my block to grow a Beatle haircut, and I buy a guitar. Can I make the girls swoon? Or at least get them to pay attention?

Yes... eventually I do and I have my first girlfriend. I am hopelessly devoted to her. I am "in love" and fascinated by the feminine "other".

I play many more roles as time passes... math major... psychology student... singer/songwriter... academic... drop-out... hippie... L.S.D. explorer... artist.... spiritual seeker... husband... father... mountain man... computer expert... corporate manager... manic or awakened one... corporate dropout... displaced worker... schoolteacher... expat... retiree... gringo... surfer... writer... musician... Kirtan leader... but who I am really?

In that group in India, all the roles and identities are exposed, and then my mind simply gives up trying to create an identity. What remains is a glowing, bliss-filled, love-exuding mystery that I take to be my authentic self. After that, all that is required is some polishing. Expressing that which remains, Ram Dass says in his continual meditation these days, "I am loving awareness."

In Advaita Vedanta, the Indian philosophy of non-dualism, it is said that "I am not a person." It means that this sense of being a separate entity is an illusion created by a false identification with "self" as object. The truth, according to those espousing this philosophy is that "I" am really awareness itself... a sort of field of being... a unified field of energy that knows, loves and contains all that is in existence. I sense the truth of this... and continually try to capture the essence of the idea in the songs that I write and the way that I live my life, day by day. [19]

***

I'm inspired by these words from the thirteenth century mystic poet, Jalaluddin Rumi, who expresses the inexpressible so beautifully. He says, "There's a field, beyond knowing and not knowing. I'll meet you there." [20]

***

The challenge that Ram Dass put to us so many years ago comes back to me now, as I am faced with the discipline of not being attached to any patterns whatsoever, the discipline of standing nowhere, of having no definitions I can cling to: no reference groups, no identifications, no self-concepts, and no models. Am I ready to face that kind of discipline?

At some point, consciousness expands to see itself more clearly, and the definitions and self-concepts drop by themselves. So do the questions. That's the moment, Osho says, when one attains to wisdom. The journey to attaining that wisdom is sometimes referred to as the pathless path, or simply the road of life. We're all travelers on this road. [21]

***

And now I end this epitaph with the last words to leave Mahatma Gandhi's lips... "Ram Ram." [22]

Acknowledgments and
Disclaimers

I wish to thank all the teachers and fellow travelers that have touched me along the path and all those whom I have loved and who have loved me. The path would not have been the same without you. What follows is a partial list of those people more or less in order of appearance in my life:

Thanks to my mother for her loving encouragement, my father for his lessons in living and my brother Laird for showing me how to love the world. Thanks to Dr. Seuss for teaching me about the imagination and Carl Sagan for reminding me of the wonder of the universe. Much thanks to Aldous Huxley, Timothy Leary, Richard Alpert and John Lilly for being the pioneers in mind expansion, and of course Richard Alpert again who would take the name Baba Ram Dass and be my first guide into Eastern Mysticism. Thanks to Carlos Castaneda for stretching my definition of what is possible, Joseph Campbell, J. Krishnamurti, Herman Melville, Eckhart Tolle, Adyashanti, Tim Freke, Leonard Jacobson and Jeddah Mali to mention just a few of those whose writings and talks have inspired me, and thanks to Osho for giving me my name and guiding me on the path to freedom. Thanks to my writer's group, especially Mary Serphos and Deborah Brackman for listening to my story and encouraging me to keep going. A special thanks goes to those teachers in addition to Ram Dass in whose company I have had the good fortune to have been: Trogyam Trungpa Rimpoche, Pir Vallayat Khan, Yogi Bhajan, Swami Rama, Swami Satchidananda, all the disciples of Osho that I have met, and the therapists at the Osho Commune in Pune, those I have met who are involved in the *Miracle of Love* work, John Ruskell and the Aspire Foundation of Sacramento, all the wonderful Sufi's involved in the *Dances of Universal Peace*, Gangaji and Pamela Wilson. A heart-felt thanks to all the people who have loved me and helped me open my heart, especially to Prem for teaching me about love and truth, and to my beloved Chantal for being a steady and loyal companion in my latter day adventures and for always keeping love interesting. Thanks also to Chantal for spending those endless evenings listening to my tale and giving me invaluable feedback. A special thanks to the musicians and singers who have taught me so much about the Bhakti path: Krishna Das, Jai Uttal, Miten and Deva Premal, and Snatam Kaur to name just a few. Thanks so much to Prartho Sereno for her inspired painting that is the cover of this offering, and finally a heart felt thanks to all of you who took the time to read this book.

Now, here's the disclaimer. Writing an autobiography is tricky, especially when most of the characters in it are still living. The first thing to say is that although this book is "non-fiction," all thoughts and feelings are strictly the author's. Remember that anything I say about another person, says more about me than it does about them. Also, I have changed some of the names of the people in the story to protect their privacy, and although the events are "true", they are only relatively true, biased by my own perception and memory. Note, also, that much of the dialogue has been fabricated to aid in the telling of the story. It is my sincere hope that I have not hurt or offended anyone in the telling of this story, and if I have, please forgive me. I can only tell it as I see it. And now, in parting, let me say to all of you, may your own journeys be full of unexpected turns.

Love and blessings,

Jashanananda
August 2013

Note: A collection of original songs that accompany this book can be downloaded by going to Facebook page "Chantalananda".

Original Song Collection

1. Being Buffaloed
2. Wouldn't You Know Part 1
3. Wouldn't You Know Part 2
4. Olivia - Chapter 17, page 3
5. Wouldn't You Know Part 3
6. Riita Vepsalenin
7. Wouldn't You Know Part 4
8. Morningsun Mountain
9. All On My Way to Forever
10. The Veil is Lifted
11. Wouldn't You Know Part 5
12. New Love
13. Ashes
14. His Shoes
15. Jack in the Box
16. My Scottish Girl
17. California Rain
18. Hello Myself
19. Everything That Is
20. I'll Meet You There
21. The Road of Life
22. Ram Ram